THE STATE UNMASKED

ITS LONG BETRAYAL OF OUR YOUTH
AND
OUR FUTURE

DR. JOE BUTTLE

(a long-suffering friend)

HOW DID IT GET LIKE THIS? EDUCATION IN ITS
HISTORICAL AND POLITICAL PERSPECTIVE

Pen Press

First published in Great Britain by Pen Press

All paper used in the printing of this book has been made from wood grown in managed, sustainable forests.

ISBN13: 978-1-78003-046-3

Printed and bound in the UK
Pen Press is an imprint of Indepenpress Publishing Limited
25 Eastern Place
Brighton
BN2 1GJ

A catalogue record of this book is available from
the British Library

Cover design by Jacqueline Abromeit

Verified sources of images used:

Kidbrooke School:	source: VADS
James Callaghan:	source: wikipedia commons
Kenneth Baker:	commentisfree.guardian.co.uk
David Young:	source: wikipedia commons
Bexley Academy:	source: Bexley Business Academy

This book is dedicated to Robert Owen, educationist, entrepreneur,

founder of the Cooperative Movement - and millowner extraordinaire

CONTENTS

Vocational Education: the academic/vocational dilemma
The New Vocationalism: national vocational qualifications
(NVQ's)
14-19 Learning : still getting it right!
Can "vocational education" be educational?
Mixed Messages

The Rise of Neo-Liberalism
The Attack on Public Services: New Public Management
Edubusiness:
    the commercialisation of education;
    the privatisation of education;
        Education Action Zones
        City Academies: "The Schools of the Future"
        Trust Schools: the 2005 White Paper
Comprehensivisation

Religious, Aristocratic, Business and Working-Class Interests
The State Interest and the Reproduction of the Socio-Economic
Order

Two Cultures
The Aristocratic Curriculum (Intrinsic):
    education for its own sake: subjects as bodies of knowledge

The Bourgeois Curriculum (Instrumental):
> Utilitarianism; Spencer's "Education for Survival".

A Person-centred Approach: Educating Interests

What is Education For?

The Material World:
> reproduction of the workforce; the examination system;
> changing needs of the economy;
> material deprivation
> the classroom as target-setting production line;
> consumerism; happiness and the therapeutic school

The democratic deficit

Democratising education:
> the school context: transparency, porosity, flexibility
> the curricular and pedagogic context:
> negotiation vs prescription
> common concerns as core of negotiated counter-curriculum;
>> the nature and organisation of work;
>> personal well-being:
>> society and citizenship

(a) Making Waves - or Ripples
> challenging the technical curriculum: "Opening Minds"
> challenging the IQ dogma : alternative pedagogies
> challenging the closed school: citizenship revisited; the student voice
> challenging fixed-term schooling: the "Learning Society"
> representative democracy: representing whose interests?
> participatory democracy : lessons from Porte Alegro

(b) Hegemonic Barriers:
> corporatism and consumerism
> technicism: psychometrics and neuroscience

(c) Where Now ?
> failures in delivery;
> internal contradictions: ideologies in conflict

the corporatist approach
the humanistic approach

TIMELINE

1798   First monitorial school
1802   Health and Morals of Apprentices Act
1819   Factory Act
1830   Whig government
1832   Reform Act: middle class enfranchised
1839   Committee of Council for Education established
1840   Tory Government
1846   Whig-liberal - radical coalition
1852   Department of Science and Art founded
1856   Education Department established
1861   Newcastle Commission Report ("sound and cheap" elementary
       education for the lower orders)
1862   "Revised Code" (for elementary schools)
1864   Clarendon Commission (public schools)
1867   Reform Act (male artisans enfranchised)
1868   Taunton Report (endowed schools)
1869   Elementary Education Act (Forster) school boards set up
1874   Tory government
1876   Schooling compulsory up to age of ten
1880   Liberal government
1884   *Reform Act (most remaining adult males enfranchised)*
1886   Tory Government
1892   Whig government
1893   School-leaving age raised to 11
1894   Tory government
1899   School-leaving age raised to 12
1902   Education Act (Balfour)
1906   Liberal government   Labour party founded Trade   unions
       recognised
1917   Secondary Schools Examination Council (SSEC) established
1918   Education Act (Fisher)
1926   First Labour government Hadow Report (on adolescents)
1930   Hadow Report (primary school children)

1935	Tory government
1938	Spens Report
1943	Norwood Report
1944	Education Act (Butler)
1945	Labour government
1947	School leaving age raised to fifteen
1951	Tory government General Certificate of Educa (GCE) launched
1962	Schools Council created Certificate Secondary Educa approved
1964	Labour government
1965	10/65 Comprehensive school plans requested
1970	Tory government
1972	School leaving age raised to sixteen
1974	Labour government
1976	The Great Debate
1979	Tory Government
1982	Schools council abolished TVEI introduced
1984	General Certificate of Education (GCSE) approved
1988	Education Reform Act National Curriculum Ofsted established
1997	Labour Government
2006	Education and Inspection Bill Trust schools
2010	Academies Bill

PREFACE

Given that mass education is a focal point of our enquiry into the present malaise afflicting our society, it is inevitable that the State, as the provider of that education, should come under scrutiny and pose some interesting questions. For example, is the State as monolithic and unchanging as it might appear to the casual observer. The size of the State is clearly a source of robust division along the political spectrum, with the political left wing favouring a Welfare State providing for the less fortunate in our society, and the right wing demanding a rollback of the State with minimal financial support for public services.

Another potentially contentious role of the state which will be exposed in the following narrative is that of "honest broker", mediating between competing interests and conflicting forces. This aspect will be of particular concern here. How, for example does the State mediate between the religious and the secular interest, or between the business and the environmental interest? How is the education interest perceived and protected ? Is it possible for "education" to be conceptualised in a neutral, philosophical context or will it constantly be redefined to meet material contingencies ?

In terms of the structure of the book, the educational role of the State is categorised in three phases:

as acting reactively to "subversive" working-class pressures, in order to protect the social order and deny poor children, by various legitimating devices, access to equality of educational opportunity;

by colonising the curriculum and exercising increasing control over the educational system in order to deny what are perceived as revolutionary forces within the teaching profession;

finally by selling out to corporate capitalism, whereby education becomes increasingly commodified and values changed from the intrinsic to the instrumental: in short with education being fundamentally redefined.

Such are the issues raised in the course of this enquiry. The method employed is that of the historic dynamic, where the impact of competing forces can be studied over time, and explanations given increased authenticity..

INTRODUCTION: Why and How I am Writing This Book

"When a population is distracted by trivia, when cultural life is redefined as a perpetual round of entertainments, when serious public conversation becomes a form of baby-talk, when, in short, a people becomes an audience and their public business a vaudeville act, then a nation finds itself at risk; culture-death is a clear possibility."
(Neil Postman, "Amusing Ourselves to Death" op cit)

I write this book from a growing concern at the creeping decline of our way of life and the gradual and dangerous disappearance of its civilising values (ironically at a time when the concept of the "Good Life" is being more widely discussed). Concern is now increasingly shared at the growth in this "social malaise", with different interpretations provided for the phenomenon and alternative explanations sought. For example, Wilkinson et al (R.J. Wilkinson and K. Pickett op cit. See also Department of Health Report (2010) "Fair Society and Healthy Lives") explore correlations between the following dysfunctional criteria:

income inequality, mental health, life expectancy, obesity, violence, imprisonment/punishment and social mobility.

From 50 "person-years" of international epidemiological studies, they come to the conclusion that the over-riding factor in all these dysfunctions is the extent of inequality in a society, suggesting a possible causal link. It is also worth adding at this point that, not only are we the most class-divided society in Europe, but this inequality is reproduced through a "public-school" system, where the top jobs go, not merely to old boys of these private schools but to the top 1%!

In contrast to such statistical analyses, this book offers a blow-by-blow historical account of this malaise, interpreted and broadly characterised in our adult population by:

> political apathy, economic illiteracy, environmental naïvety, individual materialism,
> over-reliance on the State, as well as a general cultural "dumbing down".

This malaise can also have serious and far-reaching national and global implications. For example, in the reaction to the potential threat of global warming, there are currently three prominent positions:

(i)   a culture of denial, where the claims by climate scientists are flatly rejected and climate change explained by natural processes;

(ii) the environmental movement, which seeks to curb carbon emissions in order to counter the effects of industrial activity. For example, the Green Party seeks an initial reduction of 10% in carbon emissions, leading to a 90% reduction from 1990 levels by 2030;

(iii) the Dark Mountain project, which argues that the economic system cannot be tamed without it collapsing, as it relies on perpetual growth. According to this, it is important therefore to think about how we are going to survive the inevitable collapse and learn from our experiences.

These alternatives require momentous decisions to be taken and demand an involved, educated and well-informed populace, capable of critical evaluation of evidence - not one which has been schooled along the lines described in the following chapters.

This adult population is also apparently indifferent to the steady erosion of our civil liberties and the extension of social control in the name of personal and national security, whilst subscribing to a society which is increasingly depressed, divided, unequal, undemocratic and corrupt - in short, a society lacking the solidarity, spirit and knowledge necessary to counter the awesome challenges lying in wait. (Although paradoxically - and giving some grounds for hope - well-publicised events supporting "good causes" can attract a motivated public in its millions, a paradox worth further study). In the light of all this, obvious questions suggest themselves: "How did it get like this?" and "What can be done about it ?" It is in attempting to answer these questions that the role of the State will be subjected to close scrutiny.

One evident starting-point in such an enquiry lies with the younger generation and their various formative experiences, formal and informal, in growing up. It would be reckless to expect direct cause-effect relationships in such complex cultural matters but, given that one of the principal aims of education is "preparation for adult life" (1) one line of enquiry is clearly the state education system itself . It is nothing short of extraordinary that enquiries by political parties into education seldom if ever depart from the superficial, leaving the roots unexplored, a matter which will be looked into later. But it should be borne in mind that the very concept of "mass state education" is contentious, with some arguing that working class people operate in an oral culture (see Bantock op cit) and that any attempt to provide formal education will prove to be counter-productive. As will become clear on reading this book a more generous and hopeful assumption of human potentialities is taken here.

The first thing that strikes one on looking at the work of the Education Department is its lack of vision or direction, as evidenced by a frenzy of contradictory and incoherent reforms, both in terms of general policies and detailed guidelines for teachers (2) As a recent Nuffield 14-19 Review points out, the rapid rate of new initiatives, targets and short-term measures fail to get at deep-seated problems and so lead to a general cultural impoverishment. (This frenzy of initiatives is paralleled by the frequent changes in the official title of the Department - changes which I have declined to accept, so that throughout the book I refer to the "Education Department", whilst the various aliases used over the years can be found in an Appendix)

Such an unacceptable situation can hardly be blamed on penury. State education now costs almost £1.2 billion per week and the amount spent per pupil has increased by 48% in the past decade. There are also 35,000 more teachers than ten years ago, giving a total of three-quarters of a million workers in schools today, including assistants. The public naturally demands results from such investment, and the government misses no opportunity of trumpeting the success of its educational reforms, invariably using selective test and examination results as the sine qua non for educational success, as well as generously massaging statistics where relevant.

So let us use some different criteria to assess the efficacy of the system:

- a recent poll of over 400 children in 10 countries has revealed that in terms of international awareness British 11-16 year-olds came bottom with a ranking of 2.17 out of a score of 1 to 7;

- in the past three years, according to the Programme for International Student Assessment, England has fallen from ninth to nineteenth in terms of pupils' attainment in mathematics - behind Liechtenstein and Iceland;
- whereas in 2001, England ranked third in the Progress in International Reading Literacy Study (Pirls) by 2006 it had slumped to 19th.
- nearly 230,000 pupils are classified as persistent absentees, missing more than 20% of school, with a hardcore of truants amounting to 6% of the school population;
- 15,000 15-16 year-olds fail to register for their final year, whilst 70 000 pupils go missing from GCSE examinations;
- more than a quarter of 16-18year olds are neither in education nor training (a group awarded its own acronym NEET).

The government's response to this problem, as usual, is punitive rather than constructive. Initially, it spent £900 million on anti-truanting measures, including using the police force to round up roving truants, but to very little effect. So the police have finally called it a day and pulled out of the scheme. Now the government proposes to punish the parents of hard-line truants with up to a 3-month prison sentence or a £2500 fine. The implications are clear: as far as the government is concerned, educational success is measured by examination certificates based upon an academic curriculum; and a lack of commitment is blamed on the student (and is regarded as a punishable offence) rather than an occasion for self-examination on the part of those designing and administering the curriculum. In short, instead of focussing upon such aspects as "Love of Learning " it remains with the "Strength through Suffering" school of thought.

So much for cold statistics. What of the human dimension? There are doubtless some teachers struggling to survive who are not sorry to see truanting on the scale described above. According to a new report by the teachers' union NASUWT, which for two years followed 75 newly - qualified teachers ("the most talented generation of trainees ever", according to the Training and Development Agency) teachers face a daily routine of verbal abuse with little support from management. One teacher who had had enough said:

> *"I no longer have the confidence to stand in front of a class. I would love to teach – however this job is 25% teaching, 75% crowd control"*

Another who was still fighting the good fight described one incident to the researchers

> *"A child decided he did not like me or Science, ran around the room verbally abusing me, climbed under the table and ripped his book up, tried to snatch his report, then attempted to escape the classroom through the window."*

The government's response? "Actual improvements can only happen at the front line". In other words, that's the teachers' problem.

At least delinquent truanting children are unlikely to be worried by the prospect of examinations. Not so those earnest students concerned to do well. A parent, Jenni Russell, provides a personal example:

> *"In the Spring of this year, my diligent 16-year old came back from school to tell me she was about to study the Vietnam war for her GCSE. 'Good' I said enthusiastically, 'I've got some interesting books you could read'. Her eyes widened in alarm. 'I think I should leave that until after the exam, because you know that stuff you gave me on human rights? Well, I did really badly on that paper in the mocks, cos my teacher said I'd put in a lot of irrelevant stuff.' Examination boards freely admit that people who know more than the syllabus demands find it harder to do well...An English teacher who has been teaching for two decades and who has been responsible for a sharp rise in exam passes since she joined her comprehensive says 'At GCSE our children go into exams incredibly well-prepared but by God are they bored"* (3)

It is not always just a matter of boredom. There is evidence, for example, that high-achieving girls in top schools are increasingly prone to emotional distress as they try to outperform their peers in a highly competitive environment – particularly if being pushed by ambitious parents.

These children - allegedly the most tested in the world - are coming towards the end of a school career which has seen them exposed to continual quantitative assessment. From the moment of entry into the system, a child is subject to "foundation stage profiling" with 13 early learning goals, ranging from "dispositions and attitudes" to "emotional and creative development". At the request of the Qualifications and Curriculum Authority (QCA) numerical scales were devised and so far, over the 13 early learning goals, girls have been shown to be +12 or 13% points ahead of boys. Well done, girls! Even Ofsted, the government's inspection body, is highly critical of the scheme, claiming that it is a waste of teachers' time, is too complicated for parents to understand and does not prepare children for Year 1.

No matter. SATS (standard attainment tests) have been given to children at the ages of 7,11 and (currently) 14, with the government, in the face of widespread criticism, repeatedly expressing its determination that, in some form or other, they are here to stay. It does not take a genius to work out that, contrary to empty government rhetoric, tests and examinations lead the curriculum, rather than the other way round, with teachers teaching to the tests, rather than educating their pupils. An interesting comment is made by the head of an independent school from his experiences of interviewing children from the state sector for admission to his school:

> *"The very principle militates against educating children. Youngsters are being prepared to pass SATS. Each December we interview youngsters seeking admission at 11. My heart bleeds as I hear what has been chopped from their curriculum in Year 6...it's commonplace to hear youngsters who are being taught no art, music, geography, history or technology." (4)*

Further consequences of the government's obsession with quantitative testing are spelt out by John White, president of the National Association of Headteachers :

> *"The current system doesn't recognise the achievements of less academic children and often turns them off education...The government has taken the joy out of teaching and the joy out of education." (5)*

The "student voice" has been silent until now but recently attempts have made by, for example, Ofsted and the Joint Area Review, to learn something of pupil opinion. The findings include the following:

> 4/5 would like to learn about jobs and working life and for lessons to be fun and interesting;

1/4 are worried about bullying;
1/3 cite examinations as their greatest stress factor. (6)

It is clear from this, and other evidence, that there is considerable pupil alienation in our schools - making the idea of lifelong learning little more than a fantasy. And the curriculum on offer in our schools, apart from turning children off education, does little to prepare them for the daunting challenges facing them in the adult world.

What of the wider social context? Recent research indicates that whatever social mobility there was in a system dominated by the public schools has now virtually dried up: Britain along with the USA are at the bottom of the league of advanced countries in terms of social mobility (the Scandinavian countries are at the top). In other words the life chances of children in this country depend largely on the social class into which they are born. In this respect Britain is as socially divided as it was in the nineteenth century, with children of the upper classes gaining the social and educational advantages of attending public schools and middle classes shopping around for the "best" state schools and even moving house or acquiring a religion in order to qualify for access.. On the other hand, poor children attend so-called "sink" schools, fail in terms of school criteria and retain the family position at the bottom of the pile. In this way is the social hierarchy maintained. So education, insofar as it is seen as an agent for providing equal opportunities, is clearly failing.

Such problems are often dismissed and rationalised away as "facts of life"; for example, that middle class genes are superior to those of the working class. It is even possible from this standpoint to blame the dysfunctional nature of our education upon the fact that we are offering working-class children the wrong type of education and attempting to turn sows' ears into silk purses. But a more optimistic view of children's potential capabilities is taken here:

> *"We begin with the hypothesis that any subject can be taught effectively in some intellectually honest way to any child at any stage of development. It is a bold hypothesis and an essential one in thinking about the nature of the curriculum. No evidence exists to contradict it; considerable evidence is being amassed which supports it".*
>
> *(Jerome Bruner: "The Process of Education" op cit)*

But whatever one's assumptions, there is no hiding the fact that the education system is failing our children, and we need to ask the question once again: "Why is it like this?". But various obstacles stand in the way of our understanding, not least an unquestioning belief in the sanctity of the curriculum and its associated pedagogy and evaluative processes. It is therefore necessary to undermine these beliefs by a process of "problematisation". For example, by taking the curriculum as problematic and showing that, instead of school knowledge being superior, absolute, and unchanging, it takes on this appearance because of its instant a-historical synchronic ("snapshot") quality . To destroy this illusion, it is necessary to take a diachronic ("time-lapse") approach, in order to explore the historical dynamic of mass schooling since its inception, exposing those forces which, since the beginning of the nineteenth century, have shaped - and continue to shape - the education system : not only in terms of the form and nature of the school curriculum and access to it, but even in terms of the definition of education. Once the education system has been made problematic in this way, and the various policies and vested interests within a conflict model of society made explicit, it is possible to make more sense of the educational changes taking place today and to appreciate their wider significance.

For example, the education interest and the state interest have just collided with the publication of a highly critical independent 3-year enquiry ("The Cambridge Primary School Review") involving 31 interim reports and 820 written submissions. It is particularly critical of the extreme centralisation of education and its micro-management, leading to the deprofessionalisation of teachers and the neglect of the non-core curriculum. It recommends delaying the entry of children into the formal curriculum until the age of 6 and the replacement of SAT's with teacher assessment. The Education Department, by way of anticipation, set up its own in-house enquiry ("The Jim Rose Review"). Whilst this is to some extent a humane document, loosening the strangle - hold of subject teaching, it does not question the fundamental values and political interests underpinning the present system. But it does enable the government to claim that it is putting in place some of the recommended reforms, as well as piloting a "school report card" scheme. Its other responses are unworthy of a government department, describing the suggested abolition of SAT's as "completely counter-productive" and dismissing other suggestions as "out-of- date" and a "backward step", even proposing that children should enter school in the September after their fourth birthday (thus failing to take up the challenge posed by "top-of–the league" Finnish schools, where formal education begins at 7, and where the official policy is "trust the teacher"). But along comes a new government with a different ideology and the Jim Rose Review is abandoned. C'est la vie!

Such are the tensions existing between interested parties to the education system which it is one of the tasks of this narrative to reveal.

Shape is given to this enquiry in various ways. As the narrative has unfolded, the role of the State has become the major part of the enquiry, and it has been possible to identify three major phases (a) the State on the back foot conceding as little as possible to working-class demands (b) the State dominant, taking over complete control of the curriculum and its appendages, and (c) selling out to corporate capitalism. The final section of the book is reserved for challenges to the resultant status quo.

To provide further shape, "interest" is taken as a focussing concept, whilst "curriculum" is conceptualised as technical, practical or emancipatory (7). To avoid the woolliness surrounding much educational discourse, the clear primary educational focus here is upon the development of personal and moral autonomy in a democratic context, together with its many practical implications - in short, by making the focus the education of the "whole person". There is nothing particularly original in this conception : the Czech monk and educationist Comenius was writing the following, three and a half centuries ago:

> *"Our first wish is that all men should be educated fully to full humanity ..... young and old, rich and poor, men and women…….in a word, all those whose fate it is to be born human beings……Our second wish is that all men should be wholly educated in all things which perfect human nature". (The Great Didactic, 1657)*

If this was no more than wishful thinking at the time on the part of Comenius, it at least draws attention to the question of whose view of education prevails, and why it should be so, a question which this book seeks to answer.

In the course of exploring educational developments in the last two centuries, I have attempted to provide concrete examples of the abstractions pervading educational discourse and to present a human face to historic events, in order to avoid what might otherwise appear to be a wholly deterministic and remote account. In similar vein I conclude by considering those "real" practical curriculum initiatives which promise to meet some of the problems summarised above, whilst at the same time challenging the prevailing hegemony.

I have written this book with the general reader as well as the specialist very much in mind. I have therefore kept it as brief and jargon-free as possible, and avoided the historical minutiae which might detract from the main thrust of the book. I have also attempted to introduce some humanity into what otherwise might be a sterile account by allowing the actors at the centre of the drama to speak for themselves. The overall approach, then, is broad brush rather than scribe's quill and whilst accepting the limitations of such an approach, I make no apology for it. I see the overwhelming priority as helping the public gain some understanding of what is happening to our education system, rather than engaging in scholarly discourse. For those wishing to follow up events and arguments in more detail I have provided extensive notes, references and bibliography.

Finally, I wish to acknowledge the sterling efforts of those unappreciated teachers who, despite the oppressive measures of Ofsted and the incoherent bureaucracy of the DfES have maintained their sense of mission to educate the children in their charge. I also wish to acknowledge my debt to all those who have attempted - not always successfully - to advance my education: colleagues, students and authors. Among the latter, I owe a special debt of gratitude to Brian Simon for bringing educational history alive for me through his perceptive and provocative analyses. And I am particularly indebted to Robin Watkins MA for his enthusiastic help with this project, without whose support this book would never have reached the press . It would be remiss of me not to mention the splendid library facilities of Suffolk County Council, and the excellent service provided by the Halesworth branch. It remains to sincerely thank my wife Christine and daughter Francesca for their patience and technical help in producing this book.

REFERENCES

1. The aim "preparation for adult life" illustrates the shortcomings of some of the guidelines emanating from the Education Department . Without any attempt to spell out in detail what "adult life" implies, it is little more than a slogan, providing little help to the teacher in the classroom.

2. The frenzy of initiatives from the current Education Minister, for example, reveal an ambivalent attitude towards the role of the teacher – how much control should be imposed and much autonomy allowed. Whilst on the one hand a "licence to teach" will involve 5-yearly checks, the flagship national Literacy and Numeracy strategies are to be abolished, along with SAT's for 14- year olds - the one initiative implying firm central control and the other an increasing tolerance of personal and professional judgement. Other initiatives from a busy and ambitious Minister provided with a safe seat, include the replacing of league tables by report cards and specification of the text books to be used. The fact that this particular Minister was educated privately and trained as an economist and has no practical experience of classroom teaching, raises the important issue of the source of authority for such ministerial decisions.

3. Guardian, August 25 2005

4. Lancashire Evening Telegraph Sept 16 2005

5. The Times, 20 September 2005

6. See, for example, Guardian November 16, 2007

7. After Habermas. The rough criteria are as follows:

technical : objective positive knowledge; rule-following; external control;
practical : subjective, interpretive knowledge; personal understanding and judgment;
emancipatory: critical; empowering. (See S. Grundy op cit)

PART ONE

THE RE–ACTIVE STATE : DEFENDING THE SOCIAL ORDER

AND KEEPING THE WORKING-CLASS IN ITS PLACE

The following chapters show how the State staged a series of tactical retreats in the face of working-class demands for "Equality of Educational Opportunity" in order to defend emerging class and economic divisions, culminating in both a tripartite secondary education system and fudged comprehensivation.

CHAPTER ONE

THE CONTEXT OF MASS SCHOOLING: REVOLUTION AND SOCIAL UNREST

*"The greatest improvement in the productive powers of labour…
seem to have been the effects of the Division of Labour"
(Adam Smith)*

*Political, Scientific, Ideological, and Industrial Revolutions
The Enlightenment : Authority under Threat
The Factory System and the Rise of Industrial Capitalism
Urbanisation and the Breakdown of the Social Fabric
The "godless poor"; religious monitorial schools to the rescue;
£20,000 from the State*

In order to understand the significance of the events described in subsequent chapters, it is necessary to appreciate the social, political and economic context in which these events have taken place. Whilst this is the purpose of this chapter, it should be borne in mind that there are no absolute and clear-cut starting- points for historical narratives; for example, attempts had been made to provide schooling for the poor well before the initiatives described here.

Scientific Revolution and the Enlightenment

This attempt to explain how and why the school curriculum acquired its present form begins at the turn of the nineteenth century, although its roots lie further back in history. The social order of ruling class and labouring poor had been maintained by an Establishment made up of a Parliament of landed gentry (Tories and Whigs) and the Anglican Church. Whilst a sovereign Parliament legislated, the Anglican Church legitimated, giving divine authority to man-made arrangements:

"the rich man in his castle,
the poor man at his gate,
He made them high and lowly,
and ordered their estate."

But this status quo of an apparently stable and unchanging way of life was beginning to undergo profound challenges, traceable back to the Scientific Revolution of the seventeenth century. This Revolution, by advocating an empirical experimental method in the sciences backed up by careful observation in order to discover the laws of nature, demanded that truth be based upon reason rather than faith, turning the prevailing Aristotelian orthodoxy on its head, and challenging the very basis of religious belief.. (1)

A conflict with the Church was now inevitable and it was provided on the continent both by the dramatic confrontation between Galileo and the Vatican, and by the Enlightenment, whose chief characteristics were anti - clericism and a belief in natural and moral laws to be revealed through science. These ideas were given wide dissemination through the multi-volume Encyclopedie ("A Reasoned Dictionary of the Sciences, Arts and Trades") which had, among its contributors, Voltaire (1694-1778) who was not only the chief continental agent for promoting British empiricism, but also a savage satirist, reserving most of his venom for the Catholic Church and the monarchy. (2) In a letter to Frederick the Great, for instance, he wrote:

"Christianity is the most ridiculous, the most absurd and
bloody religion that has ever infected the world",

whilst for his public satires, he spent time in the Bastille.

It is important at this point to remind ourselves, in view of the fact that we are here examining the impact of various forces upon the course of mass schooling, that mass schooling did not enter an ideological vacuum. For instance the Enlightenment had a profound effect upon the educational ideas of the French philosopher Rousseau (1712-78), who in turn was influenced by the ideas of the philosophers Plato and Locke. Reacting vigorously against Catholic doctrinal instruction, especially of the catechism, he put forward a counter-approach based upon the natural unfolding of the child's faculties in the sequence "sensation-memory-understanding", with the child discovering from experience and with minimal intervention from the tutor. In other words, Rousseau's was a developmental approach and provided yet another model of education available to the State in the period with which we are concerned.

By now, a spirit of subversion was also becoming widespread. In this country, Thomas Paine (1737-1809) was, through his writings, to have a massive influence on the working class movement throughout the nineteenth century. His demands included the liberation of the poor from their misery by creating a democratic society. And in his "Rights of Man" he proposed an enlightened plan for the abolition of poor-rates, for financial assistance and for educating poor children:

> *"By the operation of this plan, the poor laws, those instruments of civil torture, will be superseded. The hearts of the humane will (no longer) be shocked by ragged and hungry children and persons of seventy and eighty begging for bread. The dying poor will not be dragged from parish to parish…Ye who sit in ease…and who say to themselves 'Are we not well off?' have ye thought of these things?" (3)*

Paine's conception of democracy relied upon a genuine representation of the people, denying the hereditary principle and with it the monarchy. So popular had Paine's writings become (the "Rights of Man" had sold between one and two hundred thousand copies in its first three years at a cost of 3s. per copy) that they were celebrated in a parody of the national anthem:

> *"God save great Thomas Paine*
> *His 'Rights of Man' explain*
> *To every soul*
> *He makes the blind to see*
> *What dupes and slaves they be*
> *And points out liberty*
> *From pole to pole"*

But Paine had not finished writing his revolutionary tracts. Emigrating from England in 1774, he wrote a pamphlet "Common Sense" in which he advocated both independence for the American colonies and a republican state. He was clearly a dangerous man, so it was not surprising that on his return to England, he faced a charge of treason. Fleeing to France, he was imprisoned by the bourgeois masters of the French Revolution. Whilst in prison, he wrote his "Age of Reason" in which he launched a bitter attack on organised religion from his perspective of a Deist (that is, a person whose belief in God is based in reason rather than divine revelation). As far as Paine was concerned, bishops were toadies of tyrants, and churches were set up both to terrify and enslave mankind and monopolise power and profit. He went on:

> *"the person they call Jesus Christ, begotten they say by a ghost which they call holy, on the body of a woman they call a virgin...Were any girl that is now with child to say that she was gotten with a child by a ghost, and an angel told her so, would she be believed ?" (4)*

It was by such polemic that Paine made enemies of the Church as well as the State. But in so doing he brought together various strands of radical thought which, allied with the popular response throughout the country, posed a major threat to State and Church.

The Ideological and Industrial Revolutions

But other - even more potent - threats to the established order were developing, both ideological and industrial. The former was given momentum - if not actually launched - by Adam Smith in 1776 with his "Wealth of Nations", which advocated the division of labour in a laissez-faire economy motivated by self-interest. Thus was a moral economy, with regulations based upon equity, law and tradition giving fair prices, just wages and customary rights, replaced by a political economy. Smith's message was, however, generally optimistic: he predicted a progressive economy and continuing increase in wealth, leading to an increase in the happiness and comfort of the lower orders.

On the other hand, Malthus' message in his 1798 "Essay on Populations" was much more ominous. Pointing out that whilst population increased geometrically, the food supply only increased arithmetically, he argued – with the force of "natural laws" behind him - that there would be no substantial material progress (especially as the growth in manufacturing would lead to a decline in the number of workers on the land and hence a fall in agricultural productivity) and that all the poor could look forward to was a future of misery and vice.

These two opposing versions of the new political economy provided the arena for contested policies both on the Poor Laws and the provision of state schooling. Malthussianism claimed that population could be held to the level of the food supply only by preventive measures, such as delayed marriage, or "positively" by starvation and war. The logical outcome was thus the total abolition of the Poor Law, in sharp opposition to the provision of the necessities of life for those previously seen as the "holy poor". These arguments and counter-arguments would underpin the political struggles outlined in future chapters.

It has been plausibly argued in very broad terms that this period represented a transition from an eotechnic – based on wood, wind and water - to a paleotechnic civilisation - based upon iron, steam and fossil fuel. This latter civilisation reflects the increasing confidence of man to alter his environment by technical means, flowing from the scientific revolution and the possibility of applying scientific knowledge to industrial problems. The main motive force behind this Industrial Revolution was provided by the steam-engine and because of this and the insights it provides into this industrial culture and the future both of children's schooling and technical education, I will provide a little detail about its development.

The first point to make is that the development of the steam - engine was essentially progressive, building on the work of others, in response to serious social and technical problems. For example, James Watt himself built upon the ideas of the blacksmith Newcomen, who had worked on the pressing problem of the flooding of Cornish tin mines in developing his atmospheric steam - engine. But because the hot cylinder of the Newcomen engine had to be repeatedly cooled to condense the steam (in order to create the vacuum necessary for atmospheric pressure to drive a piston) the system had very low efficiency. In 1763, James Watt, a trained instrument-maker, was given the task of repairing a model Newcomen engine belonging to Glasgow University. Not only did Watt repair the model but he familiarised himself with the principles underlying it. He recalls walking across the Green in Glasgow in the spring of 1765:

> "I was thinking upon the engine when the idea came into
> my mind that as steam was an elastic body it would rush

into a vacuum and if a communication was made between the cylinder and an exhausted vessel, it would rush into it and might be there condensed without cooling the cylinder...I had not walked further than the golf-house when the whole thing was arranged in my mind". (5)

Watt was regarded as the first industrial entrepreneur, but he was soon followed by others. The invention of an efficient source of power led to a remarkable and profound transformation of the industrial landscape (in a process akin to "adaptive radiation" in the evolution of living forms). Together with Matthew Boulton, Watt developed the steam-engine in order to power cotton mills. Textile machinery was quickly developed for use in these mills to take advantage of this new source of power and to speed up the process of spinning and weaving: for example, Hargreaves' spinning jenny, Arkwright's water-frame and Crompton's mule (so-called because it was a hybrid of the other two). Watt's steam-engine was also adapted to provide the air-blast in the blast furnace, improving the quality of the iron and enabling an iron railroad to be built to accommodate Trevithick's steam tramway - replacing horse-drawn carriages and shortly to be followed by Stevenson's famous "Rocket". A canal system was also being developed, part of a coherent transport system involving Macadam's road improvement. No longer was it necessary for mills to be built next to running water; coal for steam - engines could be readily transported to where it was required. (6) In short, the ramifications of Watt's invention were immense, transforming the industrial landscape and culture of this country. There were also important educational implications arising from the work of these industrial entrepreneurs. They were essentially practical men, and were seen as such by businessmen, who consequently placed less emphasis upon education (and children's schooling). The term "practical", in the days before sophisticated divisions of labour, did not exclude the theoretical (as witness the contribution Watt made to the caloric theory of heat in his work on steam-engines). In other words, there was - within the same person - a fruitful integration of theory and practice. But with the capitalist division of labour accompanying industrialisation, came a separation of what was conceptualised as mental and manual labour, with profound implications for education, as we shall see in subsequent chapters.

The Factory System and the Rise of Industrial Capitalism

The inventions of the Industrial Revolution enabled vital components of production to be brought together into a powerful economic unit. The efficiency and mobility of steam-power enabled several textile machines as well as the workforce to be sited under the same roof in factories. Large amounts of capital were of course required to underpin this enterprise. Fortunately vast amounts had been accumulated in the previous century from the rapid growth in overseas trade and from slavery, leading to the emergence of a new bourgeois class. Factory owners were thus able to finance both the building works, expensive machinery and raw material. Apart from ownership of the product, they now had complete control over the worker's space and time through constant surveillance.

The cultural significance of this change in the relations of production from a feudal to a capitalist system and to the concept of mass education, is hard to overestimate. (7) There was now a hierarchical separation of mental and manual labour (conception and execution) with manual workers performing the same routine task in what was now a process of mass production, and with surplus labour appearing as profit. Instead of the craftsman having control over his working procedures, he was now alienated from both them and the product of his work. (In truth, the transformation was not as complete or clearcut as this: managers were intermediate in the hierarchy between master and operative, and some craftsmen were still required to maintain and repair machinery.) The principle of competition also replaced previous regulatory processes, with the result that manufacturers were always on the lookout for cheap labour, which often meant competition with schools for child labour. In summary, then, the new but rapidly expanding capitalist system had the following characteristics:

- workers sited under one roof, subject to constant surveillance and control;
- a hierarchical separation of routine mechanised operations;
- a competitive ethos in the search for maximum profit by lengthening the working day and reducing wages.

Social Consequences of Capitalism: the Working Class and Urbanisation

Apart from the technical changes outlined above there was also a profound social transformation echoing the relations of production. Capitalism could not exist without the availability of workers to exploit and this exploitation provided the workers with a means of identification. In other words, a working class was steadily emerging in place of the status system which had existed hitherto, in opposition to a developing middle class of factory owners, financiers and employers. Factories were being concentrated in the economically most advantageous areas in terms of production and distribution, with an inevitable concentration of the workforce. This migration of workers to industrial towns and the return of soldiers from the French wars, together with the rapid growth of the national population (over 1% annual growth) led to the phenomenon of urbanisation, with several important consequences. For example, the bringing together of workers into close proximity, as opposed to their previous dispersal throughout the countryside, enabled them, through a recognition of common interests, to develop into a more cohesive and coherent working class.

PERCEPTIONS OF CAPITALISM : the Academic and the Factory-worker

Andrew Ure, professor of chemistry and natural philosophy at Anderson College, Glasgow, following his travels around factory districts:

> "The blessings which physico-mechanical science has bestowed upon society has been dwelt too little on, while on the one hand it has been accused of lending itself to the rich capitalists as an instrument for harassing the poor and of extracting from the operative an accelerated rate of work… in the factory the driving force leaves the attendant nearly nothing at all to do, certainly no muscular fatigue to sustain, while it procures for him good unfailing wages; whereas the non-factory worker having everything to execute by muscular exertion, makes in consequence innumerable short pauses and earns proportionally low wages." (8)

John Fielden, inheritor of a cotton-spinning factory:

> "As I have been personally involved in the operations of factory labour for forty years…my experiences teach me to scoff at those who speak of labour in factories as 'very light'…I well know from my own experiences that the labour now undergone in the factories is much greater than it used to be. The

curse of the factory system and the avarice of masters has prompted many to extract more labour from their hands than by nature they were fitted to perform…A Dr. Ure, it now seems, is trying not to get the manufacturers down to ten hours a day but to lengthen the period to fifteen or sixteen hours a day, by telling us that some of our competitors work that long" (9)

But urbanisation, apart from enabling workers to associate more easily, had other consequences - not least for poor children. The environment was inevitably degraded by the concentration of coal-burning energy systems and their associated factories. Whilst this degradation offended the poetic nostalgia for an imagined pastoral Golden Age ("dark, Satanic mills ") there were more serious effects. In the absence of building codes, jerry - built tenements and cottages were concentrated in monotonous rows without adequate sanitation. A sanitary inspector, Edwin Chadwick, gives a "flavour" of the prevailing conditions:

> *"The various forms of epidemic (are) propagated chiefly…*
> *by decomposing animal and vegetable substances…close*
> *and overcrowded conditions prevail among the population*
> *in every part of the kingdom…the formation of all habits of*
> *cleanliness is obstructed by defective supplies of water…*
> *it appears that the greatest proportion of deaths occurred*
> *from the above specified and removable causes" (10)*

Dr. James Kay, who under the name of Kaye-Shuttleworth was to become an important figure in nineteenth century mass schooling, develops the picture from a nutritional point of view:

> *"physical energies are exhausted by incessant toil and*
> *imperfect nutrition….domestic economy is neglected,*
> *domestic comforts are unknown. A meal of the coarsest*
> *food is prepared with heedless haste and devoured with*
> *equal precipitation. Home has no other relation to him*
> *than that of shelter….from which he is glad to escape…*
> *he sinks into sensual sloth or revels in more degrading*
> *licentiousness" (11)*

It is easy to regard the working-class as homogeneous. The Manchester mill-owner (and co-worker with Karl Marx) Friedrich Engels, gives a more differentiated picture:

> *"The better-paid workers...have good food...meat daily and bacon and cheese for supper...descending gradually... until on the lowest rung of the ladder, among the Irish, potatoes form the sole food. All this presupposes that the workman has work. When he has none he eats what is given to him or what he can beg or steal."(12)*

But apart from the starving unemployed stealing food in order to survive, there was the sharp rise in serious crime associated with rapid urbanisation and the breakdown of communities. In the 50 years from 1750 to 1800, the population is estimated to have grown from eleven to sixteen million, whilst crime quadrupled. The political climate was extremely volatile, with revolutionary fervour on the continent. And many workers including the Luddites turned destructively upon the machinery they had come to hate. The Prime Minister, Spencer Perceval, was assassinated and there were rumours of plots to kill the entire government. The State's response was swift and repressive: it introduced the Bloody Code, by which over 200 crimes were punishable by death. It was left to the other members of the Establishment, the Church, to adopt a more constructive approach and to respond to demands for "gentling the masses" by introducing a system of mass schooling.

Mass schooling of the working-class: the "godless poor"

Religious charity schools for the poor had been in existence for some time, the best known being those run by the Society for the Promotion of Christian Knowledge (SPCK) to spread Christianity among the "godless poor" through the rote learning of the Book of Common Prayer, the Psalms and the Anglican catechism. But friction between the Anglicans and the philanthropists on the boards led to their eventual decline. In any case, many working-class parents declined to accept charity and preferred to pay a few pence per week to private establishments such as Dame schools, which often involved little more than child-minding in an old woman's house, until the child, often as young as seven, went to work in a local factory. The poet George Crabbe immortalised Dame schools in verse:

> *"Yet one there is, that small regard to rule*
> *Or study pays, and still is deemed a school;*
> *That where a deaf, poor, patient widow sits*

And awes some thirty infants as she knits-
Infants of humble, busy wives, who pay
Some trifling price for freedom through the day" (13)

A Dame School

Sunday schools provided another opportunity for poor children to obtain some schooling. These were often provided, not by the Anglican Church, but by Methodists and other Dissenters. Freed from dominance by the Establishment, they became both integrated into and a focus for the working-class community, by providing opportunities for amateur operatics and dramatics, bring-and-buy sales and bazaars. As far as the curriculum of such schools was concerned, the emphasis was upon reading, possibly writing and religious instruction. A library was often provided, where the books could range from "Robinson Crusoe" to "Paradise Lost". They were even credited with providing a literate proletariat. Of course, in the absence of a national system and the presence of inspectors, quality in all schools at this time could vary widely.

Ragged schools, as the name implies, were provided for the poorest of the poor, a situation described by the Reverend William Gurney in evidence to a Parliamentary Committee in 1816:

> *"We found there were a great many who did not go to any*
> *school, the reason assigned in some measure for it was*

their ragged condition and their being unfit, from their great poverty, to appear decently at any school...But there are a great many mendicants in our parish and the more children they have the more success they meet with in begging...We tried the experiment (of) giving clothes to some of the most ragged in order to bring them decent to school; they appeared for one Sunday or two, and then disappeared and the clothes disappeared also". (14)

Ragged schools were charitable institutions set up to provide free schooling for destitute children. At one point there were about 190 such schools with 20,000 children. They provided a very elementary education, together with various social (and progressive) welfare activities like running penny banks (!) and operating soup kitchens and clothing clubs. Not qualifying for government grants, ragged schools declined, particularly after the state provision of schooling.

Monitorial Church Schools (pupil/teacher ratio 1000/1)

It is clear from the above that schooling for the poor was very patchy and of uneven quality. And some Sunday schools had been essentially taken over by working-class radicals and had developed subversive tendencies. It was therefore necessary, with urbanisation and the accompanying social disorder, that the Church - under repeated attack from radicals following in the tradition of Voltaire and Thomas Paine - should seek both to re-establish its authority and instil some Christian qualities into these unruly working-class children.

"Cometh the hour, cometh the man" - in this case two men, of differing Christian persuasions: Andrew Bell, an Anglican clergyman, and Joseph Lancaster, a Quaker. Both Bell and Lancaster introduced – apparently independently – a wonderfully economical solution to the problem of mass schooling in tune with the capitalist ethos of the times. It became known as the monitorial system, whereby older boys were trained to teach the younger. In 1798 the Quaker Lancaster opened a school in Southwark, using this basic principle. He received financial support from the Royal Lancasterian Society (subsequently the British and Foreign School Society) whilst the Anglican Bell was financed by the National Society for Promoting the Education of the Poor in the Principles of the Established

Church. These monitorial schools can be seen as the first examples of faith-based education, providing a contentious precedent for the future.

But perhaps the most obvious departure from previous schools was that instruction in the monitorial system was provided in one enormous room, sometimes containing up to a thousand children, largely boys, under the scrutiny of a single schoolmaster. The brighter pupils were made monitors, coming to school early so that they could receive instruction from the schoolmaster, which they, in turn, passed on to groups of ten children, seated round long desks. The overt curriculum was confined to reading, writing (copying letters first in sand and then on slates) and arithmetic – with possibly needlework for girls. It is important to appreciate that in pre-capitalist society, knowledge for working people was tacit (unwritten and implicit) and was transmitted experientially, either formally through apprenticeships or informally by working alongside others, in the fields or the home. Now children in monitorial schools were confronted with written and explicit knowledge based upon the philosophy of NeoPlatonism (a synthesis of Platonic and Christian thought, glorifying the "Word"). Written propositional knowledge, often learnt by rote, was to be the basis for formal education and, together with the invention of the text-book, has persisted up to the present day, whether in public/private or state schools.

What was it like to be at the receiving end of this mass production system? One former pupil recalls his experiences:

> "Right up the school through all the six standards…you did almost nothing except reading, writing and arithmetic. What a noise there used to be! Several children would be reading aloud, teachers scolding, infants reciting, all waxing louder until the master rang the bell on his desk and the noise slid down to a lower note and less volume. Reading was worst. Sums you did at least write on your own slate, whereas you might wait the whole half hour of a reading lesson while boys and girls who could not read stuck at every word. If you took your finger from the word that was being read, you were punished by staying in when others went home. To remain in school was the thing above all others that the children did not want to do." (15)

There was also a covert curriculum at work here. Children were being familiarised with the future demands of a hierarchical industrial system, working in large groups and following rules, such as accepting the authority of those above and working to the clock. Insofar as the reading material was Biblical, children were also learning the principles of Christianity and (theoretically) acquiring desirable moral traits, including the Protestant work ethic. At a deeper level, they were also probably learning that important knowledge was written, handed down from above, to be learned by rote and of little relevance to their everyday lives.

It is a measure of the growing pervasiveness of a capitalist culture that the monitorial system should reflect the factory system, with its command structure, its division of labour, its strict rule - following and its economic efficiency. It was widely applauded by politicians and industrialists alike on the grounds of its systematisation of labour applied to intellectual purposes, and its cheapness. In other words it was recognised as a piece of social machinery of its time, with the potential to make a considerable contribution to the new capitalist system. The monitorial system has even been hailed as the English elementary school of the nineteenth century.

But under the surface there was bitter rivalry between the Quaker Lancaster and the Anglican Bell camps, which eventually erupted in accusations of plagiarism against Lancaster and a charge that his schools were a menace to Christian education. Now with the Anglican Church solidly behind it, Bell's National Society went from strength to strength, absorbing the remaining SPCK schools and expanding from 52 schools (8620 pupils) in 1812 to 3670 schools (346,000 pupils) in 1830. Mass education - voluntary and Anglican - was now a reality, but with this massive expansion came the question of who should meet the rising costs.

The Role of the State: £20,000 to the monitorial schools

The State had sought to maintain stability and the social order through the repressive measures described above. Now it was faced with the thorny question of whether it should subsidise voluntary schooling. State involvement in education is an issue which divides political right and left to the present day with, on the one hand, a laissez-faire "hands - off" policy of non-State intervention and, on the other, the need for social control. There was considerable hostility in Parliament, then, to any proposals that the State should finance in any way education of the masses. There was also hostility from the Anglican Church, fearful of losing its monopoly over mass schooling, as well as from those mill-owners who wanted children to be in their factories and not in schools. There was even the remarkable objection (given the stunted curriculum of the monitorial school) that an educated populace could pose a threat to the social order. For example, in a Commons debate, one member gave voice to these fears:

> *"However specious in theory, the project might be of giving education to the labouring classes of the poor, it would be prejudicial to their morals and happiness; it would teach them to despise their lot in life; it would enable them to read seditious pamphlets, vicious books and publications against Christianity; it would render them insolent to their superiors". (16)*

Children of the Industrial Revolution

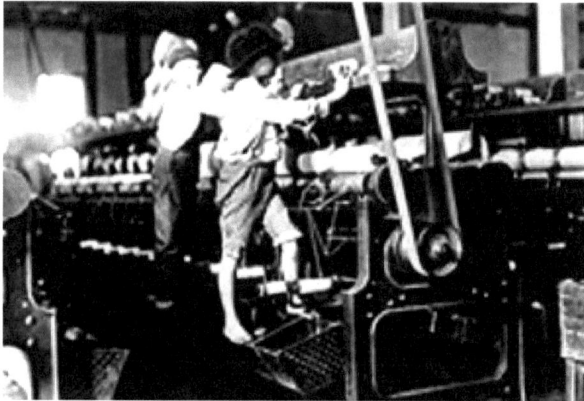

Child Labour

In the end state intervention came almost by default, through government concerns to improve the conditions of child labour in factories. The first Factory Act (1802) – the Health and Morals of Apprentices Act – was primarily concerned with improving the conditions of children working in factories, but it also required that children, in the first four years of their "apprenticeship" be instructed in reading, writing and arithmetic, and that they attend a Sunday service, to be conducted by a local Anglican Minister.

In the end, it was largely an academic exercise, since no inspectors were appointed to enforce the Act.

But at least the principle of state intervention in mass education for the poor had been established and was now on the Parliamentary agenda. But such was the hostility from various interest groups that a series of Education Bills were lost, even though a parliamentary committee had found a wide disparity in the provision of schooling for the lower orders, as well as widespread abuse of philanthropic endowments. The arrival of a Whig government in 1830, however, led to the 1832 Reform Bill which, apart from enfranchising the middle classes, also provided impetus for educational reform. The following year, the momentous step was taken by the government to vote £20,000 to the British and National Societies for school buildings, thus establishing de facto recognition of the principle of state intervention in mass education. Perhaps even more significantly, in 1839, a forerunner of the present Education Department, the Committee of Council for Education was set up with Kaye-Shuttleworth as secretary.

We have already encountered Kaye-Shuttleworth as a doctor working with the poor in northern cities. He now made a considerable contribution to improving the quality of the schooling they received. For example, inspectors - who had to be "men of respectable origins and university training" - were appointed to ensure that schools qualified for the Parliamentary grant; and £10,000 was allocated for the foundation of a national college for the training of teachers. (But once again denominational interests interfered and eventually the money was distributed on the basis of £50 per student to either monitorial society.) Kaye-Shuttleworth was also contemptuous of what he called the "monitorial humbug" of the Bell-Lancaster system and was anxious to provide formal training for teachers. He devised the system of pupil-teachers to replace monitors, whereby the most promising elementary pupils, of at least 13 years of age, were apprenticed to the headmaster for a period of five years and examined by inspectors every year. (17) [Kaye-Shuttleworth's work also provides a healthy reminder - in the face of current deterministic explanations - that individuals can still be capable of effecting fundamental social change.]

By now the government had allocated £500,000 towards elementary education, four-fifths towards the Church of England National Society, a bias which moved the Liberal spokesman, John Bright, to remark: "we have found no step taken by the government which has not had a tendency to aggrandise the Established Church." Indeed, the Anglican Church, with increasing financial support from the State, had by now established a commanding influence over mass schooling. And the understanding that religious thought occupied a supreme position over all things educational was revealed in certain official documents of the time:

> *"no plan of education ought to be encouraged in which intellectual instruction is not subordinated to the regulation of the thoughts and habits of the children by the doctrines and precepts of revealed religion." (18)*

But the schooling being offered consisted of no more than the rote learning of the 3R's based upon Biblical material. It could be argued that this amounted to indoctrination rather than education, producing an uncritical submissive public, in the interests of both Church and State. Yet contemporaneous with these developments were some challenging radical curriculum initiatives representing other interests. These will be the subject of the next chapter.

NOTES AND REFERENCES

1. Its most celebrated theorist and proselytiser was Francis Bacon. He attacked Aristotelian logic on the basis that its deductive use of unproven general statements was redundant and did not further our knowledge. His scientific method was institutionalised in the shape of the Royal Society and given substance through the investigations of Isaac Newton.

2. Voltaire exposed for example, the symbiotic relationship between monarch and Church. The Church taught that all the King's authority was given to him by God; in return the King supported the authority of the Church. He ridiculed priests as tellers of fairy tales and as unscrupulous knaves who oppressed and enslaved the multitude.

3. Tom Paine (1969) The Rights of Man. Penguin Harmondsworth

4. Tom Paine. The age of Reason

5. Transactions of the Newcomen Society 1996-97 vol. 68

6   It has been claimed that the success of these practical men led to a complacency so far a technical education was concerned. The second phase of the Industrial Revolution saw a greater penetration of industrial processes by science of a far more sophisticated character then hitherto, requiring both the appropriate technical and scientific knowledge as well as the ability to apply it. No longer would common sense and practical ability suffice. It was a failure on the part of (a classically-trained) government to recognise this development that led to Britain's subsequent industrial decline.

7   A,Clayre (ed) (1977) Nature and Industrialisation O.U.P. Oxford

8   op cit

9   op cit

10 op cit

11 op cit

12 F. Engels (1969) The Conditions of the Working Class in England in 1844. Panther.

13 quoted in H.C. Barnard (1947) A History of English Education from 1760 ULP. London.

14 S. McClure (1965) Educational Documents. Methuen. London

15 June Purvis in Goodson op cit.

16 Davies Giddy, cited in Barnard op cit.

17 Kaye-Shuttleworth, with the help of a partner, opened Battersea Normal School in 1840 as a teacher-training college to develop intellectual proficiency and a knowledge and method and skill in

the art of teaching. Training Colleges quickly mushroomed and by 1845 there were 22 Church training colleges.

18. Instructions to Inspectors 1840 in McClure op cit.

CHAPTER TWO

1800 – 1870 : "EDUCATION" SORTED IN THE NEW CLASS SYSTEM

> *"We need have no hesitation in pronouncing it (the 1862 Revised Code) to be mechanical in conception, mechanical in means and mechanical in results ...they could not in the nature of things be other than they are" (Joseph Payne (1872) "Why are the Results of our Primary Instruction so Unsatisfactory?")*

Owenism: Robert Owen and his remarkable school
Utilitarianism: "happiness" on the agenda
Working Class Radicals and "Really Useful Knowledge"
Reaction of the State:Confirming the New Social Order
Schooling of the Poor: the 1862 Revised Code
The Working-class Voice: Trade Unions and the Demand for Reform
1870 Education Act: establishment of national system of school boards

Educational Models Available to the State

Although the monitorial system – with its emphasis upon the rote learning of inert knowledge - was the chief instrument for mass schooling for much of the nineteenth century, there was no shortage of curricular alternatives being advanced. Many of these put to shame both the curriculum of the time and subsequent developments. I shall look in this chapter at some of these – and also at the State's response. Because of the sheer impact of this giant of a man and his abiding influence upon social reform throughout the century, as well as the insights it provides into life in the early nineteenth century, I shall describe the life and ideas of Robert Owen in some detail.

Owenism – the utopian socialism and cooperative philosophy of Robert Owen

Robert Owen (1771-1858), mill-owner, educational pioneer, founder of infant schooling, and arguably the prime mover of the Cooperative and Socialist movements, was the precocious son of a Welsh saddler and ironmonger, who at the age of 10, found himself seeking his fortune in London with 40 shillings capital. There he was apprenticed to a draper and, apart from acquiring spinning skills, was able to acquire experience of how the cotton market operated in those heady days of early industrial capitalism. He was, for example, able to borrow £100 to start a business making spinning machinery and to accumulate capital at the rate of £300 per annum. At the age of 20 he became the manager of a large spinning mill in Manchester with 500 employees. In 1800 came the development which was to mark out Robert Owen as a true radical: with his Manchester partners he bought the great spinning mill in the village of New Lanark. It was here that he was able to put into practice his many radical ideas, including those on child labour and education. Admittedly his first two partnerships were problematic, including businessmen who could see no point in wasting profits on social reform, but his third partnership, including Quakers and Utilitarians like Jeremy Bentham, was far more productive.

Unlike modern bureaucrats, Owen had a vision. All Owen's ideas, following those of the Enlightenment, were underpinned by his unshakeable belief in rationality, that if people were rational, all would be well with the world. If this rational approach was set in a sound environment, then people of good character would result:

> *"That plan is a national, well-digested, unexclusive system for the formation of character and the general amelioration of the lower orders. Train any population rationally and they will be rational…The national plan for the formation of character should include all modern improvements of education…and put into practice from infancy." (1)*

And rationality for Owen implied a culture of cooperation (or "union" as he often called it):

> *"We renounce the principle of individual competition...*

as being the greatest obstacle to the production and distribution of wealth, to the formation of a superior individual and national character, and to the well-ordering and good government of people...We shall therefore, as soon as the means can be obtained, exchange the principle of competition...for the principle of unlimited union" (2)

It was probably because of his confidence in the ability of knowledge and reason to overcome all obstacles and his a-political stance, that Owen never really understood the class struggle, putting it down to ignorance and irrationality. Similarly, he entertained an incomprehensible respect for the ruling class all his life. In other words, running through his life was the naivete often associated with Utopianiasm and he was often conveniently dismissed in these terms.

Owen's Ideas on Child Labour

Owen was appalled by the conditions under which children and adults laboured in many factories, and was determined to bring the attention of Parliament to this state of affairs. In the course of collecting evidence to help with the preparation of a Factory Bill, he visited several factories throughout the country. Here are some of his recollections:

"Children were admitted into mills at six and sometimes five years of age. The time of working, winter and summer, was unlimited by law but usually it was fourteen hours per day...with but half an hour's interval for the midday meal which was eaten in the factory. In fine yarn cotton mills they were subjected to this labour in a temperature usually exceeding seventy-five degrees, and in all the cotton factories they breathed atmosphere more or less injurious to the lungs, because of the dust and minute cotton fibres that pervaded it...It need not be said that such a system could not be maintained without corporal punishment. Most of the overseers openly carry stout leather thongs and we frequently saw even the youngest children severely beaten." (3)

Although Owen was ambivalent in his attitude towards the governing class, he freely associated with members of Parliament; one such association with Sir Robert Peel, M.P., father of the future Prime Minister, was to prove particularly important. Peel was a typical mill-owner, taking children from the workhouse as a source of free labour and employing them under such unhygienic and oppressive conditions, that increasing numbers were dying from fever. In an attempt to retain his competitive edge, Peel agreed to introduce a bill which Owen had drafted, prohibiting the employment of children under ten in textile factories, reducing hours to ten and a half for all under 18. It was vigorously resisted by manufacturers and it was not until 1819 that a mutilated bill finally passed through Parliament. Owen, although disgusted by the actions of both Tories and Whigs, was prepared to explain it away in typical fashion:

> *"In this and in all other cases between the tyranny of the masters and the sufferings of their white slaves, the error is in reality in the system of society, which creates the necessity for tyrants and slaves, neither of which could exist in a true and rational state of Society"* (4)

Owen's Ideas on Education

In keeping with his views on child labour, Owen refused to employ any children under ten years of age in his own factories. Instead, he built a new school to accommodate up to 600 pupils. Infants of 2 to 5 remained in school for only half the time; otherwise lessons were from 7 till 9, 10 till 12 and 3 to 5. The school was open in the evening for adults and older children, and throughout the year to the general public. According to Owen, thousands came annually to see for themselves how children were taught by his approach.

Owen had initially been so impressed by the monitorial system of Bell and Lancaster that he generously subsidised it. But as he became more familiar with various educational theorists, he changed completely from a supporter of mechanical methods to learning based on understanding. The following is an extremely brief summary of his educational principles, some of which would even to be seen progressive two centuries later

> *"The first instruction which I gave (the teachers) was that they were on no account ever to beat any of the children, or to threaten them in any manner of word or action, or to use abusive terms; but were always to speak to them with a pleasant countenance and in a kind manner and tone of voice...children in these schools should be trained systematically to acquire useful knowledge through the means of sensible signs, by which their powers of reflection may be habituated to draw accurate conclusions from the facts presented to them...and will supersede the present defective and tiresome system of book learning...It was most encouraging and delightful to see the progress which infants and children made in real knowledge without the use of books...each child will receive a general education early in life, which will fit him for the proper purposes of society, making him the most useful to it and most capable of enjoying it...Before he is twelve years old he may with ease be trained to acquire a correct view of the outline of all the knowledge which men have yet attained...He will only then have any pretensions to the name of a rational being." (5)*

ROBERT OWEN'S NEW LANARK CURRICULUM

Reading - from the most interesting books available in line with the principle that children should never be directed to read what they cannot understand.

Writing - in current hand writing, initially copied from short sentences linked in content with other subjects and then from dictation.

Arithmetic – children taught to understand both the value and the nature of arithmetical processes.

Natural history – short lectures to about 40 children, with illustrations, based upon animal, vegetable and mineral with later refinement . Children encouraged to express opinions and ask for further explanations.

Geography – similar to natural history; lectures dealing both with land and water features of the earth, followed by a study first of continents and then countries. Older children, when given latitude and longitude able to locate country and predict its features.

History – ancient and modern history illustrated by large maps showing the Stream of Time. Children encouraged to make connections between different events and other subjects.

Religion – children acquainted with the works of the Deity, in a factual rather than a doctrinal manner, and embracing practical moral principles.

Singing – for children above 5 or 6 years of age, singing both by ear and from musical notation, using a small selection of simple airs. Vocal performers in the evening school sometimes joined by the village instrumental band.

Dancing ("the devil's work" according to his Puritan opponents) – dances varying from scotch reels, country dances, and quadrilles taught as a pleasant, healthy, natural and social exercise.

Owen's ideas fell on fertile ground: hundreds of cooperative societies sprang up throughout the country - many with day and Sunday schools - linked together through the British Association for Promoting Cooperative Knowledge. Education was seen to be of fundamental importance to the cooperative movement and by the end of the 1830's Halls of Science for the education of adults in scientific, economic and political affairs were springing up, also with day and Sunday schools for children - and typically including other activities such as parties and dancing .

Owen could have been speaking to today's politicians as well as anticipating current research findings when he makes the following observations (quoted in E.J. Hobsbawn op cit) :

> *"The primary and necessary object of all existence is to*
> *be happy, but happiness cannot be obtained individually;*
> *it is useless to expect isolated happiness; all must partake*
> *of it or the few will never enjoy it "*

But Owen's predilection for organisation eventually led to his overstretching himself. Some of his community experiments failed and his attempts to accommodate rationalism and religion satisfied no one. The rationalist element was indeed absorbed into the flourishing secularist movement, with the Halls of Science being converted into Secular Halls. But Owen's vision of mutual cooperation was increasingly at odds with the Zeitgeist of ruthless competition. However he had left a legacy of cooperative and socialist activity and a radical alternative to the prevailing educational orthodoxy, as well as a vision of a future society.

It should be noted, in view of subsequent developments, that Owen's was a private educational innovation. It could be said to be in the human interest, springing from an individual's imagination, values and dynamism, and receiving no support from the State. Without being overtly political, it was necessarily concerned with the education of the working class. The next example, in contrast, derives from a middle-class philosophical movement.

Utilitarianism: "the Happiness of the Greatest Number"

The social revolution accompanying the technological, led to the emergence of a well-defined middle class system, made up of merchant bankers and industrialists. The motivation behind both the commercial and industrial elements of this new middle class was the concept of utility, identified as the generation of profit and the accumulation of capital. It was the intellectual wing of the bourgeoisie, the philosophical radicals, who under the leadership of Jeremy Bentham identified "utility" with "value" and concluded that the only absolute values in nature were pleasure and pain. Happiness was thus the supreme good. This philosophy of utilitarianism held that those actions are good in proportion to the happiness produced (leading to the simplistic slogan "the greatest happiness of the greatest number").

Utilitarians believed in a universal secular scientific education for all, which would develop character and lead to increased happiness. Such an education - and here is the rub - would also supposedly lead to an enlightened view of political economy and the acceptance of the present division of labour as in the best interests of all. The outcome of this would be that the labouring class would not have as much time as the bourgeoisie to develop their "intelligences" and would therefore not qualify for occupying responsible positions in society. Thus, whilst working-class children were provided with elementary schooling only, those of the middle class were offered secondary education. It was left to Bentham to propose a secondary school curriculum. Having thoroughly examined the various fields of knowledge, he devised the following curriculum for a secular secondary school to be taught in five sequential stages. (see below)

Jeremy Bentham (1748-1832) – born in London into a Tory family. A child prodigy, he entered Oxford from Westminster at the age of 12. He trained as a lawyer but never practised. Instead, he became a social reformer but his actions on social reform give the lie to the superficial picture of a benevolent utilitarian. For example, the poor, instead of being in a 'state of grace' were "burdensome". He even designed a 'pauper utopia': a private company with authority over 500 industry-houses for one million paupers. Every inmate would be under constant supervision and benefits would be paid only to those who entered an industry-house. On his death, his body was preserved and kept in a wooden cabinet at University Collage.

STAGES IN JEREMY BENTHAM'S SECONDARY SCHOOL CURRICULUM

(1) the 3R's, descriptive and classificatory (mineralogy, botany, zoology)
(2) mechanics, chemistry, physics (plus some history, geography and languages)
(3) application of above to technology (mining, surveying, architecture, husbandry)
(4) health (preserving and monitoring)
(5) mathematics (6)

What is of particular interest here in a culture of rote-learning is the incorporation of theory: the learning context was to be active and experiential in accordance with what was called "associationism" theory (7). With its selection and arrangement of content and its theoretical stance it might be regarded as an early attempt at rational curriculum planning. But it was not without its contradictions: for example, it was to be taught by a mechanical monitorial method. But in the end it failed to attract sufficient financial support and was vigorously opposed by the Church because of its secular nature. But it served as a model for the future, for those members of the emergent middle class searching for a suitable school for their children.

Working Class Radicals and their Ideas on Education

It makes more sense when talking of pre-industrial England to talk of working classes rather than the working class, since workers were tied to different guilds or trades and celebrated their cultures through separate rituals and leisure activities – and there were also wide variations in literacy. But the coming of industrial capitalism meant that, in the towns at least, there was a commonality of interest through the universalised relations of production.

There was also the common goal of universal suffrage, and the need to establish effective networks of communication. Even as early as the 1790's literate artisans were demanding parliamentary reform, and forming themselves into Corresponding Societies for the purpose of disseminating their ideas. For example in 1792 the London Corresponding Society was set up and organised conventions to establish networks with other reforming groups around the country. A petition articulating their various political demands obtained the support of 6,000 people. For their trouble, some members were arrested, charged with sedition and sentenced to transportation. Such a growing network of articulate working-class radicals making political demands posed a clear threat to the authority of a nervous government, at war with France. It suspended Habeas Corpus in 1794 and in 1799 passed the Corresponding Societies Act, making all such societies illegal and bringing to an end their organised activities - but despite this the dissemination of radical literature continued.

Such was the political context which working-class radicals had to negotiate - or be punished by a tyrannical government. That so many were able to make their views known to an increasingly wide audience and raise their political awareness is a tribute both to their tenacity and courage, and to their belief - following the Enlightenment and Thomas Paine – that rationalism and science were the way forward to a free and just society. The stories of these working-class radicals (and only a few are mentioned here) provide an inspiration for all those who labour under injustice and hardship.

Perhaps the most influential of these in the development of working-class identity and solidarity, through his fiery and polemical pamphleteering and his constant ridiculing of authority, was William Cobbett (1763 – 1835).

William Cobbett was the son of a tavern-owner and originally a Tory sympathiser who became radicalised by the poverty he saw around him and by the appalling factory conditions. He became the voice of the working class. In 1802, he started his own newspaper the Political Register and by his style and tone effectively related to working -class people.

Cobbett came to be regarded as the creator of a radical intellectual culture, despite the unsystematic nature of his thought. Because of this and the immense influence he exerted upon the working-class (as well as the government) I shall give a couple of extracts from his Political Registers to illustrate the power and style of his writing and as a reminder of their relevance to today's society:

COBBETT ON "TAXES AND PARLIAMENTARY REFORM"

"I have laid before you the real causes of your sufferings…..they have arisen from the taxes and loans; those arose out of the wars; the wars arose out of a desire to keep down reform; and a desire to keep down reform arose out of the borough system, which excludes almost the whole of people from voting at elections…..If the Members of Parliament for the last fifty years had been chosen by the people at large annually, do you believe that we should have expended one thousand millions in taxes raised during the wars and another thousand millions which is now existing in the form of DEBT….the only effectual remedy is to obtain such a parliament chosen annually by the people, seeing that they all pay taxes".

COBBETT ON POLITICAL ECONOMY

"They speak of 'redundant production' and observe that this admits of 'no adequate remedy' except that of diminution of supply or increase in demand…They speak of the 'inconvenience' arising from 'abundance'. Did man before ever hear of 'abundance' being an'inconvenience'? Did man hear the word 'redundant' applied to the products of the earth? Did man ever hear of a remedy being wanted for an abundant crop?…It required the existence of paper money to put it into man's mind to venture upon paper such combination of words. The system of paper money is full of monstrousness. It destroys the very mind and thoughts."

It was by the use of such accessible polemic, then, that Cobbett's Political Register became the main newspaper of the working-class, circulation running at 40,000-60,000 copies each week in 1816-17. Faced with the increasing popularity of what it saw as subversive newsprint, the government raised the tax to 4d a copy. So Cobbett published his paper as a pamphlet and sold it for 2d. Having already spent two years in Newgate Prison for sedition, and believing the government was about to arrest him again, he fled for a while to the USA, where he continued to publish his Political Register. On his return to England he became M.P. for Oldham and devoted his time in Parliament to attacking the Poor Law. There was also Cobbett the family man and his efforts to educate his own children make interesting reading. (10) He died in 1835.

Cobbett's Political Register was far from being the only radical literature available to the working-class. A tradition of self-education was developing, where newspapers etc. were eagerly sought by workers as a means of their becoming acquainted with new ideas and arguments. As mentioned earlier, the seminal ideas, apart from those of Cobbett, can be traced back to Thomas Paine and the Enlightenment with a belief in the fundamental importance of science, based upon experiment and reason rather than faith and dogma.

These seminal ideas were to bear fruit in the remarkable educational initiatives of Richard Carlile:-

RICHARD CARLILE (1790-1843) was born in Devon in 1790, the son of a shoe maker. He became apprenticed to a tinsmith and from his own harsh experiences and his reading of Thomas Paine's works, became such an enthusiastic radical that he would walk up to 30 miles a day selling such weekly papers as the Black Dwarf. For reprinting and publishing Paine's and other's writings he spent over three years in prison, writing the first twelve volumes of his periodical "The Republican". In all he spent over nine years in prison, a testament to his political will and indefatigability, as well as a tribute to his refusal to be cowed by authority. Not surprisingly, in view of all his tribulations, he died in poor health at the age of 52.

RICHARD CARLILE'S IDEAS FOR A SCHOOL CURRICULUM

"Instead of devoting time to the study of a dead language and superstition, children should be taught
>   reading and writing
>   the use of figures
>   astronomy (to expose the futility of religious views of the universe)
>   geography
>   natural history
>   chemistry

the aim being:
>   that children may at an early period of life form correct notions of organised
>   and inert matter, instead of torturing their minds with metaphysics and incomprehensible dogmas about religion. Instead, they should learn Science by experiment and observation, and Morality by example." (11)

Another remarkable working-class radical concerned with the education of poor children was William Lovett. Although radical, his radicalism took a different direction to Carlile's. There had been an implicit coalition of interests between liberal Whigs and working-class radicals working for an extension of the franchise. But the 1832 Reform Act had betrayed this perceived coalition, not only in solely enfranchising the middle class, but giving rise to a government as reactionary as its predecessor. It not only resisted demands for improved working conditions and compulsory state education but continued to suppress the radical press. Even the promise of utilitarianism and its principle of the "greatest happiness of the greatest number" proved to be hollow, used for justifying the development of an enlightened middle class exercising power in the "interest" of all.

There was thus an increasing realisation that the only way forward for the working-class lay in universal suffrage. In 1838, Lovett and others, seeking this objective, launched the Chartist movement by drafting a People's Charter with the following demands:

> adult male suffrage
> no property qualification for MP's
> salaries for MP's
> secret ballots
> equal-size constituencies
> annual parliaments.

The Chartists eventually formed two distinct camps: the Knowledge Chartists, who believed the way forward lay in universal education; and the Political Chartists who favoured direct action. Lovett belonged to the former and in his Address on Education he put forward his progressive and enlightened (and prescient) ideas for a broad, secular compulsory education in infant, preparatory and high schools under local democratic control as a "universal instrument for advancing the dignity of man and for gladdening his existence." Learning was to be a step-by-step process, experiential and proceeding from concrete to abstract.

WILLIAM LOVETT (1800-1877)

Born in Cornwall, the son of a fisherman (who drowned before he was born) and a Methodist mother. Became an apprentice rope –maker at the age of 13, changing two years to be a carpenter. Sought work in London when 21 and attended the London Mechanics Institute, where he met Henry Hetherington who introduced him to the ideas of Robert Owen. Together they formed the National Union of Working Classes in 1831, which eventually led to Chartism and the drawing up of the People's Charter. He was sentenced to one year's imprisonment for alleged seditious libel during a Chartist convention. He now began to get interested in the ideas of working class education and through subscriptions from his National Association for Promoting the Political and Social Improvement of the People, was able to set up a National Hall in a disused Methodist Chapel. This included a Sunday School, a day school for 300 pupils and a centre for public meetings – which was closed after 15 years to make way, symbolically, for a music hall and gin palace. But Lovett continued to teach elementary anatomy and physiology for a further ten years.

WILLIAM LOVETT'S SCHOOL CURRICULUM

Aim:
The happiness of the individual, through mental, physical and moral development. Some control exercised by pupils over their world.

Method:
Experiential and active learning in a context of understanding and self-expression. Punishment and rote learning to be abandoned in favour of a love of learning and the development of the imagination.

Content:
Science: the laws of nature revealed through the physical sciences,
Botany and horticulture (a school garden as a resource)
Geology, zoology and astronomy
Mathematics, with practical applications
Geography: our country's physical formation, trade and manufacture
History: the progress from barbarism to civilisation
Politics and political economy
Moral and social relationships; rights and duties
Singing and dancing; development of the imagination.

"Really Useful Knowledge"

The radical curricula of Carlile and Lovett could hardly be said to be situated in the world of provided education, whether an elite education for the rich or a basic schooling for the poor. Cobbett had harsh words for both systems. He warned his readers to steer clear of classical allusions, claiming that "learned languages acted as a bar to the acquisition of real learning":

> *"When you are told that the boys at these learned schools are set to make what are called "nonsense verses" in Latin; that is to say, to place a parcel of Latin words in lines, so that each line shall contain a particular number*

of syllables (and) when you are told that a considerable portion of a boy's time is under a grave wigged pedant, when you are told this…you will wonder that any thing but a fool should ever come forth from such places."
(13)

As for state education, there was considerable suspicion on the part of the radicals at its potential ambiguity, for as Richard Johnson points out, whereas education promised liberation it also threatened subjection. (14) Schoolmasters were variously seen as tyrants and spies, relying upon punishment to maintain their authority. Working-class radicals took the view that education was a political enterprise and they therefore rejected middle-class ventures as potentially oppressive.

This rejection is well illustrated by their reaction to the Society for the Diffusion of Useful Knowledge. This was set up in 1826, largely at the behest of the Whig, Henry (Lord) Brougham, with the proclaimed object of imparting useful information to all classes. The society was overseen by a committee made up of no less than 40 VIP's and the publications included libraries of useful knowledge, penny magazines maps and almanacs. William Cobbett, as usual, was both perceptive and dismissive:

> *"I come now to your society for the diffusion of useful knowledge, at a meeting of which you and Lord Althorp were, the other day, beplastering yourselves with praises. This, like all the rest of the "education" schemes is a combination for the purpose of amusing the working classes, and diverting their attention from the cause of their poverty and misery." (15)*

The aim, then, of the radicals' version of "really useful knowledge" was to oppose capitalist and paternalistic notions of utility. Knowledge for the working class was to be practical and directly relevant to their lived experiences. Informal methods of teaching were to be preferred, in the great outdoors as well as the classroom. Content would include:

- political economy, seen as a way of removing poverty and a means of understanding the labour theory of value;
- social science based on the Rights of Man and Owenite principles of cooperation;

- natural science, literature and locally employable skills should also be taught.

These ideas, for the political empowerment of the labouring poor, were developed by means of travelling lecturers, and diffused through the radical press and educational networks. But in the absence of a base in Parliament or influential advocates, the impact of the "really useful knowledge" project was limited and tended to be the result of individual enterprise rather than collective endeavour. Not only this, but steps were taken by the Establishment to actively suppress any enterprises considered to be socially and politically subversive, as the following extract shows.

The Science of Common Things – Education or Subversion?

In relation to the above, David Layton (16) gives a fascinating and insightful account of a radical approach to the teaching of science to elementary schoolchildren. The Rev. Richard Dawes, Rector at Kings Somborne from 1837, taught children about the "Science of Common Things", that is, things which interested them at the present time as well as those likely to interest them in the future. For example, their clothing, how it was manufactured etc; the articles they consume, from whence they come; the nature of the products of the parish, which they helped to cultivate. Having aroused the children's interest, Dawes was able to move on to explanations of expansion, pressure, the action of pumps etc.

As for his method of teaching:

> *"In subjects of this kind and to children, mere verbal explanations are of no use whatsoever; but when practically illustrated by experiment, they become not only one of the most pleasing sources of instruction but absolutely one of the most useful." (17)*

Dawes' course was greeted with enthusiasm by school inspectors, one of whom made vigorous attempts to disseminate it. Yet Science was excluded from the grant-earning subjects later to be prescribed in the Revised Code of 1862. Layton explains its demise in Darwinian terms:

> *"Here was no crumb of upper-class education dispensed to the children of the labouring poor. Instruction was related to a culture which was familiar to them and provided opportunities for the use of reason and speculation by drawing upon observations which pertained to everyday life……(they had become) casualties in a process of natural selection as the educational environment had become more progressively defined". (18)*

Hodson and Prophet (19) challenge this interpretation. They quote Lord Wrottesley, who was chairman at the time of the Parliamentary Committee of the British Association. He described an incident in a pauper school, where he asked the class for an explanation of the action of a pump:

> *"...a poor boy hobbled forth to give a reply. He was lame and humpbacked and his wan emaciated face told only too clearly the tale of poverty and its consequences. – but he gave forth so lucid and intelligent a reply to the questions put to him that there arose a feeling of admiration for the child' s talents.....*__it would be an unwholesome and vicious state of society if those comparatively unblessed with nature's gifts should be generally superior in intellectual attainments to those above them in station__*". (20)*

Wrottesley clearly regarded schooling as a means of maintaining the status quo and as an agent of social control. It was not until 1882, twenty years later, that Science was admitted to the grant-earning subjects of the elementary school, and then it was to be in a "pure" form, aimed at developing various intellectual abilities, rather than being grounded in the cultural experiences of the working class.

So much for the remarkable educational initiatives emerging from the working-class in the first half of the nineteenth century, initiatives which make our present approach to mass schooling seem reactionary and oppressive. In today's language they would be categorised as belonging to the world of private enterprise in competition with the public sector. So what would be the "public" response of the State?

The Reaction of the State: Educational Confirmation of the new Class System

During this period the only intervention by the State into mass education was the subsidy to the Church monitorial schools by means of the Committee of Council (Education Department). Kay-Shuttleworth, the secretary of this committee, believed that anything short of national provision would prove to be inadequate. And, of course, working men's associations had been calling for a national system of education since the 1830's. On the other hand, religious sects had been eyeing each other suspiciously lest the State bounty should favour one rather than the other. With regard to the curriculum, there was clearly disquiet in some quarters that the educational initiatives described above could educate the lower orders above their station in life. Let us see how the state responded to what might be seen as a fundamental challenge to the status quo.

Schooling of the Poor: the Newcastle Commission of 1861 and the 1862 Revised Code

The State was more concerned with financial than curricular matters: disquiet was being expressed at the sharp increase in Treasury grants to voluntary bodies, rising from the original £20,000 in 1833 to £663,000 in 1858. The response was twofold: on the one hand the Committee of Council was merged with the Science and Art Department in order to administer these grants and, on the other, the Newcastle Commission was set up under the chairmanship of a member of the ruling class, the Duke of Newcastle, a wealthy landowner. The terms of reference were as follows:

> *"to inquire into the present state of popular education in England, and to consider and report what measures, if any, are required for the extension of sound and cheap elementary instruction to all classes of the people"* (21)

A survey of elementary schooling was thus carried out, which led to the conclusion that there was little cause for concern, because compared with other countries, there seemed to be sufficient voluntary places available, thus weakening demands for a national system. The most notable recommendation to be accepted by the government was the notorious system of payment by results. The fleshing out of these proposals was left to the vice-president Robert Lowe and he made the most of this opportunity to put his principles into practice: a national, state-assisted and inspected system of elementary education for the poor. The curricular results of this exercise are seen in the Revised Code of 1862, where there were to be six graded yearly "standards" for the teaching of the three R's.

ROBERT LOWE (1811-1892) born albino, son of a Nottingham rector. Educated at Winchester and Oxford, where he took a 1st in Classics and a 2nd in Mathematics. Called to the Bar in 1842 and went to Australia, where he became a member of the New South Wales legislative council. Returning to England in 1850 he worked for the Times before being elected to Parliament. In 1859 he became vice-president of the Committee of Council on Education where he took a hard line on financial matters and introduced the system of "payment-by-results".

ROBERT LOWE'S 1862 REVISED CODE (FIRST NATIONAL CURRICULUM)

	Standard 1 ►	Standard V1
Reading	Narrative in mono-syllables ►	**A short ordinary paragraph in a newspaper, or other modern narrative.**
Writing	Form on black-board or slate, from dicta-tion, letters (capital and small) manuscript. ►	Another short ordinary paragraph in a newspaper or other modern narrative, slowly dictated a few words at a time.
Arithmetic	Form on blackboard or slate, from dictation, figures up to 20; name at sight figures up to 20; add and subtract figures up to 10, orally, from examples on blackboard. ►	A sum in practice, or bills of practice.

Schools were to be financed directly by central government, with grants going directly to the managers, rather than the teachers. Being a free marketeer, Lowe demanded "value for money" and as he told the House:

> *"I cannot promise the House that this system will be an economical one or promise that it will be an efficient one, but I can promise that it shall be one or the other. If it is not cheap it shall be efficient; if it is not efficient, it shall be cheap. Hitherto, we have been living under a system of bounties and protection, now we propose to have a little free trade" (22).*

This Revised Code can be seen as a determined effort on the part of the State to gain systematic centralised control over the disparate schooling at the time, with school boards being responsible for the maintenance of elementary schools and the regular attendance of pupils. It can be argued that this represented the first National Curriculum, an idea not to be resuscitated for over a century. It also represented a dereliction of duty on the part of the State in ignoring the educational models available in favour of a policy of indoctrination and social control.

It needs to be borne in mind that, apart from the curriculum models described above, the idea of mass education had been taken seriously on the continent for some centuries with various theoretical approaches. The 17th century Czech pastor Comenius took what we might now call the "epistemological approach" (theories of knowledge) with his beliefs in the "unity of experience" and the "comprehension of all nature" ; whilst a century later the French writer Rousseau's approach was psychological with his notions of stages of child development (physical-intellectual-emotional) to be matched by appropriate learning activities. But the United Kingdom was not to be seduced by such distractions: the emphasis in this country was to be a-theoretical with its emphasis upon "education for social control" - and so it has remained to the present day.

Robert Lowe was aware that his proposals were controversial, so they were slipped into the Commons as a Minute on the last day of the Parliamentary session. But controversy there was in plenty. Religious bodies complained bitterly that Religion was not one of the three R's, since there was no stipulation in the Revised Code that biblical material be used in the development of literacy. And educationalists like Matthew Arnold and Kaye-Shuttleworth pointed out that a universal system was inappropriate, given the wide disparity in social and economic circumstances in which elementary schools were located. But despite the various objections, the Code of Regulations made by the Committee of the Privy Council on Education was revised in the light of Lowe's recommendations and they remained in force for the next thirty years, subject to further, relatively superficial, revision (for example, in 1882, a Standard 7 for elementary science was introduced).

Education of the Rich: The Clarendon Report of 1864

By the middle of the nineteenth century, a capitalist counter-culture with its competitive ethic, was challenging a complacent status quo. Competitive examinations were replacing corruption and nepotism for entry into such public professions as civil and military service. And the new proprietary schools, established to meet the need of the middle classes for a utilitarian rather a gentry curriculum, were proving so popular they were attracting clients who might otherwise have sought a public school education.

It was in this context, and with increasing disquiet over the possible abuse of endowments, that, in 1864, a Royal Commission under the chairmanship of the Earl of Clarendon was set up to inquire into the nine "great" public schools, the nature and application of their endowments, and into the system and course of studies pursued therein. The Earl was of the opinion that reform was urgently needed because the current inefficiency of the public schools was threatening the social order, with lower classes receiving a superior education. A detailed investigation into these schools was therefore carried out, with cross-examination of (sometimes hostile) witnesses. Science and technology were by now playing a large part in the cultural and commercial life of the country and the Great Exhibition of 1851 had provided them with a public platform. It was thus inevitable that some of the witnesses should be eminent scientists, who argued for a prominent place for Science in the public school, on the grounds both of its value in training the mind and the necessity for the ruling class to be aware of scientific developments. In its report the Commissioners did acknowledge the value of Science in cultivating:

> *"the faculty of observation...the power of accurate and rapid generalisation...the mental habit of method and arrangement (and the accustoming of) young persons to trace the sequence of cause and effect". (23)*

Nevertheless the Commissioners reaffirmed the supreme position of a classical education at the heart of the public school curriculum. Recommending that more attention be paid to content rather than form, it held that:

> *"the classical languages and literature should continue to hold the principal place in the course of study, (since) they supply some of the noblest poetry, the finest eloquence, the deepest philosophy, the wisest historical writing".(24)*

It was thus recommended that classics take up half the available time, with science being allocated one-eighth, along with mathematics, foreign languages, music, history, geography and English. So much for curriculum content. As for pedagogy, the quality of teaching was generally found to be unsatisfactory, with idle teachers producing idle students with empty and uncultivated minds.

With regard to the abuse of endowments, each school was to submit a scheme for a more representative governing body made up of men conversant with the requirements of public life. The governing body was to take responsibility for the curriculum, teaching and the administration of endowments. There should be open competitive examinations for Foundation scholarships, clearly favouring boys from private preparatory rather than elementary schools. As Brian Simon puts it: "the Commissioners had done what was required of them and had done it well". (25) That is, they had assimilated the expressions of public unease by a process of limited accommodation of "modern" subjects, whilst ensuring the children of the ruling classes still had access to a "superior" education, marking them off from the rest of society.

What to Do with the New Middle Class: The Taunton Report of 1868

It remained to investigate the remaining schools: the endowed (grammar) and the new proprietary schools. Given the disquieting findings of the Clarendon Report regarding both the quality of teaching and financial administration in the public schools, the Schools Inquiry (Taunton) Commission was required to look at both educational and financial aspects. The outcome was a very thorough investigation, using both written and oral evidence, of over 800 grammar and proprietary schools in every area of the country. The commissioners came to the overall conclusion that, whilst the work of the endowed schools was very unsatisfactory, the educational character of the new proprietary schools (established to meet the needs of the emerging middle classes for a broad curriculum) was good.

But the most revealing aspect of the Report concerned its attitude towards endowments. Setting its face against the idea of a free education, it took the view that endowments were made in the national, rather than the individual interest. What it called wasteful "indiscriminate gratuitous instruction" was the result of the current situation, resulting in slovenly management and irregular attendance, doing no favours to poor children "enjoying" their endowments. The poor in monitorial schools usually paid for their schooling. Why then, it was argued, should poor children get a free education in what were supposed to be middle class schools. (26) So free education and the current endowments system were to be abandoned, to be replaced by competitive "exhibitions" (These naturally favoured middle-class children. In any case headmasters developed all sorts of tricks to keep the poor at a distance, well away from their schools).

The Commission then carried out a very interesting if presumptuous exercise, based upon the rapidly evolving middle classes, of differentiating the desirable secondary schools into three grades, according to social background, the wishes of the parents and the age at which they were prepared to keep their children at school. It was, in other words, an exercise in confirming the developing social structure through educational arrangements.

But it was to be an academic exercise only. The Taunton Report was followed a year later, in 1869, by the Endowed Schools Act which ignored its curricular recommendations. Instead, three Commissioners were appointed to investigate and reorganise the charitable trusts of the endowed schools. This they did with vigour and enthusiasm, acting on the principles that:

- there should be no free education;
- an application of endowments becomes increasingly needful as the education becomes higher;
- it was invidious that poor children had to pay for their elementary education whilst the favoured poor could receive a higher education by means of endowments;

another example of the state taking from the poor to give to the rich.

These three reports, then, all compiled by members of the Establishment, served the following functions:

- they provided reinforcement, through educational arrangements, for the new social order of upper, middle and lower class;
- they provided legitimation for a classical education for upper class boys, thus sustaining the position of the landed gentry at the apex of the social hierarchy, remote from the daily concerns of the industrialist and artisan;
- they recommended differentiated secondary education for the middle classes;
- they ensured that poor children were given a basic elementary schooling with very limited prospects of advancement into secondary education.

Whilst the government could claim that these recommendations were in the public interest, they were in fact in the interests of the upper class, using education as a means of underpinning the new social order and providing a domesticating schooling for the poor. This was certainly not the reform that the working class had been demanding. The government was clearly treating what was still a fragmented working class with indifference, if not contempt. We need then to find out how the working-class was organised at this time and what direction its struggles were taking.

The Working-class Voice: Trade Unions and the Demand for Reform

As the nineteenth century progressed, industrial capitalism was being increasingly acknowledged as a fact of life, and artisans were coming to terms with the fact that their interests might be better served by economic bargaining as well as through universal suffrage. They therefore began to form themselves into groups depending on their particular trade. There were now two major working-class forces for change by the 1840's: the new trade unions demanding better working conditions and the Chartists demanding universal suffrage. The latter organisation reached its peak in 1848, with a series of mass meetings across the country (half a million at Salford it was claimed) and a proposed march on the House of Commons. The government, still rejecting the Charter, was now fearful that the revolutions on the continent would spread to Britain. The army was brought in, arrests were made and even more repressive measures introduced, including the transportation of those workers seen to be organising themselves, such as the Tolpuddle martyrs. From then on the militancy declined and internal divisions in the Chartist movement developed (for example, between the knowledge and political wings). With the economy prospering, there was a continuing loss of popular support and an eventual demise of the movement. As the Duke of Wellington – apparently indifferent to the state's draconian measures - had observed: "The English are a very quiet people".

But as Chartism declined, so the trade union movement flourished through "New Model" Unionism. The increasing sophistication of industrial processes led to an "aristocracy of labour" with skilled artisans organising themselves into highly centralised unions, and with full-time officials employed to negotiate with the bosses and recommend strike action when negotiations had irretrievably broken down. But it was becoming increasingly clear that economic bargaining was not enough, that it was necessary to agitate for political reform and universal suffrage . In response to increasingly strident demands, respective governments from the mid-1850's had introduced a series of Reform Bills designed to give "respectable skilled" artisans the vote. But these Bills had either been withdrawn or run out of time. It was the defeat of the 1866 Reform Bill, which would have extended the franchise to respectable working men whilst excluding the "unskilled and feckless", which caused a split in the ranks of the Whigs. The defeat of the Bill led to the resignation of the Cabinet, to be replaced by a minority Tory government. The following year, in 1867, Disraeli, now Prime Minister of a minority government, introduced yet another Reform Bill, designed to redistribute seats in favour of large industrial towns and to add another million voters to a household franchise of £10. The continuing opposition to the "rule of the ignorant" (with the prospects of the end of free trade, the destruction of property and even war) was again articulated by Robert Lowe:

> "If this House means to maintain the great power and influence which it exercises over the executive, it must beware of putting itself on too democratic a foundation. If you form your House solely with a view to numbers, you will destroy the element out of which your statesmen are made.....Once give the men the votes and the machinery is ready to launch those votes in one compact mass

*upon the institutions and property of this country…….
If you want venality, if you want ignorance, if you want
drunkenness….or if on the other hand you want impulsive,
unreflecting and violent people, where do you look for
them? Do you go to the top or the bottom"? (27)*

Disraeli did not, however, share these fears; he was able to maintain unity
within his own party whilst dividing the opposition. The Reform Bill was
thus finally carried and an Act put in place, to the relief of politicians of all
colours, anxious that the matter be settled once and for all.

It is one of the ironies of history that Robert Lowe, repeatedly using "the
rule of the ignorant" argument for his continuing opposition to reform,
should have ensured the power of this argument through his small-minded
educational policies and his Revised Code. But he finally acknowledged
that it was necessary now to provide compulsory education for children of
the working class.

> *"I believe it will be absolutely necessary to compel our
> future masters to learn their letters ….. to qualify them
> for the power that has passed into their hands" (28)*

But as usual there was no attempt to spell out in any detail what "learning
their letters" might be or what qualities might be imparted which would
qualify them for future roles.

And Lowe's anxieties concerning "education for democracy" have remained
unresolved to the present day.

He went on to argue that because power was now passing out of the hands
of the upper class, they must preserve their social position through a
superior education and recover some of their influence by means of a wider
and more enlightened cultivation. We shall see in subsequent chapters how
successfully the ruling class was able to maintain this position.

Aside from the political arguments, though, a pressing problem was creeping
up on the government, with urbanisation increasing much more rapidly
than the provision of schools. Something had to be done about providing
widespread schooling for the masses.

The Education Act of 1870: a national system of school boards

In 1868, a year after the Reform Act, there was a general election and a new party – the Liberals – assumed the reins of power. (This new party had been formed in 1859 from Whigs, disenchanted free-trader Peelites and Radicals.) One of the first problems facing it concerned the precise nature of educational reform. In the prevailing climate of capitalist laissez-faire opinion there was considerable resistance to further state intervention. And the Anglican Church was anxious to protect its vested interest in its faith schools. On the other hand, the Trades Union Council, at its second congress in 1868 demanded that schooling should be unsectarian. The Anglican Church, alarmed at these working-class demands for a non-sectarian education system, set up a National Education Union to lobby for a denominational system. So the educational interests of various sections of society were becoming more clearly articulated.

Politicians were equally divided, using different issues to justify their position. For example, the Liberal Arthur Roebuck championed the cause of national popular education on the grounds of democratisation:

> "I wish the people to be enlightened that they may use the power well which they will inevitably obtain. If the parents be able to give their children sufficient education, then they should not be compelled to send them to the national school. If, however, they should be unable or unwilling to give them such instruction, then the State should step in to supply this want, by compelling the parent to send the child to a school of the State." (29)

The Tory Robert Lowe, still holding on to his reactionary position, unsurprisingly reflected a different political ideology, fearing a bureaucratic and centralised system with too much power on the one hand and a subverting of the order of things by the extended franchise on the other. He favoured the status quo, praising:

> "the invaluable superintendence of the gentry and the clergy, the zeal of religious conviction, the harmony with the present state of society and the standard already reached" (30)

and fearing that these would be sacrificed if the instruction of the poor were placed in the hands of "indifferent and incompetent local bodies or of a central government".

So, apart from the question of who was to receive provided schooling, there was the fundamental issue of who was to provide it. This question of voluntary/private or state/public provision - which separates the political right from the left to the present time - meant that the government, given the strength of feeling in opposing camps, would have to step warily.

Inevitably, the government compromised, stressing that the bill to be introduced was essentially a case of "filling the gaps" rather than developing a completely new system, with as much assistance from parents as possible. There were still to be opportunities for voluntary effort, school fees and private endowments. To meet the varying demands of pressure groups, Gladstone's Education Minister, W.E. Forster, adopted a Dual System in his Education Bill. On the one hand, the religious interest was satisfied by a 50% grant from the Education Department to voluntary schools. On the other, a secular system was to be consolidated by the setting up of school boards throughout the country, thus "filling the gaps". School boards were to be elected, empowered to build schools, raise a rate and to charge fees (although they had the power to issue free tickets in cases of need) and to compel attendance between the ages of 5-13. Inspection of schools was essential, although now there was no denominational requirement placed upon inspectors. With regard to pupils, they could withdraw from religious instruction on conscience grounds, and no particular religious denomination was to be taught. In his speech to the Commons, Forster made it clear what the imperatives were behind the initiative:

> *"what is the purpose in this Bill? Briefly this, to bring elementary education within the reach of every English home…We must not delay. Upon the speedy provision of elementary education depends our industrial prosperity. It is of no use to give technical teaching to our artisans without elementary education…Upon this speedy provisions depends also…the good safe working of our constitutional system…now that we have given (the people) political power we must not wait any longer to give them education". (31)*

In other words, both the business and democratic interests were to be met - theoretically.

The 1870 Education Act has been hailed by some as a major development in mass education – and blamed by others for falling standards. It must be remembered, though, that there were no corresponding developments in the Revised Code, which had to be taught by its strict rules, if payment was to be claimed. Matthew Arnold, chief inspector at the time, made it clear what he thought of the Revised Code in his report of 1867, comments which are still relevant at the present time:

> *"The mode of teaching ...has certainly fallen off in intelligence, spirit and inventiveness since my last report. It could not well be otherwise...A change in the Department's regulations, by making two-thirds of the government grant depend upon a mechanical examination, inevitably gives a mechanical turn to the school teaching....In the game of mechanical contrivances the teacher will in the end beat us, and it is now found possible, by ingenious preparation, to get children through the Revised Code examination...in reading, writing and ciphering...without their really knowing any of these three matters". (32)*

Matthew Arnold's damning report is a comprehensive indictment of the effects of the Revised Code on elementary schooling. It would seem that Forster was either naïve or disingenuous in his above instrumental justifications of the Education Act. Even if by some miracle, elementary schooling did produce functionally literate people, there was at the time no technical teaching provided to build on this.

By 1876, half of the school population was under compulsion. (33) As far as the private/public division went, whilst only 20% of the schools were board schools in 1880, the figure had increased to 46% by 1900. But the absence of free schooling was proving a bone of contention with the working class: it was argued that fees of 2d to 8d per week with an income of less than £1 per week in a large family represented real hardship, and in any case encouraged absenteeism. The Establishment gave its usual response - that it was "degrading" for respectable people to accept free offerings from the State. But continuing pressure from groups like the TUC eventually led to special "fee-grants" being introduced in 1891, so that elementary schooling was now virtually free (although it was not until the Fisher Education Act of 1918 that fees were finally and officially abolished). Another factor lessening the impact of the Act was the continuing employment of children in factories. Although the worst excesses described earlier had been banished, pressure from employers (and, it has to be said, some parents) ensured that child-labour continued on a half-time basis until employment under the age of twelve was finally forbidden under the 1918 Education Act.

What can be made of the developments described in this chapter? The differentiated class system which had developed in the nineteenth century was to be underpinned by official government reports legitimising an education system where the upper class was educated privately at public schools, receiving an "elite classical education" whilst the lower class children received an elementary schooling based upon the 3R's. Enough examples have been given in this chapter of alternative radical forms of schooling promising to produce a genuinely educated working-class. But this was clearly the last thing the government wanted: it was in the interest of the state and the ruling class to underpin the new social order and so the emphasis was upon social control and domestication, rather than intellectual emancipation. So far as the Anglican Church's interest were concerned, whilst Religion was not a prescribed subject in the Revised Code, biblical material provided the substance of elementary schooling and it was to receive continuing generous financial support from the tax-payer.

The rhetoric of a differentiated educational system, with quality depending upon class, is one thing; the reality is another. We have already seen how one inspired elementary teacher achieved results with poor children so remarkable that they were seen as threatening the status quo. And some teachers and subject experts worked the Revised Code system by introducing educational innovations within existing curriculum space. It remains to explode the myth of "elite classical education". From accounts provided by former public school boys, it appears that the upper class was receiving just such a series of rote-learning and stultifying experiences as children in elementary schools. Former student D'Arcy Thompson describes his experiences at one public school, beginning at the age of seven with a 'portentously bulky' Latin grammar:

> *"The syntax rules, in the edition presented to me were,*
> *for the first time, rendered mercifully in English: those*
> *for gender and quantity remained in the old Latin; and*

the Latin was communicated in a hideously discordant rhythm. Over the years we went systematically through and through that book; page after page, chapter after chapter. It was all unintelligible, all obscure." (34)

So much for the overt official curriculum. The hidden curriculum of the public schools was doubtless at work, helping to develop qualities appropriate for subsequent entry into the upper echelons of society, such as social mores, self-belief and an unquestioned right to lead a life of privilege.

But it is clear that the State was putting social and political considerations before the educational interest.

In short, the differentiated educational system resulting from the above Reports was symbolic rather than substantive. It was certainly not in the interests of the working-class, for whom secondary education seemed as far away as ever. Their continuing struggle to attain this goal provides the substance of the next chapter.

NOTES AND REFERENCES

1. Silver, H. (ed) Robert Owen on Education
2. Morton, A. L. Life and Ideas of Robert Owen
3. op cit
4. op cit
5. op cit
6. Simon, B. Studies in the History of Education 1780-1870
7. This theory assumed that all knowledge was obtained from sense impressionsandthatsubsequentideasbecameassociatedandorganised in the brain - what today we might call conceptualisation.
8. Cole, G. D. H. and Margaret Cole (eds) The Opinions of William Cobbett
9. op cit
10. Cobbett, like several of his contemporaries, sought to educate his own family. The 1931 Report of the Consultative Committee on the Primary School describes his "project method", rejecting current methods of organised book drill. This involved his engaging their interest in the work he was doing on his smallholding and allowing them to discover that this could not be done without "book learning" Similarly, "calculations about farming methods forced arithmetic upon us: the use, the necessity of the thing led us to the study".
11. Roger, L. Sociology of Mathematics and the Cultural Divide: Ideologies of policy and practice. 1750-1900 Roehampton Institute.
12. Simon, B. op cit
13. Cole op cit
14. Johnson, R. (1981) Really Useful Knowledge; Radical education and working-class culture 1790-1848 in Dale, R. et al Politics, Patriarchy and Practice vol.2 Falmer /UO Press. Basingstoke
15. Cole op cit
16. Layton, D. (1973) Science for the People
17. op cit
18. op cit
19. Hodson, D. and Prophet, R.B. Why the Science Curriculum Changes; evolution or social control ? School Science Review Sept 1983
20. op cit
21. McClure op cit
22. Briggs, A. op cit
23. McClure op cit

24. op cit
25. Simon op cit
26. op cit
27. Winter, J. (1976) Robert Lowe. University of Toronto Press. Toronto.
28. Simon op cit
29. Barnard op cit
30. Briggs op cit
31. McClure op cit
32. op cit
33. At the same time, a surprising number of working-class parents sent their children to private schools, for a number of reasons. As with Dame Schools, they did not wish to accept what they saw as charity, they had more control over events, so that teaching was less authoritarian and more informal - and they belonged to the local community.
34. Barnard op cit.

CHAPTER THREE

SECONDARY EDUCATION FOR ALL; "A THREAT TO THE SOCIAL ORDER"

"I am not one of those who throw blame on the School Boards because they have in many cases trespassed on the territories of secondary education.....But frankly I must add that these authorities for primary education have exaggerated their capacity for dealing with secondary education." (A.J Balfour, Prime Minister)

Working the System: Higher Grade Schools
The 1888 Cross Commission: "back-door" secondary education made illegal.
The 1902 Education Ac : selection by ability conceded ; the end of School Boards.
1904 Regulations protect the new social order with two curricula:
*   pastoral for elementary schools*
*   academic for secondary schools.*
The Labour Movement Grows up and get a louder and clearer voice.
The First World War and a feeble 1918 Education ("Part-Time") Act: "plus ca change"

Working the System : Higher Grade Schools

The 1870 Education Act has been hailed as the greatest breakthrough in popular education, with its provision for democratically-elected school boards across the country. But it fell far short of the aspirations of working-class radicals. In the first place, the schooling was oppressive; nor was it free (except in exceptional circumstances) with cases of fines and even imprisonment for non-payment. Neither was it secular, with a dual system operating for school boards and voluntary denominational organisations.

This dual system illustrates the compromises which had to be made to accommodate various interests and pressure groups. For example, the National Education League, made up of Liberals, non-conformists and trade union leaders, demanded, amongst other things, unsectarian schooling. Robert Applegarth, co-founder of the League and trade union leader, accused Forster of conceding too much to the church party:

> *"When I told him that the League would surely fight him on the religious difficulty he was creating, he tartly replied: "Then they will have to fight" (1)*

Conflicting interests were also revealed in the attenuation of the 1870 Act by the continuing demand of mill-owners for cheap child labour and their opposition to any schooling which took the child out of the factory. In fact, as mentioned earlier, it was legally possible to operate a "half-time" system until the 1899 Act put a stop to it; and a part-time system until the 1918 Education Act outlawed it.

But one of the most significant features of the 1870 Act was its support for a continuing demarcation of upper and lower social orders through elementary and secondary schools. Indeed, some endowed grammar schools even began to aspire to the status of independent boarding - schools, by shaking off their obligations to the local community. One common device was to hive off the sons of tradesmen ("the lower-class element") into separate day schools, thus giving exclusive use of the boarding - school to the "sons of gentlemen". Such schools were not only able to acquire "public" school status, but received the ultimate accolade of being admitted to the Headmasters' Conference.

At the other end of the social scale, radicals bitterly criticised the method of drilling in elementary schools, producing submissive children accepting of a capitalist morality. They demanded technical education and training in reasoning, memory and observation and set about working the system to slacken the grip exerted by the 1861 Revised Code.(2) As a result, the 1867 Revised Code was extended to include grammar, geography and history, for which grants were available. And four years later, mathematics, science and languages were added to the curriculum. School boards, recognising the reservoir of ability, began to manipulate the system by allowing pupils to stay on longer in so-called Higher Grade Schools, whilst some schools exploited the situation further by organising their higher work to conform to the grant arrangements of the Science and Art Department ("organised science schools"). So by 1881, 5% of the school population was in the age-range 12-14. Even more enterprising school boards went as far as centralising the system, by grouping higher grades together to give "central schools". Such was the progress being made, that when Commissioners carrying out their investigations for the 1882-4 Samuelson Technical Education Report visited Manchester Central School they were able to report:

> "The results of science teaching in this school are well worthy of note. Out of a total of 320 boys, 276 have passed Standard VI and are taught physiology, chemistry, sound, light, heat, magnetism and electricity, geography, mechanics and French" (3)

The 1888 Cross Commission: an end to all this

Such schools were becoming increasingly popular with middle-class parents and posed a clear threat to the health of both grammar and voluntary schools. Indeed, it was following complaints from Roman Catholics led by Cardinal Manning and backed by the Church of England, that the Cross Commission was set up in 1888 to:

> "inquire into the workings of the Elementary Education Acts in England and Wales". (4)

The resulting committee was stocked with churchmen, including Cardinal Manning himself. One of their recommendations was that grants be increased and that those grants to voluntary schools be paid from the rates, giving them equal opportunities with the school boards. The Report also agreed on the eventual abolition of payment-by-results and the provision of improved facilities for the training of teachers (replacing pupil-teacher centres with training colleges). Despite hearing several witnesses argue cogently for a completely secular schooling, the Commissioners came down on the side of all children receiving religious and moral training through the medium of elementary schools.

As indicated above, the elementary/secondary divide was being blurred by certain radical and enterprising elements working to subvert the principles of the Education Act. To counter this, the Cross Commission suggested that the curriculum of higher elementary schools be restricted in such a way as to avoid it trespassing upon the secondary school curriculum, seen as catering for the needs of an entirely different class and receiving continuous instruction until sixteen or eighteen. In the end, a majority report recommended that the curriculum of the elementary school be reined in, with more attention being paid to handwriting, practical arithmetic, and learning poetry by heart, as well as "good and economical cookery", and some simple physiology.

In this respect, the commissioners were true to form, revealing a surprising indifference to the 1884 Royal Commission on Technical Instruction's expressed concern (from such evidence as that provided by the 1851 Great Exhibition and the subsequent Paris Exhibition of 1867) to the effect that our technological competitiveness was declining with alarming rapidity. (5) It was left to Bernhard Samuelson, chairman of the above Commission to propose the introduction of a system of higher elementary and technical schools in order to introduce a "practical and scientific spirit" in pupils. (6) But the government was still unmoved by such arguments - it was clearly more concerned to maintain the status quo. But these proposals were underpinned by what became known as the Cockerton judgement (7), subsequently enshrined in law, which disallowed any expenditure on higher elementary schools, thus severely constraining the attempts by enterprising school boards to extend the educational opportunities of less fortunate children.

The attitude of the working-class to such developments and its requirements for educational reform are well-illustrated by the remarkable testimony of Thomas Smyth, a plasterer by trade, a manager of evening classes and a representative of the London Trades Council. In the face of hostile questioning by the Cross Commission he made the following observations. On board schools:

> "We are called upon, through taxes and rates, to help maintain and pay for them and we feel they are our own."

On free education from elementary school to university:

> "We feel that it is necessary to have all the roads to education open, free and unfettered to the people."

On religious instruction:

> *"It is liable to become the reflex of the teacher's own dogmatism, however guarded against, and there is a widespread feeling against religious teaching being given in schools supported by the rates and taxes". (8)*

But the Cross Commission was concerned to limit rather than extend the education of the poor. The voice of the working-class once again went unheeded, with the government determined to use the differentiated structure of the education system to underpin the hierarchy of social class through a corresponding hierarchy of knowledge. Plus ca change!

The 1902 Education Act: "SELECTION BY ABILITY"

The voice of the working class grew louder with the enfranchisement of most working males in the 1884 Reform Act. And the position of secondary education in the national education system was still far from settled. So the Tory government, in its 1902 Education Act (after its landslide re-election in 1900) put part of the blame for the incoherence of secondary education upon the school boards. The Prime Minister, A.J. Balfour, introducing the Bill in the Commons, made these comments about school boards, before announcing his intention to abolish them in favour of what came to be called local education authorities (LEA,s):

> *"these authorities for primary education have exaggerated their capacity for dealing with secondary schools…the normal and healthy growth of a true scheme of secondary education has been inevitably warped…I am not one of those who throw blame on the School Boards because they have in many cases trespassed on the territories of the secondary schools…there was a great vacuum to fill. If we are considering the whole field of secondary education no mere addition of higher classes at the top of the elementary schools will carry out the objects we have in view." (9)*

It was clearly a major concern of the Tory government to address the interests of the Anglican Church. Abolishing the school boards was one step towards securing the future of the voluntary sector. But Prime Minister Balfour went further than this, drawing attention to what he called the

> *"deplorable starvation of voluntary schools...after all their great efforts...the voluntary schools are in many cases not adequately equipped and not as well fitted as they should be". (9)*

He thus took the highly controversial step of agreeing to provide financial support from the rates, reforms which meant that tax-payers would be paying for the upkeep of faith schools in a persisting dual system of state and voluntary schools.

But the major problem remained: the access to secondary education. In what had now become a minefield, the government passed the responsibility to local authorities, authorising them "to supply or aid the supply of education other than elementary " - for which purpose they were empowered to charge a rate of 2d in the pound. Out of this tentative approach have come some fundamentally important developments. For example, there emerged the contentious educational principle that entry should be confined to those children seen as able to benefit from a secondary education. This principle of "selection by ability" tended to be implemented in the form of scholarship examinations for elementary schoolchildren (plus payment of fees by parents deemed able to pay).

This was of course widely interpreted as a device for maintaining the class divisions in education. The Labour movement and other interested parties therefore continued to work for the development of higher elementary education as a genuine alternative to secondary education. Eventually the government conceded the principle and permitted pupils able to follow 4-year courses between the ages of 11 and 15 to pursue these in higher elementary or central schools, where the curriculum had a commercial or technical emphasis. But the crunch came with the rule: no external examinations, thus ensuring that these schools could not compete with secondary schools in terms of status or credibility.

1904 Regulations: Two Curricula: Elementary (pastoral) and Secondary (academic)

This new principle of "selection by ability" could be interpreted in different ways. On the one hand, it could be argued that the working-class were winning their struggle for secondary education. On the other hand, it might be claimed that access to secondary education for the select few was a way of revivifying the ruling class by hybrid vigour – and there was also the possibility that this select band might take on aristocratic values and become genuine members of the upper class.

It was important for the State, therefore, to ensure there was no loosening of the barriers built into the social order. It was Sir Robert Morant, the permanent secretary of the new Board of Education (formed from the merging of the Education Department, the Science and Art Department and the Charity Commission) who solved this problem by developing separate curricula for elementary and secondary education in such a way that not only would the social order be maintained but the changes would not easily be undone.

In the case of the 1904 Elementary Code, the curriculum took the following form:

MORANT'S AFFECTIVE ELEMENTARY CURRICULUM

Purpose:
> "to form and strengthen the character and to develop the intelligence of the children entrusted to it and to make the best use of the school years available, in assisting both girls and boys, according to their different needs, to fit themselves, practically as well as intellectually, for the work of life" (8)

Human Attributes:
- moral: strengthening of character; self-control, perseverance
- utilitarian: fit themselves for the work for the work of life
- physical: healthy development of their bodies
- cultural: familiarity with the literature and history of their own country
- intellectual: develop intelligence, reasoning ,observation
- personal: develop special gifts.

Pedagogy:
> each teacher should think for himself (sic) and work out such methods of teaching as may use his powers to the best advantage.

There are several admirable features of this curriculum in purely educational terms. It moves away from the rote learning underpinning "payment-by-results" previously characterising elementary schooling. And the role of the teacher would now involve practical judgements as well as technical rule - following. But – apart from its acceptability to employers of the workforce - this "affective" (10) curriculum ensured that elementary schooling still had both low status and social credibility. - and was not in any way a preparation for secondary education.

That this curriculum was designed to confirm the low status of elementary schoolchildren was underlined by Morant's 1904 Regulations for Secondary Schools which could be conceptualised in the following terms:

MORANT'S COGNITIVE SECONDARY CURRICULUM

- English, Geography and History- not less than 4 and 1/2 hours per week
- Science and Mathematics - not less than 7 and 1/2hours
- Language - not less than 3½ hours (preferably Latin if more than 1 language- where two languages are taken and Latin is not one of them, the Board will be require to be satisfied that the omission of Latin is for the advantage of the school).
- Manual work and physical exercises.

It can readily be seen that this secondary school curriculum was to be tightly prescribed in terms of subject labels roughly along the lines of the public school, with no reference to its possible utility (apart of course from preserving social divisions). It has been described in fact as a clone of the public school curriculum. It ensured once again that secondary education would be more concerned with producing cultured gentlemen than technologists, following in the footsteps of the "great public schools" as described in the Clarendon Report 40 years earlier. [But as the Spens Report put it several years later (see next chapter) it "failed to take note of the comparatively rich experience of a practical and quasi- vocational type which had been evolved in Higher Grade Schools"].

Corelli Barnett was more forthright:

> *"The Arnoldian public school, with its high-minded emphasis on religion and the classics, and its late Victorian successor's vaunting of team-games and imperial patriotism not only helped to create a non-technological intelligentsia and governing elite, but also served as a baneful model for the reformed grammar schools and, after 1902, for the new state secondary schools". (11)*

(Whatever the explanation, despite the many educational reforms, the UK slipped from world leader economically in 1870 to fifteenth place a century later.)

To summarise, Morant, contemptuous of the working class, had by his Revised Code and Regulations cleverly drawn new lines of demarcation between elementary and secondary education, which could only be breached by deserving "bright" children passing the scholarship examination. But in introducing this new concept of "selection by ability", the government was storing up a considerable amount of trouble for itself - as we shall see in the next chapter..

The Labour Movement Grows Up and Develops a Louder and Clearer Voice

The developments described above were a far cry from the demands of working-class radicals for a free, secular education from nursery to university open to all. The fact that so little account had been taken by previous governments of working-class demands pointed to a lack both of coordination and political influence from the various radical organisations. But in 1868, voluntary associations of trades councils and unions combined, for their own protection and welfare and to amplify their voice, to form the Trade Unions Congress, with an educational policy, to be repeated continuously, of "equal opportunities for all". And the 1880's were noteworthy for the emergence of a number of a left-wing parties [H.M. Hyndman's Social Democratic Federation, with the aims of universal suffrage and nationalisation of the means of production and distribution; Keir Hardie's Independent Labour Party with the main objective, now that skilled artisans had the vote, of getting some working-class people into Parliament; and an intellectual Fabian Society, dedicated to gradualist reform and increasing efficiency.]

But the lack of progress made by such fragmented groups, and attacks by the government on trade union rights, led to the realisation that collective action was the only way forward. On February 27, 1900, representatives of the various groups met in London and passed a motion to establish

> *"a distinct Labour group in Parliament, who shall have*
> *their own whips, and agree upon their policy, which*
> *must embrace a readiness to cooperate with any party*
> *which for the time being may be engaged in promoting*
> *legislation in the direct interests of labour ".(12)*

Thus was the Labour Representation Committee formed. In the 1900 General Election, two members were elected to the House of Commons. By 1906, this number had increased to 29 and at this point the name of the organisation was changed to the Labour Party.

The clear message of the 1902 Act was that elementary education was essentially for the lower orders, in preparation for manual work, whilst the children of the upper classes were to have an "intellectual" secondary education, fitting them for the higher reaches of society. This separation was to be assured by the abolition of elected school boards and the invoking, where necessary, of the Cockerton judgement. What was seen as the retrogressive character of the 1902 Act aroused furious opposition. The TUC held conferences to protest against the abolition of school boards and sent out circulars urging members to put pressure on their M.P.'s to vote only for councillors opposing the bill. (A reminder that political groupings are not monolithic was provided by Sidney Webb, founder- member of the Fabian Society, who went against the party line by supporting the abolition of school boards on the grounds of administrative efficiency, a split exploited by the Tory party to the full).

But such reactions to the 1902 Bill, including Labour demands for free secondary and technical education (and Nonconformist objections to the idea that they should be compelled to pay for the teaching of the Anglican creed through State endowments) were ignored by the Tory government, more concerned at the time with the demands of other interest groups.

Ultimately the TUC produced, in 1905, its own Education Bill: "to promote the improvement of Education and the Physique of Children attending Elementary Schools", with the following requirements:

secular instruction,
secondary and technical education for all who desire it,
at least one free meal a day, and
the appointment of a medical officer,

the cost to be borne both by the Exchequer and by the restoration of those educational endowments which had been stolen from them.

But before the TUC Education Bill could be presented to the government, the Tories, under Balfour, had been ousted from office in the 1906 Election, with Liberals gaining 377 seats, Tories 157 and Labour the substantial number of 53. It was, then, a very different Parliament to which the TUC Bill was presented on 2 April, 1906. A week later the government introduced its own bill, but this dealt only with the sectarian aspects of the 1902 Act. It was of little consequence, since it was thrown out by the Lords. Despite furious demands by all left-wing groups for a secular education, an amendment in the Commons in favour of secular education was defeated by 477 to 63, an indication of the strength of opposition to any suggestion of the removal of religious instruction from state schools.

However, with a Liberal government in office, the Labour Party was rewarded with some success. In 1907, the scholarship system for entry into secondary school was rationalised and extended. A grant of £5 was awarded for each student admitted, provided the school admitted no less than 25% of the school population as free scholars by an entrance test. Although this was still seen as controversial by those more radical elements demanding a staircase not a ladder into secondary schooling, it represented to reformists some sort of victory for continuing agitation. The government - doubtless mindful of lessons to be learnt from the poor physique of those fighting in the Boer War a few years previously - also went some way to meeting those welfare demands in the TUC Bill. In 1906 an Education (Provision of School Meals) Act enabled local authorities to supply school meals out of the rates; the following year another Act required local authorities to institute medical examinations and by 1911 there were 900 medical officers. On the other hand TUC pressure for an inquiry into the endowments system and for the abolition of half-time working for children was unsuccessful.

The First World War and a feeble 1917 Education (Part-time) Act

The Labour movement constantly repeated calls for a free, full-time secondary education for all until, in 1914, hostilities provided a diversion. The First World War had several implications for the British educational system: the deficiencies in technical education compared to Germany; and the surprising contribution elementary school children showed they could make to the war effort, by working on the land. (13) Lloyd George, when he replaced Asquith as Liberal Prime Minister, quickly resolved to implement a programme of educational reconstruction. In 1916, he set up the Lewis Committee "to consider what steps should be taken to make provision for the education and instruction of children and young persons after the war". The Committee came to the conclusion that, not only was public education after elementary school a part-time affair, but there was very little of it. The Report continued with these radical and stirring words:

> "What, then, are the remedies? But there is only one remedy .....nothing less than a complete change of temper and outlook on the part of the people of this country as to what they mean, through the forces of industry and society, to make of their boys and girls. Can the age of adolescence be brought out of the purview of economic exploitation and into that of the social conscience? Can the conception of the juvenile as primarily a little wage-earner be replaced by the conception of the juvenile as primarily the workman and citizen in training. Can it be established that the educational purpose is to be the dominating one ?" (14)

But the Report did not follow the implications of its own rhetoric by recommending secondary education for all. Instead, it recommended early legislation to establish a uniform elementary school leaving age of 14, and attendance for not less than eight hours a week at day continuation classes from 14 to 18. No curricular recommendations were made, nor was there any recognition of the effect of these proposals on social structures. The working-class interest was still not being taken seriously.

In 1917 H.A.L. Fisher, President of the Board of Education introduced his Education Bill, by acknowledging the contribution of elementary children to the war effort:

> *"If anyone had doubted the value of our elementary schools, that doubt must have been dispelled by the experience of the war"*

He then took up the theme of the Lewis Report that the industrial workers of the country are entitled to be considered primarily as citizens, but this was firmly set in the reactionary context of the current social stratification:

> *"There is a growing sense that...the industrial workers of the country are to be considered primarily as citizens and as fit subjects for any form of education from which they are capable of profiting. I notice also that a new way of thinking about education has sprung up among the more reflecting members of our industrial army. They do not want education only in order that they may become technical workmen and earn higher wages. They do not want it in order that they may rise out of their own class, always a vulgar ambition, they want it because they know that in the treasures of the mind they can find an aid to good citizenship (and) a source of pure enjoyment." (15)*

Fisher is here patronising the workforce in the most blatant fashion. And his words proved to be empty. Although he appears to be advocating a broad, intrinsic - even an academic - education for the future workforce, his Act revealed this as pure humbug. Once again this did not stretch as far as secondary education for all – nor were there any relevant curricular recommendations. But he did announce the abolition of fees in elementary schools, a uniform and compulsory raising of the school-leaving age to 14 (eventually introduced in 1920) and the extension of school life at both ends by empowering LEA's to provide nursery classes and by the introduction of free day continuation schools up to the age of 16. But the Act is perhaps best remembered for its abolition of half-time working. (it became known as the Half-Time Act) and the emergence of industry as a force to be reckoned with. The organisation of industry into lobbying groups with a louder voice was now under way and one of these groups, the Federation of British Industry (forerunner to the CBI) made it abundantly clear that these developments were not in its interests:

> *"Industry is unable to bear the burden of releasing juvenile labour for eight hours a week...only a small*

minority of children are able to benefit by secondary
education... creating (as in India) a large class of persons
whose education is unsuitable for the employment which
they eventually enter" (16)

This was an early intimation of the growing tension between the business and education interests. It was now clear that the government would have to take the business interest more seriously. In the face of what was now an organised lobbying group the proposal for continuation schools was dropped from the final Bill. But, to meet increased expenditure, LEA's were allocated a 50% grant from the Treasury, which however was reduced by a third in 1921 because of financial stringencies.

In the end, whose interests had been met in the Bills described in this chapter? From one perspective, it could be said that the interests of the working-class were satisfied by a scholarship system which allowed access to secondary education for those able to benefit. The Anglican Society was given financial security and a compromise was reached with industry whereby – although part-time working was abolished - continuation schools were not proceeded with . But the State had sustained - by ensuring that any concessions were relatively minor - both the social order and its reproduction, through the differentiation of knowledge along class lines.

The Labour movement at the time was not slow to see the implications of the Fisher Act. At the 1918 Labour Party conference, a resolution was put forward expressing dissatisfaction with

"a system condemning the great bulk of children to
merely elementary schooling, with accommodation
and equipment inferior to that of secondary schools, in
classes too large for efficient instruction...and which,
notwithstanding what is done by way of scholarships for
exceptional geniuses still reserves the endowed secondary
schools...to the sons and daughters of a small privileged
class".

As far as working-class radicals were concerned, the struggle for mass secondary education was clearly far from over. It would now be accompanied by the battle-cry "Equal opportunities for All." How "equality" was to be defined and implemented in subsequent educational reorganisation is the subject of the next chapter.

NOTES AND REFERENCES

1. Lawson and Silver op cit
2. Mary Waring (in Goodson op cit) describes how the presence of the famous scientist Thomas Huxley on the London School Board was instrumental in science being
    introduced into London elementary schools. Problems facing this initiative included
    the lack of suitable teachers and the kind of science being taught. In the end a tradition of individual practical work had become established.
3. B. Simon op cit
4. McClure op cit
5. The Devonshire Report of 1875, for instance, on public and endowed schools revealed an alarming indifference to the role of Science in a modern curriculum. Of the 128 schools replying to requests for information, only 63 taught any Science at all (30 of these without a regular slot in the timetable) and only 13 had any laboratories.
6. The subsequent Technical Instruction Act empowered local authorities to raise a 1 penny rate in order to supply or aid technical and manual instruction.
7. H.C. Barnard op cit
8. All extracts from B. Simon op cit.
9. McClure op cit
10. Psychologists for their own convenience (and lately that of the marketing and advertising men) divide human behaviour into three domains: the affective consisting of feelings, emotions, interest etc; the cognitive, consisting of thinking, comprehension, knowledge etc.; and the conative – action, intentionality, willpower etc.
11. www.victorianweb.org/history/barnett.html
12. Simon op cit
13. This, and the fact that illiteracy had virtually disappeared is a corrective to the view that elementary schooling had only negative effects.
14. McClure op cit.
15. op cit
16. Simon op cit
op cit

CHAPTER FOUR

SECONDARY EDUCATION FOR ALL: THANKS TO A NEW SOCIAL SCIENCE

> *"All humans are equal but some are more equal than others" (after George Orwell)*

Adolescence Comes of Age: the Ground-breaking Hadow Reports
The Beginning of the End for the ElementarySchool: the birth of the Primary School
The Equality Principle and Secondary Education:
  (a) the Spens Report: Psychometrics to the Rescue;
  (b) the Norwood Report: Men of Gold, Silver and Bronze: thanks be to Providence
The 1944 Education Act and the Reality of a Tripartite Secondary System

Fisher, in introducing the 1918 Education Act, appeared to not only give a more generous interpretation of education but to express a desire to extend its availability to all children:

> *"We assume that education is one of the good things of life which should be more widely shared than has hitherto been the case amongst the children and young persons of this country. We assume that education is of the whole man, spiritually, intellectually and physically and it is not beyond the resources of civilisation to devise a scheme of education...from which the whole youth of the country, male and female, may derive benefit." (1)*

This high-flown rhetoric may have given the impression that a good secondary education for all young people was just around the corner. But the reality was far different. The 1921 Census showed that whilst 55% of 11-16 year olds were in elementary schools, only 7% were in grant-aided secondary schools. In September, 1918, shortly after the passage of the Act, the Trades Union Congress, whose membership had doubled to four million in the period from 1909 to 1914, called once more, in its Annual Report, for equality of educational opportunity, to be realised by the expansion of free common secondary and higher education. But there was no consensus – even on the political left - on what form equality of opportunity might take. The principle of "selection by ability" had divided the political left, with the Fabian Sidney Webb – a strong supporter of the scholarship system for selecting the cleverest children to go to grant-maintained secondary schools - merely wanting this system extended to 200 places a year.

The current system of elementary and secondary education, with separate populations, reflected the economic and social order of manual and mental labour. But events were unfolding which were to put fresh pressure on this state of affairs. An integrated system, with all schoolchildren proceeding into secondary education, would present a serious challenge to the social order, a challenge which the state had so far sidestepped with a series of tactical retreats. Although Labour had produced a pamphlet "Secondary Education for All" (with its intellectual high priest R.H. Tawney, as the prime mover) when it came to power in 1926 it still declined an immediate challenge. Instead it asked the Consultative (Hadow) Committee of the Education Department to review the experiments which had been carried out with post-primary education, with a remit which specifically excluded consideration of secondary education:

> *"to consider and report upon the organisation, objective and curriculum of courses of study suitable for children who remain in full-time attendance at schools, other than secondary schools, up to the age of 15" (3)*

Adolescence Comes of Age: the Ground - breaking Hadow Report

But perhaps the government, in setting up this committee, got more than it bargained for.The report of the Hadow committee is highly significant for many reasons. In the first place the committee was clearly aware of current psychological findings on child development; so the tone of their report is different from any of their predecessors in regarding children as subjects with their own biological and psychological needs, rather than as objects to be manipulated. The very title of their Report, "Educating the Adolescent" is indicative of this shift of emphasis. It begins with a literary flourish:

"There is a tide which begins to rise in the veins of youth at the age of eleven or twelve. It is called by the name of adolescence. If that tide can be taken at the flood and a new voyage begun in the strength and along the flow of its current, we think that it will 'move on to fortune'"
(4),

before reviewing the evolution of the elementary into "higher grade" schools and the incoherent results of experiments with post-primary education (central schools, junior technical schools, higher elementary schools and pupil-teacher centres). The Committee then ignored their remit by using psychological evidence in order to justify the transfer of children from the elementary school at the age of 11 or 12 to either :

grammar (currently fee-paying secondary schools) to at least the age of 16;
modern (currently central schools) with at least a four-year course;
senior classes, for pupils over the age of 11 not going to either of the above.

Having acknowledged the existence of adolescence as an important and major component of human development, the Committee concluded that the "new environment should be adjusted as far as possible to the interests and abilities of each range and variety." The enlightened and ambitious ends they had in view included:

- the forming and strengthening of character;
- the training of the tastes which will fill and dignify leisure;
- the awakening and the guiding of the intelligence,

with the curriculum of modern schools and senior classes being "realistic" and "practical". Insisting that modern schools and the children in them should not be seen to be inferior to grammar schools, the committee insisted on parity of teacher qualifications and staffing levels as well as standards of equipment, and recommended the school-leaving age be raised to 15.

This Hadow Report was important for several reasons:

(1) it had brought into the public domain issues of child and curriculum development - if in rudimentary form ;

(2)   it had used these issues to justify the existence of a secondary stage of education:

> *"The word "secondary" is in many ways an admirable one. It suggests clearly and precisely the essential fact that the concern of the secondary school is with the second stage of education. 'Primary' and 'secondary' carry their meaning on their face and set the relations between the first and second stages of education in the right perspective" (5)*

an argument the government would find difficult to refute;

(3) it also made some very enlightened comments on the potential dangers of industrialism, which education could counter to make industry more effective:

> *"Industrialism has its grave effects on national life. It demands, only too often, a narrow specialisation of faculty; it produces only too readily, a patterned uniformity of work and behaviour; and it may, unless corrected, infect the minds of men with the genius of its own life. Education can correct industrialism, by giving to the mind the breadth and fresh vitality of new interests, and it can also make industry more effective." (6)*

The Beginning of the End for Elementary Education: "The Primary School"

In short, the Hadow Report, by drawing upon psychological evidence, had made a compelling case for the separation of schooling into primary and secondary stages. It received widespread approval and in 1928, the Board of Education published a pamphlet urging local authorities to adopt its proposals. In the same year it set up another consultative committee, once again under Hadow and with a majority of the former committee members

> *"to inquire and report as to the courses of study suitable for children (other than infants) up to the age of 11 in elementary schools". (7)*

The resulting report, with the pre-emptive title "The Primary School", is a remarkable document, not least for the detailed follow-up to the basic idea of child development presented in the previous Report. Interviewing almost 100 witnesses and calling upon available psychological evidence, it takes a comprehensive developmental approach to children's growth, particularly in the age range 7-11 years. For example:

- physical development: muscular/skeletal, auditory; visual etc.
- mental development, in the areas of attention; memory; imagination; reasoning etc.
- emotional development: i.e. motivation; changing interests.

(The Committee accepted that studies in child development were at an early stage and suggested further detailed investigations for this age-range.)

The organisational implications of the above included a separation of the age-range 5-7 and 7-11 into different departments, and because of different rates of children's development in the latter age-range a separation of the more from the less advanced children – although there was no suggestion that the sexes should be separated.

The "child-centred" approach of the Report received perhaps its most revolutionary expression – and the one for which it is best remembered - when turning to the curriculum which:

> "is to be thought of in terms of activity and experience rather than knowledge to be acquired and facts to be stored". (8)

It gave expression to these ideas by recommending the use of topics rather than formal subjects (e.g. a school garden for nature study, and weather records for geography), as well as new approaches like the "project" method in both practical and concrete contexts. Its progressive and humane character is further revealed by its emphasis upon dancing as a form of physical culture, and craftwork as a means of liberalising closed rule-following activities.

The committee recognised that such a break from the traditional curriculum would make daunting demands, not least in terms of classroom discourse, upon the teacher. The Report therefore recommended that teachers should have general rather then specialised qualifications and have served a probationary year; they should also spend most of their time with the same small class of children. The comparison with the monitorial schools of a century earlier, with their enormous class sizes, is stark - here the Committee argues that the maximum class size for a Hadow primary school should be no more than forty. (9)

It was through its obvious concern for children's welfare that the Committee introduced a new environmental perspective on mass education, arguably to develop into the sociology of education. Through surveys conducted in wealthy (Dulwich etc) and poor (Lambeth etc) boroughs of London to explore the correspondence between poverty and educational retardation, they revealed that whereas in the poor districts, educational retardation was of the order of 20%, in the wealthy areas, it was no more that 1%. Whilst accepting a possible genetic component, they also pointed to malnutrition, poor hygiene and health, as well as linguistic deprivation as factors in underachievement in school, before making suggestions on the detection and education of mentally retarded children. It is in the context of such variability of pupil intake that the Report concludes (compare the current system of league tables):

> *"We cannot too strongly deprecate the tendency to base*
> *a comparative estimate of the efficiency of schools upon*
> *the class lists of a selective "free place" examination".*
> *(10)*

Things would never be the same after these two ground-breaking Reports (although their educational ideas were to be in constant tension with those defining schooling in terms of social control.) They had:

(1) brought the child nearer to the centre of the stage ;
(2) introduced psychological and sociological factors into the equality/ inequality equation;
(3) clearly defined state education as a two-stage process: primary and secondary.

They had in fact signalled the demise of elementary schooling and provided legitimation for a new conception of state education, with "primary" and "secondary" forming an integrated system. [This narrative, however, repeatedly raises the question "Which educational model becomes the preferred option and why?" The notion of "child-centred education", for example, was to become the straw man in the continuing struggle between progressives and reactionaries, as we shall see.] So the prevailing social order was again under threat. Let us see how the State reacted to this new challenge.

The Equality Principle and Secondary Education :

(a) The Spens Report: "PsychoMetrics" to the Rescue

In clarifying the distinction between "primary" and "secondary" education, the Hadow Committee had at the same time recommended what was essentially a bipartite secondary system of grammar and modern schools as its model. In other words, it had reflected the current orthodoxy in neglecting technical education. Nor was this omission challenged very forcefully by commercial and industrial interests. But ever since the Samuelson Report, there had been growing unease in some quarters about the state of technical education in the country, and this unease led to the setting up in 1933 of the Spens Committee with the remit

> *"to consider and report on the organisation of those schools where the pupils do not remain beyond the age of 16 ".*

The Committee condemned the 1904 Regulations for making the academic curriculum the archetype for all secondary schools. It went on:

> *"We are convinced that it is of the greatest importance to establish a new type of higher school of technical character…To provide a good intellectual discipline and to have a technical value in relation to a group of industries…and as a first step we recommend that a number of the existing Junior Technical Schools which at present provide a curriculum based on the engineering industries…should be converted into Technical High Schools in the sense that they should be accorded in every respect equality of status with schools of the grammar school type".(11)*

So there would now be three types of state secondary school: grammar, technical and modern, with a recommended leaving age of 16. This separation raises the question of how children would be selected fairly and justifiably for these different routes, a question which could theoretically be answered by the Aristotelian Equality Principle: "equals to be treated equally; unequals to be treated to be unequally". But how was "equality" to be established?

The Spens Committee was clearly impressed by recent psychometric work on intellectual development:

> "intellectual development during childhood appears to progress as if it were governed by a single central factor... 'general intelligence'...innate intellectual ability. It appears to enter into everything which the child attempts to think, say or do, and seems to be the most important factor in determining his (sic) work in the classroom.. (we are) assured that it can be measured approximately by means of intelligence tests...Because these mental differences grow larger with age, different children from the age of 11...if justice is to be done require types of education varying in certain important respects"(12)

The Committee then expressed its confident belief that this selective examination at the age of 11+ was capable of selecting those pupils who had so much intelligence that they ought to receive a grammar school education. As for the others:

> "We recommend that the age of recruitment for these (technical) schools should be 11+ and that the method of recruitment should be through the general selective examination by which children are recruited for the Grammar Schools." (13)

So was born the controversial eleven-plus examination for separating unequals for unequal treatment in terms of their "intelligences". It is perhaps appropriate that a Report stressing technical education should have accepted a technicist approach to education; that is, the effecting of social control through quantitative technical means such as psychometrics.

(This is the first, but it was not to be the last time that the education system was to take a technicist approach to problems, as later chapters will show.)

The Spens Report showed more confidence in the validity of intelligence tests than subsequent evidence would justify. More recent research has indicated that there is no single general intelligence (the fashion today being for "multiple intelligences") that intelligence can be developed and that intelligence tests are culture-biased. But with the prospect that intelligence testing met a pressing social need, LEA's began to use them and the Board of Education expressed its confidence that the value of intelligence tests was higher than supposed and recommended that they be used in every examination for special places.

The assumption that children could now receive an education commensurate with their abilities gave support to a particular version of equality of opportunity. The idea that "appropriate" secondary education could now be given to all children even found some support among Labour ranks, thus weakening the claims of those radicals demanding common schools with no selection. But it was recognised that the whole edifice would collapse in the absence of what came to be known as parity of esteem:

> "If schools providing secondary education of different types are to be made equally acceptable to parents, and opportunities for entering the type of school which can best develop their particular abilities are to be made equally available to children, the establishment of parity between all types of secondary school is a fundamental requirement". (14)

(b) The Norwood Report: Men of Gold, Silver and Bronze - thanks to Providence

The Spens Report was quickly overtaken by the events of the Second World War. But the work of the Committee was supplemented by a special committee set up in 1941 under the chairmanship of the former headmaster of Harrow School Sir Cyril Norwood, with the following remit:

> *"to consider suggested changes in the secondary school curriculum and the question of school examinations in relation thereto." (15)*

The problem of school examinations was therefore firmly on the educational agenda and has remained there ever since. It is therefore necessary to briefly recapitulate the development of the examination system.

The Development of the Examination System

Examinations had become increasingly popular in the 1850's and 60's, as the capitalist competitive ethic and social Darwinism ("social survival of the fittest") replaced nepotism and corruption. In the 1850's Civil Service examinations were initiated as a means of recruitment, and in 1858, Oxford and Cambridge "Locals" were introduced for pupils from both endowed and private schools. In 1874, the first examinations for university entry were launched by the Oxford and Cambridge Joint Board, to be taken by public school boys of age 18. By the end of the century several examination boards were competing for candidates and the situation was not only fragmented but it became increasingly evident that "the curriculum was following the examination" with pupils being crammed by their teachers.

A Consultative Committee in 1911 recommended some coordination, with the result that the seven university examination boards of the time standardised their schemes in the form of a lower school (school certificate) based on a general curriculum for sixteen-year olds and a higher school (higher certificate) for more specialised subjects at 18. In 1917, the Board of Education set up a Secondary Schools Examination Council to control the standards of the various examinations. But criticism continued, both of the pressures a "grouped" examination was placing on pupils and of certain abuses which were taking place, such as some universities regarding the lower certificate as adequate for entry purposes.

This was roughly the situation which the Norwood Committee inherited and which they were required to examine. They proposed the abolition of the school certificate and its replacement by a single-subject examination as a preliminary to internal examinations run by the schools themselves. They also recommended a school-leaving age of 18 for university entrants and continued part-time education up the age of 18 for others.

But the Committee went far beyond its brief in describing the attributes of children in terms of tripartite organisation. Since these proclaimed attributes provide an insight into Establishment rationalisation at the time, they are worth quoting in some detail:

> *"English education has in practice recognised the pupil who is interested in learning for its own sake…who can grasp an argument…is interested in causes and a coherent body of knowledge…is sensitive to language…such pupils (are) commonly associated with the grammar school.*

> *"Again, the history of technical education has demonstrated the importance of recognising the needs of pupils whose interests and abilities lie in the field of applied science or applied art…he (sic) often has an uncanny insight into the intricacies of mechanism, whereas the subtleties of language construction are too delicate for him.*

> *"..(there is) still another grouping of pupils …the pupil in this group deals more easily with concrete things than with ideas….interested in things as they are…Because he is interested only in the moment he may be incapable of a long series of connected steps…abstractions mean little to him…his test is essentially practical." (16)*

We have here a classic example of "theory" being invented to fit a particular social system: these divisions are redolent of the Platonic ideals of men of gold, silver and bronze corresponding to - in economic terms - professionals, technicians and operatives. We would now recognise these descriptions as outrageously presumptuous. But at the time they served their purpose in providing legitimation for divisions of labour in the world of work - in that sense they were providential. But since these divisions are accompanied by differences of status etc. they throw into doubt the possibility that there could ever be "parity of esteem" between the different secondary courses. The next chapter will show to what extent parents accepted the Equality Principle as a legitimate basis for selection, using intelligence quotients as one of the criteria for equality/inequality and hence as justification for providing different types of schooling for their children.

The 1944 Education Act: The Reality of a Tripartite System

The Second World War, like the first, had several profound implications for the educational system. Technological shortcomings were once again revealed. On the other hand, a sense of solidarity developed, together with an idealistic feeling that life must be better after the war than it was before - "a land fit for heroes". But there was no consensus about what a "better life" entailed for schoolchildren.

The Spens and Norwood Reports enshrined a particular view of equality: that unequals be treated unequally, with different criteria for 'inequality'. Several organisations disputed this interpretation as they drew up plans for a post-war Britain. In September 1942, the Workers Educational Association, the Trades Union Congress, the Cooperative Union and the National Union of Teachers formed the Council for Educational Advance, for the:

> *"purpose of securing the swift passage of an Education Bill to provide full equality of opportunity for all children, independent of social or economic status in order to equip them for democratic citizenship and a full and happy life." (17)*

And at the Labour Party Conference in May 1942 a demand was made for a sound, comprehensive educational system. It should be noted that over the years the working-class educational aspirations had shifted from the concrete here-and-now "Really Useful Knowledge" to the abstract "equality of educational opportunity" without making clear what precisely was involved in terms of substance - although the implication was that children of the working-class should have access to the same sort of education as those of the ruling elite.

The war-time coalition government of Tory and Labour Parties also consulted widely on the future of state education and in 1943 produced a White Paper on Educational Reconstruction proposing a continuous process of education. Other matters needing to be addressed included:

the continued existence of the public schools ("two nations");
the dual system: the voluntary system was once again in a run-down state;
the control and organisation of the finally agreed system.

In the following year, the Education Bill was presented to Parliament, establishing a statutory system made up of three progressive stages, primary, secondary and further education. A Minister of Education was appointed to be responsible for the organisation and control of the education of the people of England and Wales, with local authorities under his direction. Local authorities had a duty to secure adequate provision of primary and secondary education. Tuition fees were forbidden. As for the other issues raised above:

(a) the school-leaving age was to be raised to 15, with power to delay this for two years;
(b) the dual system was retained: an increased grant was allocated to voluntary bodies, in return for more democratic representation (e.g. LEA's on governing bodies). In the State sector, religious education was to be compulsory (to an agreed syllabus) and there was to be a daily act of collective worship,
(c) as far as the public schools were concerned, a committee had been set up under Lord Fleming, but it had conveniently failed to report by the time the Education Bill was published. So the private sector was left largely untouched to carry on preparing children from the privileged classes for entry to university and top positions in society - completely at odds with the comprehensive principle.

Local authorities were charged with contributing towards the spiritual, moral, mental and physical development of the community, whilst parents had the duty to cause their children to receive efficient, full-time education suitable to their age, aptitude and ability. The government referred the contentious and electorally dangerous issue of secondary organisation to the local authorities who generally followed the lead given by the Spens and Norwood Reports and provided education for their charges - depending on the result of an 11-plus examination - in one of three schools,

- Grammar;
- Technical High;
- Secondary Modern.

Whose interests could the Education Act be said to serve? The public and grammar schools retained their privileged positions, along with their academic curriculum (the public schools even keeping their charitable status). And the Anglican Church not only received generous financial assistance from the taxpayer for the upkeep of their faith schools, but Voluntary (Controlled) schools were supported entirely by the State. So it could be argued that both aristocratic and clerical interests had been met. What of the children of the lower class? They were now entitled to a secondary education, but access was constrained in accordance with the State's definition of their capacity to benefit from it.

So the State had done it again ! Whilst it may be argued that it had met the educational demands of the working-class, it had at the same time managed to establish a tripartite school system, reflecting the increasingly-dominant capitalist mode of production, with its separation of mental and manual labour, as well as sustaining social class divisions. And the public schools system had been left untouched. In other words, it had ensured the continued reproduction of the social order.

So far as one interested party - the radical left - was concerned, although the country might have moved a long way since the early nineteenth century from elementary to secondary school, there was some way to go the final revolutionary goal of common, secular and comprehensive education.

NOTES AND REFERENCES

1. McClure op cit
2. Barnard op cit.
3. McClure op cit
4. Hadow Report "Educating the Adolescent"
5. McClure op cit
6. Hadow Report "Educating the Adolescent"
7 Hadow Report "The Primary School"
8. op cit
9. When the "bosses" (National Association of Inspectors and Educational Organisers) were asked about the optimum size of a primary school class, the figure 40-44 was recommended ("teacher personality is more important than class size"). When the "workers" (the London Teachers' Association) were asked the same question, a figure of not more than 35 was given. Arguments about class size have continued to the present day, with claims being made to the effect that class size was irrelevant - irrespective of what was being taught, and how.
10. Hadow Report "The Primary School" op cit
11. McClure op cit
12. op cit.
13. op cit
14. Barnard op cit
15. McClure op cit.
16. op cit.
17. B. Simon op cit.
18. McCulloch op cit

CHAPTER FIVE

COMPREHENSIVISATION BRINGS A NEW SET OF PROBLEMS

> *"The comprehensive ideal remains powerful. The belief that drove politicians like Crosland should drive us now. It is a passion that all children, from whatever background, are alike in their capacity to reason, to imagine, to aspire to a successful life." (Ruth Kelly, Education Secretary overseeing the City Academies programme, in lecture to Fabian Society, 2005).*

1945 – The First Postwar Labour Government - and Backsliding
A hierarchical bipartite system confirmed by examinaion:
> *the grammar school and GCE's,*
> *the secondary modern school and CSE's*

Cracks in the Façade "Down with the Eleven-Plus"
1964 – Labour in Power Again and requesting comprehensive plans with Circular 10/65
Curriculum Inertia: Where Have All the Radicals Gone?

The First Post-war Labour Government – and backsliding

The Butler Education Act received the Royal Assent in August 1944. Within a year, and with the war in Europe over, the Labour Party was elected with a landslide majority, and with a mandate from an expectant and war-weary public for radical reform. The Labour Party had, at its conferences, pledged to introduce comprehensive education. The 1944 Act had not stipulated a tripartite system but the new Ministry of Education, following the Spens and Norwood Reports, interpreted the Act along these lines, supporting its stance by issuing the pamphlet "The Nation's Schools". This argued against comprehensive schools on such grounds as the resultant unwieldy size of multilateral 11-18 schools. Once again, the claims of technical education were ignored, with technical high schools almost disappearing from the scene, in what could be seen as the maintenance of the cognitive/ pastoral division introduced in Morant's 1904 Regulations. Instead the government set up what was essentially a bipartite system, with 25% of the school population recommended for a grammar school education, and the rest being in secondary modern schools (the latter being for those members of the working -class "whose future employment will not demand any measure of technical skill or knowledge"). Admittedly, some members of the political left had accepted the principle of "selection by ability". But here was a Labour government, ostensibly representing a Labour movement with an overwhelming majority demanding radical policies, confirming the educational status quo, and accepting the spurious legitimation of psychometrics as a means of justifying its divisive policies. Not only was it resisting comprehensivisation but it was overtly reinforcing traditional occupational and social divisions. "Equality of opportunity" was being given a new interpretation. Not for the first time a voice in opposition was changing its tune when in government - and raising the question "where is the locus of power?"

This reactionary policy was reinforced with Circular 103 "Examinations in Secondary Schools" prohibiting any pupils from schools other than grammar schools from taking external examinations until after the age of 16 (rationalised on the grounds that these schools would thus be "free from the pressure of external examinations to work out the best and most appropriate education for their pupils"). Later a new more difficult single-subject General Certificate of Education replaced the grouped-subject School Certificate, with the new pass level corresponding to the old "credit", and also not to be taken before the age of 16.

It was clear that the Labour government, by placing such barriers between grammar and modern schools, was determined to maintain the present socio-economic order. The Education Minister was also at pains to assure an anxious independent sector that its place was secure within the 1944 Education Act and there was no intention of absorbing it within the state sector. It would even retain its charitable status - worth at present £100 million in tax relief! As for the direct grammar schools, they were also to be retained as a separate category.

What possible explanations could be advanced for this volte-face on the part of the Labour Party?

- after years in the political wilderness this new Labour government had no stomach for taking on the Establishment and going counter to the current educational orthodoxy with a battle for common secondary schools ("Who Runs the Country?");
- support for this orthodoxy came from psychometric claims for differential intelligences;
- many of the government who had been educated in grammar and public schools had strong loyalties to their traditions;
- education was much lower down the political agenda than it is now, and the public was more concerned with day-to-day affairs such as food and housing;
- the government was preoccupied with other major social reforms. The Beveridge Report had provided the government with the basis for the launch of the Welfare State, with its provision for social security and a National Health Service;
- and, at a deeper level, the State interest lay in reproducing the socio-economic order.

In any case, some of the educational reforms had serious practical implications. For example, the raising of the school-leaving age would require a rapid expansion in the teaching force and a large increase in the number of school buildings. It would also, according to the Chancellor of the Exchequer, threaten the national labour force. Eventually, the view of a more radical Education Minister, Ellen Wilkinson, prevailed in Cabinet, and in 1947 she was able to announce that the school-leaving age was to be raised to 15. This announcement was followed by the launching of the Emergency Training Scheme providing a one-year training course for intending teachers (chiefly ex-servicemen). To accommodate the increase in pupil numbers, a massive building operation was set in motion, including the erection of "temporary" prefabricated huts.

The 1944 Act had not stipulated the types of secondary schools which would follow from implementation of the Act. Local authorities therefore had the right to submit their own development plans, which the Minister was empowered to approve or reject, although she had already revealed her hand by publicly expressing her faith in the position of grammar schools within a tripartite system. Faced with several authorities submitting plans for multi-lateral schools, as opposed to separate differentiated schools, another Circular was issued stressing the need for any secondary reorganisation to be set within a grammar, technical and modern context. In the event, some comprehensive plans were accepted for various compelling reasons. For example, Anglesey, with its small, diverse population in a rural location, was allowed to develop a completely undiluted comprehensive system. On the other hand London County Council's ambitious and well thought-out plan for a comprehensive system was subject to political intrigue, resulting in the end in an emasculated comprehensivisation and restructuring of its schools.

KIDBROOKE COMPREHENSIVE SCHOOL

Kidbrooke School for Girls provides an interesting case study in the political shenanigans indulged in to save grammar schools. Under the London School Plan, Kidbrooke school was to become a purpose-built comprehensive school by merging a grammar, 2 technical, and two modern schools. But before the plan could be implemented, the Tory Party was in power and the new Education Minister, Florence Horsbrugh, actively encouraged local protests from interested parents to keep the grammar school open. On the strength of the subsequent show of strength, the Minister was able to refuse approval for the merger of the grammar school, so that Kidbrooke Comprehensive School lost its grammar component. As we shall see, this procedure was to be repeated elsewhere, with the result that most of the early comprehensive schools were "creamed" of their more "academic" intake.

The Secondary Modern School and the CSE

By now, technical high schools had virtually disappeared, an astonishing development given the repeated expressions of concern at the technological malaise of the nation and the widespread recognition that industrial growth required a more highly-trained technical and scientific work-force. And so far as comprehensive education was concerned, no more than 1% of the school population were in comprehensive schools. The secondary system was, in short, to all intents and purposes bi-partite (grammar and secondary modern), recalling the recommendations of the 1926 Hadow Committee. By the time the Labour Party left office, in 1951, there were no more than twelve comprehensive schools in existence and the traditional divide between grammar schools and the rest looked as secure as ever.

The Tory Party was to stay in power for the next thirteen years until 1964. Inheriting what was a tacit consensus on a bi-partite system of secondary education, it was the job of the government to make the new secondary modern system as acceptable to parents as possible and to make the notion of "parity of esteem" with grammar schools a reality. During the next thirteen years it poured large amounts of money into the secondary modern programme, so that at one stage, two schools per day were being opened. But what of the curriculum? A picture of life in a secondary modern school was depicted by a Cabinet Minister, Quintin Hogg, speaking in the House of Commons:

> *"I can assure honourable members opposite that if they would go to study what is now being done in good secondary modern schools they would not find a lot of pupils biting their nails in frustration because they had failed the eleven plus. The pleasant noise of banging metal and sawing wood would greet their ears and a smell of cooking with rather expensive equipment would come out of the front door to greet them. They would find that these boys and girls were getting an education tailor made to their desires, their bents and their requirements." (1)*

One cannot glean much about the official purpose of such schools from this thumb - nail sketch. More explicit is the Tory Party 1955 election manifesto:

"What matters in education is the development of the child's talents and personality, not the forwarding of political theory. We shall not permit the grammar schools to be swallowed up in comprehensive schools. It is vital to build up secondary modern schools and to develop in them special vocational courses, so that they and the technical schools offer a choice of education that matches the demands of our expanding economy." (2)

Aware of the growing unease over what was now becoming a socially divisive bipartite system, the government did make some concessions. Some comprehensive plans (including for some two-tier schools) were approved, providing they did not affect any existing grammar schools.

But with the school-leaving age now 15 and with more modern pupils opting to stay on there was the pressing problem of providing appropriate examinations for them. So it was that in 1958, the Education Minister of the day turned to the Secondary Schools Examination Council (hitherto responsible for GCE examinations) and gave them the brief "to look at secondary schools examinations other than GCE." The subsequent Beloe Report recommended the introduction of the Certificate of Secondary Education (CSE) to be taken in the fifth year. It was to be a single-subject examination aimed at the middle 40% and had several radical features. For example, it took the form of three modes:

- Mode 1 - an external examination on syllabuses provided by the regional subject panels,
- Mode 2 – an external examination on a syllabus devised by the school, but approved by the regional subject panels

and the revolutionary

- Mode 3 – examinations set and marked internally but moderated externally. (3)

With the further aim of engaging the less able pupils in worthwhile activities, the Newsom Committee was set up in 1961 with the contentious remit "to consider the education between the ages of 13 and 16 of pupils of average or less than average ability" (4). Having established an appropriate context, the Committee then set about what can be described as an early attempt at curriculum development:

A RECOMMENDED CURRICULUM FOR THE "NEWSOM CHILD"

Objectives

  Skills in communication (reading and writing) and calculating
  Capacities for thought, judgment, enjoyment and curiosity
  Sense of responsibility
  Initiation into the world of work, with a range of realistic and vocational
  courses broadly related to occupational interests.
  Moral and spiritual development through the corporate life of the school,
  underpinned by a corporate act of worship and religious instruction.

Content

  Practical "subjects" (the label "subject" to act as a landmark rather than a body
  of knowledge)

- Art and studio crafts
- Handicraft
- Rural studies
- Housecraft and Needlework
- Physical education
- Music
- Science, including scientific method
- Mathematics, computation and practical arithmetic.
- Humanities
- English, including drama, literature, film and television, project work
- A foreign language with emphasis on "lively communication through speech"
- History and geography; a scientific approach to factual evidence and "an ability to enter imaginatively into other men's (sic) minds".

Assessment

All pupils would receive an internal leaving certificate, including a record of achievement. The new Certificate of Education would be available for suitable pupils, with oral work and teacher assessment forming part of the examination.

Although the Newsom Committee had produced a curriculum which in the hands of competent teachers could provide a cognitive as well as an affective education, there was the implicit acceptance of the political status quo with the likely outcome that uncritical pupils would enter the labour market prepared to accept unquestioningly their place in society. It was left to the Minister for Education, when accepting the Report, to make the enlightened point, without apparent irony, that "all children should have an equal opportunity of acquiring intelligence."

Cracks in the Façade

Wastage of Talent

As early as 1946 the Barlow Report on Scientific Manpower drew attention to the enormous loss of potential arising from the current educational system:

> *"We have surveyed the results obtained in recent years on the distribution of intelligence, as measured by "intelligence tests" among the whole population and among members of certain universities. At present less than 2% reach the universities. About 5% of the whole population show, on test, an intelligence as great as the upper half of the students, who amount to 1% of the population. We conclude, therefore, that only about one in five of the boys and girls who have intelligence equal to that of the best half of university students actually reach university." (5)*

This wastage could have been attributed to the fact that a bi/tripartite system had only just been put in place. Yet thirteen years later the Crowther Report, with a remit of "the education of boys and girls between the ages of 15 and 18" (6), carried out a statistical survey of National Service recruits and showed that educational attainment and school-leaving age correlated far more closely with social background than with measured ability. (For example, 41% of all men in ability group 1 left school at 18 or later, whilst only 24% of sons of manual workers did so). This provided important evidence to refute claims that middle-class children progressed further because they were "brighter" than their working-class contemporaries. The Report recommended raising the school-leaving age to 16:

> *"We may hide, but we do not solve, teenage problems simply by letting boy and girls leave school.....(our case) rests on the conviction that all boys and girls have much to learn and that school (in the broadest sense) and not work is the place for this. 'Secondary Education for All' will not be a reality until it is provided for all up to the age of 16".(6)*

This was yet another Report drawing attention to social factors in educational achievement. Common sense alone would suggest that malnourished children in crowded homes without books or serious conversation, sleeping in cramped conditions along with other siblings, would be at a serious educational disadvantage compared to other children. But to win the argument against vested interests it was necessary to underpin common sense with rigorous sociological research. One of the many sociologists involved in this research, J.W.B. Douglas, followed the educational careers of over five thousand children from eleven to fifteen, and came to the conclusion that educational attainment was related to health, family size and type of school attended. With regard to social class:

> *"Middle class pupils have retained almost intact their historic advantage over the manual working class....the social class differences in educational opportunity which were considerable at the primary school stage have increased at the secondary and extend now even to pupils of high ability." (7)*

Credibility in selection procedures was further undermined by developments in psychology. The eminent and influential psychologist Cyril Burt had been prepared to confidently assert in the 1930's that intelligence was an:

> *"innate intellectual ability (is) inherited and not due to teaching.....general not specific, entering into all that we do, say or think and measured with accuracy and ease."*
> *(8)*

Twenty years later the situation had changed dramatically. Not only did research show that a person's intelligence quotient could be increased by as many as 14 points by appropriate coaching. Anthropologists also claimed that instead of intelligence tests being objective they were "culture-bound". And the whole area had been brought into disrepute by attempts to show that various races were superior/inferior (the 'nature/nurture' controversy.) Furthermore Burt's reputation had been tarnished by revelations that he fabricated some of his "evidence". The case against the selection of children's education at eleven was steadily acquiring objective and scientific support.

Down with the eleven-plus!

Although both grammar and secondary modern schools were granted "parity of esteem" by the 1944 Act, parents were becoming increasingly aware of the substantial socio-economic benefits conferred by a grammar school education and of the vital importance to their children's life chances of the eleven-plus examination. Pressure was thus increasing on primary school teachers to deliver, with the result that they taught to the eleven-plus examination and streamed their classes. And of course it was also important that the general public came to believe that the eleven-plus represented a valid, fair and reliable assessment of children's abilities. But its credibility was becoming increasingly undermined by the developments described above. Selection for grammar schools by the use of intelligence tests was thus becoming more and more difficult to defend. In short, the gross inequity of deciding a child's life-chances at the age of eleven, with both psychological and sociological evidence throwing doubt on the authenticity of the selection procedure, was being increasingly recognised, and parental pressure groups were forming around the country with the slogan "Down with the Eleven Plus".

So the Conservative government found itself facing growing opposition to its arguments in defence of the existing system, such as the need for gifted children to be together in a school with the appropriate learning ethos. In 1955, the Education Minister, recognising that the 11-plus examination could be a crucial election issue, attempted to draw the sting. He suggested that transfer between schools should be made easier, and that "something special", including vocational education, should be provided in modern schools. But he retained his position that comprehensive schools would only be approved if there were no damage to existing schools, and that not only should 15-25% of the secondary school population be in grammar or technical schools, but that new technical schools should be provided only in the most compelling of circumstances. So this political indifference to technical education continued, despite the number of reports underlining its importance both to the economy and its place in the school curriculum. In fact one wonders if politicians and industrialists bothered to read such reports as the excellent White Paper on Technical Education (9). It would seem that the government's prime concern was in maintaining the supremacy of the academic/aristocratic curriculum and the corresponding social order, than in the economic or student interest, even in the face of growing public hostility.

1964-1970 A New Labour Government – the Circular 10/65 "Request"

Shortly after the Newsom Report was published, there was a change of government. The Tory party was in disarray, but at the subsequent election in 1964 Labour won with a surprisingly small majority, which limited its scope for introducing radical new policies. But Labour Party conferences had repeatedly pledged the next Labour government once again to comprehensivation and this time there was popular support, if only on the negative grounds of abolishing the eleven-plus. The new Education Minister, Tony Crosland, had made his views on the educational system he was inheriting abundantly clear:

> "The school system in Britain remains the most divisive, unjust and wasteful of all the aspects of social inequality. First it denies even the limited aim of equal opportunity. Before the war it did so to an extent which seems fantastic, so that a high proportion of children had no access to secondary education of any kind. Of boys born between 1910 and 1929, only 14% of those from state elementary schools achieved a secondary education, compared with 89% of those from private primary schools" (10).

But Crosland's idealism was tempered by pragmatism in the face of the moral dilemma of persisting social injustice:

> "We are not starting tabula rasa, but with segregated schools already established and strongly entrenched... the ground ahead is studded with obstacles – the shortage of suitable buildings, the state of public opinion...What, then, can be done? First a Labour Government should explicitly state a preference for the comprehensive principle and should actively encourage local authorities to be more audacious in experimenting with comprehensive schools...Secondly, the object must be to weaken to the greatest possible extent the significance of the 11+ examination." (11)

In short, any educational radicalism was subject to what were seen at the time as practical or ideological obstacles. For example, the position of the public schools did not appear to be on the government's agenda. Nor would there be legislation or coercion. Instead, the following year, Circular 10/65 was published, requesting local authorities to submit within a year plans for comprehensivisation in accordance with one of six plans, including 11-18 schools, two-tier schools and middle schools (with a strong preference for the former). More force was added to the "request" the following year (after Labour had gained a larger Commons majority) in Circular 10/66 which declared that capital building grants would be available only for those government-approved plans. Of the early replies to the Minister's request, 50 authorities were now comprehensive, or almost so; 40 were producing plans whilst 20 (largely Conservative-controlled) expressed an unwillingness to cooperate.

But by the end of Labour's time in office many other authorities had fallen into line. 115 authorities had their reorganisation plans approved, 13 had their plans rejected and ten had failed to respond. The number of comprehensive schools had grown from 10 in 1950 to 1145 in 1970 but the national proportion of pupils in comprehensive schools remained disappointingly low:

- grammar 18.3% school population
- comprehensive 29.2%
- secondary modern 36.2%
- technical high 1.2%

Several questions remained to be answered, including the controversial one of the internal organisation of the comprehensive schools. For example, a 1968 Survey showed that only 35% of comprehensive schools used mixed ability classes in the first year, a long way from the ideal of common educational experiences.

In the absence of further decisive progress, the Labour government did in fact prepare a Comprehensive Bill, but it was overtaken by events. In 1970, the Tory party was again in office. It promptly withdrew Circulars 10/65 and 10/66 and replaced them with Circular 10/70 whose guidelines included the wise use of resources and the attention to local needs, implying a weakening of the comprehensive principle. But by now there was virtually total opposition in the country to the eleven-plus examinations Predictably, the effect of Circular 10/70 was to strengthen this opposition and Stop The Eleven Plus (STEP) campaigns were launched throughout the country, even in conservative areas – giving local councils pause for thought.

And so education reform of one sort or another moved slowly forwards, with all reorganisation proposals being dealt with by the government on a case-by-case basis - and with true comprehensives being the exception rather than the rule.

According to Benn and Simon:

> *"The net effect of both the Labour government's circular 10/65 and the Conservatives' 10/70 has been to force the demand for comprehensives down to the local level...But there is a limit to what the local authorities or the local pressure groups can do alone...It is a comprehensive system which is required, not merely a few more comprehensive schools; and only a national decision will make this possible." (12)*

But a national decision was never made.

Where have all the Radicals Gone?

Comprehensivation poses a clear threat to the efforts described earlier to maintain the existing social order. Any attempts to develop a national system were at best half-hearted and at worst obstructed by the ruling elite and the Tory party. But in what was potentially an ideological upheaval there was at least the opportunity for radicals to look afresh at the whole educational picture. In the event, the Labour Party seemed to have lost its sense of history and its zeal for rescuing the working-class from exploitative forces. The efforts of working-class radicals in developing educational ideals described at the beginning of this narrative had apparently been forgotten. For example, the radical nineteenth century demand that education should take account of the need for cooperative, experiential and active learning, in informal settings to develop critical understanding and to awaken the imagination - as well as a love of learning - were ignored. As was the constant demand for political economy to be added to the list of subjects. **This absence of a clear educational rationale was to leave comprehensive education all too vulnerable to attack from reactionary elements in our society and from those who felt their privileges threatened**.

In the end comprehensivisation became a political rather than an educational exercise. "Equality of opportunity" had been taken to mean the opportunity to receive a grammar school education. So embedded in the public consciousness were the unchallenged assumptions lying behind the public/ grammar school curriculum that even as late as 1978 the HMI document Curriculum 11-16 still propagated its values, leading to the following despairing comments by one headteacher:

> "These people have obviously read Hirst and Peters and all that. I was brought up on it myself, but all it does is look at the curriculum and find good reasons for it being there…… the truth is that most of the kids are bored out of their minds with this stuff. It's OK for those who have to put up with it for a few years to get a nice job like mine but what are the other 80% here for? Nothing in this Report is going to cause a revolution in terms of motivation…. What I am concerned about is what sort of science should we do and make it relevant to the 20th century, let alone the 21st. Teaching them about pop groups and football is no answer either. Of course, we have got to expand their horizons and offer them genuine choices in life but how do you do it? This Report is no help at all in this respect"
> (13)

This frustrated head had put his finger on perhaps the most basic problem to be revealed by comprehensivisation . Hitherto schooling had been used instrumentally to divide society into workers and professionals, with separate pastoral and cognitive curricula. Now it was essential to look again at the purposes and the concept of education and devise a curriculum which could be seen as fair and just to all people. But where was the authority and expertise for such a challenge to the status quo to come from? By a remarkable turn of apparently unrelated events, it was the government itself which acknowledged the teacher interest and provided the authority for schools to develop their own curriculum based upon the needs of the pupils. We shall see in the next chapter how well this opportunity was taken by the teaching profession.

NOTES AND REFERENCES

1. Hansard, Jan 21 1965
2. www.psr.keele.ac.uk/area/uk/man/con55.htm
3. McClure op cit
4. Half our Future (1963) Department of Education and Science . HMSO
5. McClure op cit
6. op cit
7. J.W.B. Douglas op cit
8. B. Simon (1953) Intelligence Tests and the Comprehensive School. Lawrence and Wishart
9. It was a speech given by Sir Winston Churchill, the Prime Minister, which drew attention, in a widely-reported speech, to advances by the Russians in the field of technology and technical education (to be symbolised shortly afterwards by the launching of the Sputnik into space). The 1956 White Paper on Technical Education speedily followed. It recommended an expansion of technical education at all levels. It was in clarifying what until then had been an ill-defined area that the White Paper did potentially a great service to education. It made the following important points of direct relevance to the school curriculum:
   - every technologist relies on technicians and craftsmen to translate his (sic) plans into products….much therefore depends on strengthening the base of technical education by improving the education in the schools;
   - technical education must not be too narrowly vocational or too confined to one skill or trade;
   - swift change is the characteristic of our age …. so technical studies should lead to adaptability and versatility and should therefore be grounded in the fundamentals of mathematics and science;
   - such subjects as business studies, economics, wage systems and human relations must now be given more prominence;
   - a place must be found for liberal education to protect and support spiritual and human values.
10 C.A.R. Crosland op cit
11 op cit
12 C.Benn and B. Simon op cit.
13 D.H. Hargeaves op cit

CHAPTER SIX

1965: OPPORTUNITY MISSED : "TEACHER POWER" COMES AND GOES

"We are a kind of Parliament of Education, each of us (except the Chairman) owing his membership to the wish of his constituents. So we are no bunch of stooges. We have our own headquarters, our name-plate on the door, our own budget and our own full-time staff.. If we succeed (and we mean to) success will be a long-term process of fostering a new dynamic in the schools" (Sir John Maud, chairman of Schools Council, 1965)

The State and the "Secret Garden"
A Case Study: Capitalism, Scientific Management and Educational Objectives
The Schools Council and a "top-down approach
Curriculum models
       An Objectives Model; Science 5-13
       A Process Model:the Humanities Curriculum Project
Curriculum Pluralism
Ideological Underpinnings
A Missed Opportunity: the Status Quo Inviolate

We have now reached the stage where "equality of opportunity" was expressed in terms of comprehensivisation but without the accompaniment of a comprehensive curriculum, leaving schools coping as best they could in an ideological morass. Also at this time, by a series of unforeseen parliamentary developments, what might be called the "teaching interest" was finally acknowledged. The resultant institutional autonomy led to a period of intense curriculum theorising. Although this period was relatively short, it was highly technical. I have thus pared the chapter down to the bone, but what is left I believe to be highly significant and important for the following reasons:

(a) it keeps alive those curriculum and ideological alternatives, necessary for a pluralistic society, at a time when an oppressive state is attempting to stamp out any challenges to the status quo;

(b) it focuses attention on specific social and economic forces sustaining or undermining curriculum change.

The State and the "Secret Garden" of the Curriculum

It was a Tory Minister of Education David Eccles who in 1960 brought the question of the school curriculum to the forefront:

> *"I regret that so many of our debates have had to be devoted almost entirely to bricks and mortar and to the organisation of the system. We treat the curriculum as though it were a subject about which it is not done for us to make remarks. I should like the House to say that this reticence has been overdone. I shall therefore try in future to make the Ministry's voice heard rather more often, more positively and no doubt sometimes more controversially.... As for the Ministry of Education itself, my Department has the unique advantage of the countrywide experience of Her Majesty's Inspectorate...... the section in the Report on the Sixth Form is an irresistible invitation for a sally into the secret garden of the curriculum." (Hansard. Vol 620. 21 March 1960)*

This was followed by discussions with Her Majesty's Inspectorate, and in 1962 the Minister set up the Curriculum Study Group, staffed by officials of the Ministry and HMI's and funded by the Research and Intelligence Branch of the Ministry. In other words, the curriculum was to be opened up to scrutiny by central government, presenting a clear challenge to both local authority and teacher autonomy. It was a challenge that was to be taken up vigorously, particularly as Eccles' initiative had been taken unilaterally, without proper consultation. The local authorities and the National Union of Teachers joined forces and threatened to withdraw cooperation unless a truly representative body was set up. (4) And by now the teachers, rapidly becoming an all-graduate profession, had organised themselves into associations with bargaining power. Such was the hostility generated that a new Education

Minister, Sir Edward Boyle, concluded that the Curriculum Study Group be replaced by a representative organisation. In 1963, the Schools Council for the Curriculum and Examinations was set up, and with a guaranteed teacher majority on both the governing body and all its committees, with the declared purpose of undertaking research into the curriculum, teaching methods and school examinations. **It was made clear that each school should have the fullest responsibility for its own curriculum, to be developed by the staff and based on the needs of the student**.

So, theoretically, teaching finished up with more autonomy - and more responsibility - than before! But more important was the question of "To what purpose will this increased autonomy be put" in the light of the invitation from an enlightened Education Minister for schools to develop the curriculum from the grass roots in order to meet the needs of pupils, in the context of generous funding from the State. We shall see in the next few pages how this invitation was taken up by the teaching profession and what new ideas were brought to bear on the curriculum, bearing in mind the following questions:

> where have these ideas come from ?
> which ideas outlast others and why ?

The following fascinating account provides one particular answer to the first question.

Capitalism, Scientific Management and Educational Objectives

As we have seen, mass schooling developed in England at the beginning of the nineteenth century in the image of the new factory system, with large numbers of "workers" gathered under one roof and under constant surveillance, with a hierarchical authority structure and with children obediently following instructions. These new social forces of industrial capitalism provided what has been called a "hidden" or "covert" curriculum where children allegedly learned attitudes and patterns of behaviour corresponding to the social relations of industrial production, for subsequent application in factories.

A century later, this time in the USA, new social forces of capitalism were emerging which would affect the education of future generations of British

102

children. One of these followed from the astonishing rise of the American business man at the turn of the century ("The business of America is business") and the saturation of American society with business/industrial values, out of which emerged the "Efficiency Expert". Whilst the general question now concerned ways of increasing the productivity of American industry, the specific question initiating this reform movement concerned the efficiency of the North-East railroad system. The railroads had applied to the Interstate Commerce Commission in 1910 for an increase in freight rates to compensate for wage rises. The subsequent hearing exposed the railroads to a charge of inefficient operation and the claim that it was possible through what was being misleadingly called "scientific management" to both reduce costs and increase wages.

The publicity surrounding the hearing propelled the idea of "scientific management" into the public arena and brought Frederick W. Taylor into prominence. He had been working on the "efficiency" problem since the late nineteenth century with such ideas as a "piece-rate system". Now in 1911 he brought his ideas into a coherent whole with his "The Principles of Scientific Management". Management was to be made more efficient by assuming responsibility for planning, and training selected workmen to perform clear tasks as defined by his job analysis, which he submitted to "time and motion" study to give "unit times". The essence of this development, then, was standardisation and control: each man was provided with an instruction card describing in detail what precisely was to be done, and incentives were provided through a bonus system. In other words a rigid system of objectives was to be imposed on the workforce.

Such principles led to a dramatic increase in productivity and it was not long before the state of the public schools was also being questioned. For example, in the Ladies Home Journal of 1912:

> "Can you imagine a more grossly stupid system tenaciously persisted in to the detriment of over seventeen million children and at a cost to you of over 403 million dollars a year – a system not only absolutely ineffective in its results but also actually harmful in that it throws every year 93 out of every 100 children into the world of action absolutely unfitted for even the simplest tasks in life........Yet that is exactly what the public school system is doing today, and has been doing". (1)

Whilst this may be seen as a complaint against the aims of schooling as much as its administrators, it was part of a swell of opinion which served notice on the school superintendents. Fearing for their livelihoods, they were not slow to respond: sessions at their annual general meetings invariably included (imperfectly understood) interpretations of scientific management and their relevance to schooling.

Educational Objectives

It was Franklin Bobbitt, instructor in educational administration at the University of Chicago, who, with his article "The Supervision of City Schools" in the 1913 Yearbook of the National Society for the Study of Education, really came to grips with the problem of educational productivity and rigorously applied Taylor's principles to education with his books "The Curriculum"(1918) and "How to make a Curriculum".(1924) Bobbitt took the view that education had the responsibility to prepare for 50 years of adult life rather than the 20 years of childhood and youth. He therefore analysed adult activities and transformed these into minute and explicit educational objectives. Teaching would then involve the application of standardised means to these ends. Bobbitt was also anxious that these standardisations should be quantified:

> "The ability to add at a speed of 65 combinations per minute, with an accuracy of 94 % is as definite a specification as can be set up for any aspect of the work of the steel plant….. (The teacher) needs a measuring scale in measuring his product…(so)…..she can know at all times whether she is accomplishing the things expected of her (sic) or not." (2)

Elsewhere Bobbitt revealingly observed that education was as much a shaping process as the manufacture of steel rails. (Having spent much of his working life in the steel industry he was fond of drawing analogies between steel manufacture and education.) In other words his view of education was a mechanical one with elements of social control.

The term educational objectives had now entered the educational lexicon, to be refined and developed in subsequent decades. Ralph Tyler, for example, stressed that objectives should not be concerned with the teacher's activities but with changes in behaviour of pupils. He posed four fundamental questions:

- What educational purposes should the school seek to attain?
- What educational experiences can be provided that are likely to attain these purposes?
- How can these educational experiences be effectively organised?
- How can we determine whether these purposes are being attained? (3)

Tyler came to the conclusion that educational objectives or purposes should be expressed as student behaviour with a particular content. Later Hilda Taba argued that the first move in curriculum planning should be the statement of general broad educational aims, which should then be translated into specific behavioural objectives.

The Schools Council

We have now reached the time (1960) when, across the Atlantic in England, the Schools Council for the Curriculum and Examinations was about to be born and the educational developments in the USA described above were about to be utilised. "Curriculum development" was now one of the key concepts which provided a focus for the work of the Schools Council. But such major changes do not take place in a cultural vacuum : the imminent raising of the school-leaving age to sixteen (ROSLA), although eventually postponed until 1972, held serious implications for the curriculum. Teachers would now have to teach "less able" pupils for a further year, many of whom would resent the fact that they could no longer leave at 15. Clearly, "more of the same" was not a sensible option and radical developments in the curriculum were urgently needed. In the course of its lifetime, the Schools Council launched well over a hundred "top-down" curriculum projects, some costing hundreds of thousands of pounds. What is important from a political point of view is the way the Schools Council and its projects were structured. The organisation of these projects followed a standard pattern: the Council selected a title for a project as well as deciding such matters as funding and duration; a Project Director was chosen who was allowed to select his own staff and then "get on with it". From the welter of Projects I have selected just two, of differing styles, and kept the detail down to a minimum.

A Schools Council Objectives Model: Science 5-13

This project was sponsored jointly by the Schools Council and the Nuffield Foundation and based at Bristol University over a six-year period. Its brief included assisting teachers in helping children learn and gain experience about science through discovery methods. For this purpose, account was taken of recent developments in Piagetian psychology (5) with the assumption that the children would be in one of three stages of intellectual development. An Objectives Model was used and developed logically and so thoroughly that it is worth looking at a section in some detail. (6)

SCIENCE 5-13

Broad aim (arrived at through discussions with teachers and others with wide and relevant experience)
"developing an enquiring mind and a scientific approach to problems"

This broad aim was then broken down into 8 further aims:

1. developing interests ,attitudes and aesthetic awareness
2. observing, exploring and ordering observations;
3. developing basic concepts and logical thinking;
4. posing questions and devising experiments or investigations to answer them;
5. acquiring knowledge and learning skills;
6. communicating.
7. appreciating patterns and relationships
8. interpreting finding critically

Behavioural Objectives
Finally, appropriate skills, interests and attitudes etc were defined. For example,
"the ability to discriminate between different materials". A remarkably precise numbering system was employed, incorporating three digits :

- the first digit referring to psychological stage 1,2 and 3
- the second digit to the broad aim
- the third digit to the particular objective.

Evaluation
The evaluator began work at the outset, breaking aims down into "specific statements expressed in behavioural terms" to enable the Project Team to produce appropriate written materials (for example, Working with Wood, Time, Minibeasts). She obtained her evidence by working closely with teachers in the pilot schools (informally, for example, on the process of discovery and formally through teacher reports and attitude scales); by interviewing pupils and giving them pre- and post-tests.

The evaluation was essentially "formative"; that is, to give ongoing feedback for course improvement. Not surprisingly, given that many teachers were not familiar with discovery methods, there was great variation in the grasp and application of the Project's ideas.

Materials
The final, very attractive, materials that were eventually published comprised:

> an Introductory Unit to familiarise newcomers,
> 6 Background/Resource Books for teachers, and
> 17 Units of ideas for activities through which children at different stages
> of development could reach the learning objectives.

It can be seen that the Science 5-13 Project faithfully followed the ideas set out above, arising from the organisation of capitalist working practices. The expectation would naturally be that the "objectives model" would be standard for all curriculum development. But, as mentioned above, the general pattern for Schools Council projects involved only the selection of a title for the project, its funding and duration. It was this relative openness that led to a totally different conception in the Humanities Curriculum Project, which we turn to now.

A Schools Council Process Model: The Humanities Curriculum Project

This was sponsored by the Schools Council for average and below-average secondary pupils. It had as its Director Lawrence Stenhouse, who took the Schools Council Working Paper no. 2 as the point of departure. It had the general aim:

> *"to develop an understanding of social situations and human acts and the controversial issues which they raise". (7)*

but on this occasion there was no attempt to translate this into behavioural objectives. As with all Schools Council projects, considerable attention was given to the production of attractive materials, in the forms of packs for both pupils and teachers, with a general handbook to provide guidance for the teacher on how to handle them. These materials took the form of broad themes, calculated to generate controversy:

War and Society
Poverty
Education
Relations between the Sexes
People and work
The family
Living in Cities
Law and Order

But the most important feature was the absence of a knowledge-delivery approach characteristic of a "technical" curriculum. The predominant pedagogic mode was discussive, rather than instructional: pupils and teacher would sit in a circle, facing each other, with the teacher adopting the controversial role of a "procedurally neutral chairperson" (prepared to tolerate silence rather than dominate the discussion). The teacher was also required to set a context favourable to discussion, protect divergence of view within the group, introduce appropriate evidence and take responsibility for standards of learning.

Evaluation was a major component of the development of the Project and, as with Science 5-13, commenced at the beginning of the team's work. In the absence of measurable behavioural objectives, an anthropological approach was adopted based upon case studies. The resultant feedback enabled certain parts of the programme to be modified. It also convinced the Team that an active policy of Dissemination should be pursued, rather than allowing the Word to be spread merely by diffusion. Most encouragingly (especially for the cause of comprehensivisation) the case studies revealed that there had been a serious underestimation of the abilities of the pupils involved. Less encouragingly, the demands made upon teachers in adopting radically new roles was also underestimated, so that teacher development (for example, a self-training procedure) became a prime concern.

This Project, unique at the time, could be described as a Process model of curriculum development, with the emphasis upon the exercise of the students' mental processes, rather than upon pre-specified outcomes. It provided a humanising alternative to the orthodoxy of the dominant managerial objectives model. It was not a curriculum to be "delivered", but rather "engaged in". Dealing as it was in controversial issues, the Humanities Curriculum Project became a controversial issue itself and we will return to it later.

"Curriculum" as a Subject for Enquiry

It was at the 1967 Third International Conference, sponsored partly by the Schools Council that Dr. John Goodlad, of the University of California, put the academic cat amongst the pragmatic pigeons. In his opening address, he made various demands for "curriculum theory":

- more systematic, sustained, rigorous work in centres where long-term enquiry can be pursued without activist pressure;
- work to be carried beyond verbal abstraction to the level of model-building;
- experimental schools in which to test the models.

As J. Stuart McClure, observer at the Conference recorded:

> *"The effect of Goodlad's address was to polarise at the outset some of the differences between the English and North Americans. It confirmed many of the English in their deeply-held suspicion of educational theory and their amazement that an apparently pragmatic matter like the curriculum should be turned into a topic for academic abstraction....it left many members hopping mad". (8)*

But it could be argued that the controversial nature of "curriculum theory" was a sign of growing maturity. Goodlad's address coincided with a remarkable growth of curriculum projects, as well as books, articles and disputations, all carrying the hallmarks of academic discourse. Reputations were made and empires built, as argument raged over various aspects of curriculum. It is only possible here to touch very briefly upon some of the major disputes and controversies.

Curriculum Pluralism

(a) *Rational Curriculum Planning*

The Objectives Model: a Technical Curriculum

The philosopher Paul Hirst whilst rejecting the cruder form of behavioural objectives, gives a clearcut version of this sort of planning:

"First there are the educational objectives (A) which are being aimed at.....qualities of mind, attitudes, values, skills, dispositions ...... Secondly, there is the content or the matter (B) to be employed as a means to these objectives. Thirdly, there are activities and methods (C) that are employed to achieve the objectives. As I understand it, rational curriculum planning consists of developing a course under B and C to achieve A......it is as simple and straightforward as that."(9)

The Process Model: A Practical Curriculum

But for Lawrence Stenhouse it was far from being "as simple and straightforward as that." Whilst accepting the usefulness of behavioural objectives for training in skills, he claimed that their use in the field of knowledge revealed an ignorance of the deep structures of knowledge, leading both to gross distortion and trivialisation. He further argues that it is possible to plan curricula rationally in the process model by specifying content and principles of procedure, rather than prespecifying objectives. (10) This approach, turning the prevailing orthodoxy on its head, aroused considerable hostility, not least with the idea of the "procedurally neutral chairperson" being at the heart of the matter. These two models suggest a pluralistic approach to education. It will be interesting to trace their futures in later chapters.

(b) Curriculum Content

A problem that emerges from the above approach to curriculum planning concerns the selection of worthwhile content. A philosophical approach is provided by Paul Hirst (11) who, starting from the premise that education is concerned with the development of mind, identifies the following distinct forms of knowledge, distinguished by their:

basic concepts and the structures relating them;
the characteristic techniques used in exploring and developing the forms;
and ways in which their truth claims are tested:

- Physical sciences
- Human sciences
- Logic and mathematics
- Philosophy

- Religion
- Moral knowledge
- Fine Arts and literature.

This view of knowledge, when used within an objectives framework is in great danger of becoming unproblematic. An alternative approach would regard the disciplines not so much as received knowledge but as themselves subjects for critical enquiry, in what would be hypothetical and interpretative modes. In helping the student "make increasing sense of his/her world" this particular form of curriculum would be negotiated between teacher and student, where both are involved in the construction of meaning and a concern for "truth".

(c) Curriculum Evaluation

Any responsible curriculum development has an element of evaluation built into it, the precise form reflecting the purpose of evaluation and the logic of the curriculum model. Areas of controversy would include whether the evaluation would be ongoing (formative) to provide instant feedback to student and teacher, or final (summative) for the benefit of examiners, sponsors, administrators or potential consumers. Clearly, the style of evaluation will depend upon the model of curriculum development. If it is based upon behavioural objectives, then the evaluator can obtain hard quantitative data as we saw in the case of Science 5-13 above by measuring changes in behaviour. If, on the other hand, the objectives are expressive - or the model is of the "process" type - then data will be softer and obtained by observation, interview etc. Controversy then centres on such topics as the reliability and validity of the data obtained in what is now a pluralist situation.

d) Curriculum Research

The research style adopted will depend, like that for evaluation, on the model underpinning that particular curriculum. A positivist technical model will enable evidence to be obtained and hypotheses tested by the measurement of behaviour in controlled situations.

In the case of the process model, the research emphasis is interpretative with the focus upon teacher development, since the teacher, instead of being instructor, now assumes the additional role of learner. The logical development of this approach is provided by Action Research where the teacher collects evidence from the classroom (for example, by tape or video recorders or from outside observers) in order to test implicit or explicit hypotheses. The essence of this research is the development of the self-reflective teacher: reflection upon discrepancies between collected data (which could include pupil accounts) and intentions could lead to increased self-awareness and professional development. Such is an outline of the theory. In practice, it requires a cooperative ethos, both between teacher and pupils and teacher and colleagues in an open classroom - and is extravagant in its use of resources. This type of research is, of course, treated with contempt by those wedded to technical aspects of curriculum development with the teacher as instructor. It is regarded as vague, ill-defined and not leading to definitive final conclusions. On the other hand, technical research is dismissed as superficial and trivial and incapable of leading to professional development.

Ideological Underpinnings of the Curriculum

The objectives and process models of curriculum development hint at two different ideologies, representing opposing values, beliefs and prejudices. On the one hand there is the managerial/rationalist type characterised by beliefs in:

- positivism (human behaviour similar to the behaviour of inanimate matter)
- reductionism (persons reduced to separate manageable components e.g. cognitive v. affective)
- behaviourist psychology (stimulus—required response --- reward)
- quantitative data (e.g. psychometric tests)
- objectivity
- ahistoricity (indifferent to origins)
- competition
- instrumentalism.

On the other hand, the collaborative/humanist type is characterised by beliefs in:

- phenomenology (subjects construct own reality)
- holism (the "whole person")
- developmental psychology (passage through various stages of development)

112

- qualitative data (anthropological-like case studies)
- subjectivity
- historicity (concern with origins)
- cooperation
- the intrinsic. (12)

Managerial teachers would be recognised by the way they behave as postman delivering a curriculum package; whereas the humanist type would be carrying, not the curriculum, but a tape-recorder. It should be added that with the former type a process of "reification" frequently takes place, with the curriculum regarded as object; whereas for the latter, curriculum represents a series of human interactions.

As mentioned earlier it is also sometimes helpful to categorise the curriculum as the following ideal types (after Habermas (13):

technical: knowledge seen as objective and positivist; involving rule-following and serving the purpose of social control;
practical: knowledge basis is subjective and open to individual interpretation; emphasising understanding and judgment;
emancipatory: concerned to empower the learner through the development of critical thought.

A Missed Opportunity: the Status Quo Inviolate

It is important to keep this government initiative in perspective. Although it may contain some radical elements within it, in the event the status quo was not seriously threatened: "bright" students continued with their academic subjects, took conventional examinations and passed into higher education, maintaining the social order. But the Schools Council was presented with a golden opportunity to produce a comprehensive curriculum to accompany comprehensive reorganisation and thus provide a rationale which would give the enterprise credibility and validity. One of the major objections to the work of the Schools Council, then, was that it did not devote its energies, expertise and considerable resources to the development of common curricula for all children, or to considerations of "interest" "relevance" or "needs" - or to use as a starting-point the everyday problems that teachers at the grass roots were encountering.

Understandably, in a culture of technical rationality, the emphasis was upon means rather than ends. From the start it accepted subjects as the basis for curriculum design, with subject experts represented on the various committees. Any changes would consequently involve top-down reform rather than grass-roots revolution, with members of the Schools' Council solving their own problems, rather than helping teachers solve their own perceived problems in the classroom. In any case, given that teachers are prisoners of their own schooling and professionally embedded in a technical culture of education, marked by the delivery of an official curriculum package, creative innovation was hardly to be expected. Many teachers were undoubtedly sceptical of the value of the Schools Council, perceiving their own interest as bound up with day-to-day survival, rather than with "curriculum development". But even the use made of both the imaginative and attractive teaching materials and teachers' centres provided by the Schools Council was extremely limited. It would require the force of something like government fiat to bring about a fundamental change in perceived interest - and that was not to be long delayed.

NOTES AND REFERENCES

1. I have drawn heavily in this section upon the work of R.E. Callahan and his "Education and the Cult of Efficiency", from which this excerpt is taken.
2. Callahan op cit
3. R. Tyler op cit
4. B. Simon op cit
5. see, for example, L. Stenhouse op cit
6. Science 5-13(1972)With Objectives in Mind. MacDonald Educational. London
7. L. Stenhouse op cit
8. Schools Council (1968) Curriculum Innovation in Practice. HMSO
9. Schools Council (1967) Educational Implications of Social and Economic Change. Working Paper 12. HMSO
10. L. Stenhouse op cit
11. P. H. Hirst (1974) op cit
12. W.A. Reid categorises "Rationalist" and "Humanist" in a similar way in his "Thinking About the Curriculum" (1978) Routledge and Kegan Paul. London.
13. This is an extremely simplified summary of the ideas of Habermas. See Grundy op cit.

PART TWO:

THE PRO-ACTIVE STATE

COLONISATION AND CONTROL OF THE CURRICULUM

How the State, under pressure from industry, the media, parents and the political right, extended its interest from access to education to its nature. The curriculum, local authorities and teachers were put under scrutiny, initially focussed upon "accountability" and "standards". But eventually state control was extended to a National Curriculum, with agencies for pupil testing and teacher inspection. At the same time the interests of "marketeers" were acknowledged by freeing schools from direct financial control from local authorities, the empowerment of governing bodies and the provision of school league tables to facilitate parental choice. But however radical these processes of rationalisation and control might appear to be, they did nothing to challenge the socio-economic order.

However, with the education system now rationalised and under the control of the state it was vulnerable, by virtue of its uniformity, to capture by a corporate hegemony, resulting in a comprehensive cultural transformation. Thus education was defined in economic rather than developmental terms, knowledge was seen as objective and certain, expressed in terms of targets; judgments became quantitative rather then qualitative; competition replaced cooperation, and instrumental activities were emphasised at the expense of the intrinsic. This decline in common humanity was accompanied by an increase in clinical depression amongst children and the introduction of a therapeutic dimension to teaching, with so-called "happiness" lessons and a quantified "emotional literacy".

CHAPTER SEVEN

GOODBYE TO ALL THAT: THE WATERSHED

*"To the teachers I would say that you must satisfy the
parents and industry that what you are doing meets their
requirements and the needs of the children. For if the
public is not convinced then the profession will be laying
up trouble for itself in the future."*
*(James Callaghan, Labour Prime Minister Ruskin
College speech, Oct. 19,1976)*

Forces of Reaction: The Black Papers and the Popular Press
The Government Response: legitimating central control
*   setting the agenda: standards and accountabiliy*
*   "The Great Debate": seeking or engineering consensus?*
*   bureaucratisation: data collections: Assessment of Performance Unit*
*Education Minister abolishes Schools Council and becomes chief policy
maker*
The "Upstart"("storming the citadel") TVEI and the Business Interest.

Forces of Reaction: The Black Papers

Whilst the Schools Council was busy with its ambitious, expensive and
large-scale curriculum projects, changes were taking place in the outside
world which were causing increasing unease amongst the traditionalists
and the political right. Comprehensivisation was going forward, often
accompanied by mixed ability teaching, and the Plowden Report (1)
provided legitimation for informal "child-centred" teaching methods in
the primary schools. All this was in a general context of student unrest,
with the most dramatic events being the student riots on the continent.
The media, which was now largely owned by a handful of press barons
and could be regarded as orchestrating and representing the interests of

corporate capitalism, was invariably hostile to these recent educational developments and orchestrated a campaign against "trendy teachers", ostensibly on behalf of its readers and claiming to be acting in the interests of parents and their children. Also, by now industry had organised itself into a powerful lobbying group through the Confederation of British Industry and was attacking the teaching profession for not paying sufficient attention to the business interest, with the result that too many unemployed young people were leaving school.

Eventually, in 1969, these various forces of reaction were reinforced in this country by a group of 'academics' in a series of polemical Black Papers. They were unashamedly political. Not only were copies sent to every M.P. but readers were encouraged to write to their M.P's with the rallying cry "The spirit of anti-education must be fought!" The main targets were the abandonment of streaming in favour of mixed ability grouping; the progressive informal methods implied by the Plowden Report; and comprehensive education.

On Streaming

Streaming: Standards or Equality?

> *"To the egalitarian, streaming is part of the method of training children for competitive western society. Streaming encourages able children, who are put in a high stream, to think of themselves as potential members of society's leadership, while it teaches unintelligent children that they are only destined for a position in the middle or at the bottom of the hierarchy. Streaming teaches children this fact of life and that if they wish to do well in the hierarchy they must use their intelligence and work hard". (2)*

On Progressive Methods

The Mystique of Modern Maths (3)

> *"Are we perhaps as teachers suffering from the advice of well-intentioned but misguided theorists who glibly condemn table-learning and drill in the mechanical aspects of number but offer nothing in its place which is*

half so relevant to the ordinary business of living. After all, for the great majority of the population, mathematics need not provide a skill much beyond being able to verify the grocery slip at the supermarket or to check the bookmaker's payout."

On Comprehensive Education
Comprehensive Inequality (4)

> *"The advocates of comprehensivisation make no secret of their aims...their whole campaign is now concentrated on a single issue: the use of educating as a means of breaking down the country's social structure and creating 'equality of opportunity'. What an irony it is, that the very moment when comprehensivisation has revealed its total educational and social bankruptcy in the USSR, the maddened hordes of British self-styled progressives... should be engaged in installing the same system in our country...They must not be allowed to succeed. "*

The issues raised are important and valid, worthy of serious scrutiny, rather than being the basis for a polemic. But instead of serious discussion, selective statistics are quoted to "prove" that examination results have declined with comprehensivisation, and that reading levels have fallen with informal teaching - even though few comprehensive schools were yet genuinely comprehensive and comparative data for reading scores do not always compare like with like. So it is not difficult to produce statistics giving opposing conclusions.

But the media picked up the general thrust of the Black Papers that education was in the hands of left-wing extremists sacrificing educational quality for their ideological utopian ambitions. So that when a piece of educational research by Neville Bennett (5) was published "showing" that "formal" teaching methods produced better results than "informal" (in terms of Bennett's categorisations), it resonated with the general mood and received widespread media coverage. (Bennett's work contains the weaknesses as well as the strengths of positivist research, so it was not surprising that when Bennett reworked his data some time later he came to different conclusions. On this occasion, the finding was largely ignored, since it was not what the right-wing press wanted to hear.) But at least Bennett, ironically, in the course of his research had served to confirm the impressions of HMI's that progressive teachers were in a small minority – and so did not represent a serious threat to educational orthodoxy.

Schools were also at this time coming under attack from a different direction. In the early seventies, the "deschoolers" hit the commercial market with a series of books advocating the abolition of schools, on the grounds that they were too expensive, perpetuated conformity and maintained privilege. Various ambitious alternatives were proposed to take the place of institutionalised schooling. For example, the sharing of resources in "learning networks", both of:
   (a) things: e.g. - libraries, workshops and computers etc.
   (b) people: e.g. - skill models (contacts to be obtained through directories)
        - peer groups (for the sharing of ideas and experiences)
        - professional educators (administrators, pedagogues and ill- defined leaders). (6)

It is difficult to estimate the impact the de - schoolers made on the public perception of the condition of state education, but general unease was growing, fuelled by the press, acting in the proclaimed interests of its parent-readers. For example, the Daily Express of September 25, 1975, ran the headline: "Parents Accuse Teachers of Indoctrinating Their Children With Left-wing Politics and Condemn Their Standard of Teaching". It was by now becoming a party political matter, with the Black Papers being quoted at Tory party conferences. In short, the Tory Party was increasingly being seen as the custodian of education standards and values. Furthermore, this was accompanied by a sharp rise in youth unemployment, blamed not on structural changes but on the failure of schools to equip their pupils with appropriate attitudes and skills. In short, a populist mood was being created that teachers ought to be "slapped down" and that the government should put its house in order.

Also waiting in the wings, as always, were those free marketeers, such as the Institute of Directors, who advocated the abolition of rate support, privatisation of the education system and exposure to market forces.

The Government's Response: An Exercise in Legitimation

It was important for the government, faced with a variety of opposing forces and interests, to tread warily. How this was done over the years is described in the following pages, providing valuable insights into the machinations of modern government in a representative democracy.

Setting an agenda: Standards and Accountability

The government, in the face of widespread public criticism and what were seen as the excesses described in the previous chapter, was clearly determined to move to the centre of the stage. England had a legacy of decentralised authority and a tradition had been built up that teachers should have professional control over the "what and how" of the curriculum . It was therefore essential for a democratic government constantly in the media spotlight to prepare its case well and win over potential allies by appealing to their interests, whilst at the same time outmanoeuvring its opponents. In short, any proposals from the government had to be seen to be legitimate. Since this can be seen as the start of a long-term strategy and because the processes it set in train continue to the present day, I will go into some detail in describing subsequent events.

It was a new Labour Prime Minister James Callaghan who in 1976 faced this problem. Known as "Sunny Jim" because of his emollient approach, one of his first tasks was to institute a series of briefing sessions with the Education Minister and others and request a paper on four aspects:

> primary education and the 3 R's;
> the later years of compulsory education;
> examinations; and
> the 16-19 problem.

The result was a confidential 63-page report, the Yellow Book, giving detailed criticism both of schools and the Schools Council, the latter's performance on curriculum and examinations being described as "generally mediocre". This document highlighted the following problems:

> *"an uncritical application of informal methods" in primary schools, secondary school teachers often unqualified in specialist subjects, "too ready to drop their sights in setting standards for more difficult pupils ";*
> *a failure "to develop new styles of assessment", 13-14*

year olds permitted to choose unbalanced curricula or "to opt innumbers insufficient for the country's needs for scientific and technological subjects".

It recommended a core curriculum including vocational education.

In conclusion, the memorandum made a bid for some control to pass to the Education Department:

> *"It will be good to get on record from ministers, and particularly the Prime Minister, an authoritative pronouncement on the division of responsibility for what goes on in school...the Department should give a firmer lead...nor need there be any inhibition for fear that the Department could not make use of the enhanced opportunity to exercise influence over the curriculum and teaching methods; the Inspectorate would have a leading role to play in bringing forward ideas in these areas and is ready to fulfil that responsibility". (7)*

JAMES CALLAGHAN (1912 – 2005)

Started work as a clerk in the Inland Revenue in 1929 at the age of 17. Eight years later he became a full-time union official. In 1931 he joined the Labour Party. Whilst on leave from the Royal Navy he was selected as Labour Party candidate for Cardiff South, winning a seat in 1945. He became the only person to hold all the four major offices of state.

THE WATERSHED

On October 19, 1976, the Prime Minister gave a speech at Ruskin College, Oxford, which has come to be seen as laying down a marker for a future agenda and marking a watershed in the relationships between the various partners in the education system. Having paid tribute to the adult literacy campaign and the enthusiasm and dedication of the teaching profession, he quoted Labour's father - figure, R.H. Tawney to make sure he was seen to be firmly on the side of parents:

> "What a wise parent would wish for their children, so the State must wish for all the children..........there was unease felt by parents and others about the new informal methods of teaching, which seem to produce excellent results when they are in well-qualified hands but are much more dubious when they are not". The goals of education "are to equip children to the best of their ability for a lively, constructive place in society and also to fit them for a job of work. Not one or the other – but both......In today's world higher standards are demanded and there are simply fewer jobs for those without skill...There is a challenge in education to examine its priorities and to secure as high efficiency as you can by the skilful use of the £6 billion of existing resources"... (8)

He then emphasised the fields needing extra attention:

the methods and aims of informal instruction;
the strong case for the so-called core curriculum of basic knowledge;
the proper way of monitoring the use of resources in order to maintain a proper national standard of performance;
the role of the Inspectorate in relation to national standards;
the need to improve relations between industry and education .

As expected, the speech was severely criticised by the teacher unions, but even the Times Educational Supplement was unimpressed:

> "He has gathered his Black Paper cloak around him. He has trotted out clichés from the CBI...He has whistled up weasel words to exploit popular prejudices. And he has sought to divert popular indignation from his own management of the economy."(9)

The "Great Debate" – Seeking or Engineering Consensus?

But the Prime Minister had not only entered the "secret garden of the curriculum", he had made it clear that it was now to be open to regular inspection. His speech had been an attempt to "define the situation" – it was now important to achieve an apparent consensus, so that the government's definition prevailed. To this end the so-called "Great Debate" was launched; eight one-day conferences were organised to which representatives of various organisations, including local authorities and employers, were invited and for which a background paper "Agenda for Discussion" was provided, based upon the following concerns, roughly comparable to those issues the Prime Minister had drawn attention to in his Ruskin College speech:

> Curriculum
> Monitoring/assessment
> Teacher training
> School and Working Life.

A subsequent paper sharpened up this agenda by focussing on more specific issues:

> *"What should be the aims and content of a core curriculum?*
> *Is there a case for tests in English Language and Mathematics to be taken by all pupils at certain ages?"*
> *(10)*

But the general impression from those involved seems to be that there was no genuine debate and no serious attempt to arrive at consensual positions. In the words of one observer the verdict on the Debate was "not found wanting because never tried" (11)

But what mattered for the government was both the public display of the "partners in education" apparently reaching consensus, and the right of entry of the DES into the affairs of teachers and local authorities. With teachers in its sights, the Green Paper published shortly after the Great Debate firmly placed the concept of accountability on the agenda and stressed the need, both for closer links between schools and industry and the need for a coherent and soundly-based means of assessment for pupils and schools. Note, for example, the language in the following consultative paper, published shortly after the Great Debate and confirming the right of the Department to be involved in educational matters, whilst still referring to interested others as "partners":

> *"It would not be compatible with the duty of the Secretary of State to 'promote the education of the people of England and Wales'...to abdicate from leadership on educational issues which have become a matter of lively public debate. The Secretaries of State will therefore seek to establish a broad agreement with their partners in the education service on a framework for the curriculum, and particularly on whether...there should be a 'core' or 'protected part'".*
> *(12)*

This exercise in justification had enabled the DES to present itself as a key player in matters which have hitherto been regarded as the preserve of teachers and local authorities. Maintaining the momentum of the Great Debate, Circular 14/77 addressed to local authorities swiftly followed, requiring information by the following June on the following six main points:

- arrangements for the coordination and development of the curriculum;
- steps taken to encourage appropriate curriculum balance and breadth ;
- policies for particular subject areas;
- transition between schools;
- school records;
- preparation for working life. (13)

This was intended to provide the basis for further consultations, in the course of which agreement would be sought on the nature of further action that might be necessary to develop curriculum policies and to meet national needs more effectively. (14)

Bureaucratisation: Data Collection: Assessment of Performance Unit

It was essential, if the Department were to be more involved in policy-making, to collect as much information as possible about the education system. Given the fragmented nature of this "system", this would be no easy task. Local authorities were responsible for the administration of education in their area but with no generally agreed curriculum goals or mandatory subjects. Whilst some guidance was provided by the subject content of examination boards these boards were all independent and had different regulations and syllabuses.

A prior step in the move towards central control, then, was increasing bureaucratisation of the department by the incorporation of further expertise (provided by the transfer of some HMI's from their normal duties) and the setting up of machinery for the collection of appropriate data, to be controlled and interpreted by these experts. It was decided in 1974 to set up the Assessment of Performance Unit for the purpose of national (not individual) monitoring of national standards in Maths, English, Science, Modern Languages and Technology through a "light sampling" of 1.5% of the school population. The terms of reference were:

> "to promote the development of methods of assessing and monitoring achievement and to seek to identify significant differences of achievement related to the circumstances in which children learn…….information about the effectiveness of the school system is essential for the development of educational policy and the allocation of resources." (15)

If the implications of the setting-up of APU on relationships between central and local government. were not already clear, they were spelt out in the Green Paper mentioned above:

> "LEA's need to be able to assess the relative performance of their schools in order to reach decisions about staffing and the allocation of resources. In particular, an essential facet of their accountability for educational standards is that they must be able to identify schools which consistently perform poorly, so that appropriate action can be taken". (16)

So much for local authorities. As for teachers, their powers were also gradually eroded. The Education Minister restructured the Schools Council so that no longer were there teacher majorities on committees, whilst the

1977 Taylor Report (17) on school government granted school governing bodies formal access to school activities.

By such a series of manoeuvres, the government in just a couple of years had shifted the balance of power away from teachers towards the centre, ostensibly in the interests of the consumers of education, such as parents and industry. And two new conceptual weapons had entered the armoury of the Department: accountability and standards. Not as uncontroversial as they may seem at first sight, they were to be used with great effect in the years to come.

Within a couple of years, in 1979, the Labour government had been replaced by a Tory party determined to continue with those educational reforms which would make teachers accountable to a central authority and at the same time provide parental choice by easing the grip of LEA's on the system. The new prime minister, Margaret Thatcher, appointed Mark Carlisle as her Education Secretary to oversee such reforms. He quickly introduced two Education Bills, the first "to remove the compulsion on local education authorities to reorganise their schools on comprehensive lines"; the second the Assisted Places Scheme whereby the DES paid independent schools to take selected pupils from the state sector (removing up to 15,000 pupils a year from comprehensive schools, 20% of the school population). Both these initiatives were clear examples of the restoration of selection and differentiation to state schools, reversing the comprehensive policies of the previous administration.

The Education Minister Abolishes Schools Council and Becomes Chief Policy Maker

But the Prime Minister found Mark Carlisle rather ineffective and too left-wing and replaced him in 1981 with the right-wing monetarist Keith Joseph:

> *"Keith Joseph had told me he wished to move from Industry. With his belief that there was an anti-enterprise culture which had harmed Britain's economic performance over the years, it was natural that Keith should now wish to go to Education where that culture had taken deep roots"*
> *(18)*

Joseph, in keeping with his free market beliefs, considered extending parental choice beyond the Assisted Places Scheme by introducing a voucher scheme whereby parents could exercise a greater choice of schools. He eventually dropped the idea because of possible legal complexities - much to the consternation of his right-wing colleagues.

It was also clear that, with his poor opinion of the educational system which he had inherited and with the legitimation of government intervention described above, he would attempt to take more control to himself. Subsequent events showed how firm and widespread this control was to be - in sharp contrast to the first post-war Education Minister, George Tomlinson, who famously declared "Minister knows nowt about t'curriculum". The broad sweep of his concerns emerging in the course of his tenure included:

> promotion of national agreement on the purposes and content of a broad, balanced, relevant and differentiated curriculum;
> completion of the reform of the examination system, including records of achievement;
> tackling truancy by improving the training of education welfare officers;
> setting up a new council (Council for the Accreditation of Teacher Education) for the approval of initial teacher training;
> ensuring a more balanced membership of school governing bodies.

The Schools Council was clearly an obstacle in the way of both the implementation of some of the solutions to the above problems and to the idea of central control. The Council had been both losing credibility and attracting odium in recent years, to the extent of its recommendations being ignored by the government. And when an independent investigation of its functions led to the conclusion that it was anti-intellectual and overstretched, it merely added to general complaints that it was lacking accountability, ineffective in bringing about large-scale innovation and arrogant in its relations with civil servants. The ground was thus prepared for Keith Joseph to abolish it. This he did in 1982, to replace it with two separate bodies, both accountable to him - an Examinations Council and the School Curriculum Development Council. The latter was to keep abreast of current curriculum developments and identify gaps and current needs, whilst the Examinations Council was to coordinate and supervise the conduct of examinations at 16-plus and 18-plus and monitor the activities of GCE and CSE examination boards.

With regard to examinations, it had been generally assumed that the GCE O-levels would cater for the top 20% of candidates and CSE for the next 40%. But the development of a comprehensive system of secondary education made the idea of separate examinations of different status an anomaly. Joseph therefore requested the GCE and CSE Joint Council to look into the possibility of a common examination, the General Certificate of Secondary Education (GCSE). The Joint Council, after wide consultation, produced a common format of aims, assessment objectives, course-work, and common core. Grades A-C would be the responsibility of the GCE boards and the remaining grades D-G the responsibility of the CSE boards. Syllabuses would then be constructed taking account both of general criteria and (subject-specific) national criteria.

The Minister, obsessed with the idea of "absolute standards of performance", had made it clear that he would have the final say on the composition of these syllabuses. True to his word, he dismissed attempts by the English working party to include a multi-cultural element and he rejected the inclusion of social and economic elements in the Physics syllabus. He also announced that the new GCSE examination would come into operation in 1988 and insisted that "grade-related criteria" should be included in GCSE syllabuses. For this purpose, he requested that the Secondary Examinations Council organise small working-groups to develop grade-related criteria to be presented within ten months to examination boards for inclusion in their syllabuses.

This time-scale and the Minister's inflexible attitude caused consternation among those involved. As Roger Murphy put it:

> "Grade-related criteria are an entirely new concept in the world of public examinations….they aim to provide a description of what any candidate who achieves a particular grade knows, understands and can do…As the working groups get further into their deliberations it will be remarkable if they don't stumble upon a whole range of intractable problems." (20)

Indeed the reaction of the English working group was that the task would be impossible unless changes could be made to the National Criteria. However, despite these objections, work went ahead and grade-related criteria were eventually added to the National Criteria.

Reactions to the GCSE were widespread and varied. Teachers complained that the whole exercise was rushed, that classes were too large and that resources were too limited. Traditionalists bemoaned the inclusion of what they described as "instant studies", such as business, computer and film studies, on the grounds that any education not based in traditional disciplines was liable to political manipulation. And the (surprising) continued presence of course-work (internally assessed and counting for as much as 60% in Design and Technology) was decried as an invalid contribution to a public examination, open to widespread abuse. It was the right-wing think tank, the Centre for Policy Studies, which perhaps made the most pertinent points, claiming that the difficulty of moving from a norm- to a criterion-referenced examination (21) had been grossly underestimated, a difficulty highlighted by the sometimes meaningless distinction between grades, for example, "the ability to do X" and "some ability to do X"!

What this examination shows, once again, is the relationship of education to the occupational hierarchy, with the top 20% (A to C grades) destined for the academic route and the next 40% (D to G grades) for a technical/vocational destination. The remainder continued to be a problem, in terms of not only having achieved anything from their education but not having anything to show for it - a problem which in the past had been largely ignored. But Keith Joseph, for all his monetarist economic inclinations, showed a genuine concern for the welfare of low-achieving children. In 1982, the Lower Achieving Pupils Project (LAPP) was set up "to introduce a more effective education with a practical slant" with a £2 million grant. But this innovation was clearly regarded by the State as relatively unimportant. Various schools and local authorities took up the challenge but on the whole the effect was peripheral, so that the education of the bottom 40% remained a low priority (19).

Although Keith Joseph was both intellectually and emotionally involved in problems facing the school curriculum, he was strongly opposed, unlike his successor, to any form of compulsory or national curriculum, on the grounds that emerging and useful subjects would be omitted and teachers put in a straitjacket. In the end, the neoliberal Joseph, exhausted by his constant wrestling with educational problems and with the demands of the teaching unions, was ready in 1985 to step down. Some insight into his concerned state of mind is provided by the following revealing extract from an interview he gave on leaving office:

"We have a bloody state system I wish we hadn't got. I wish we'd taken a different route in 1870. We got the ruddy state involved. I don't want it. . I don't think we know how to do it. I certainly don't think Secretaries of State know anything about it. But we're landed with it. ...We've got compulsory education, which is a responsibility of hideous importance and we tyrannise children to do that which they don't want, and we don't produce results."
(Quoted in C. Chitty op cit)

It will be for historians in the future to assess the contribution he made to the education system, but even now it is possible to point to the irony that, whilst Joseph was grappling with the problem of the disadvantaged 40% of the school population, it was the Department of Employment which was nearer to providing a solution, with its eye-catching and well-resourced Technical and Vocational Education Initiative..

The Upstart: "Storming the Citadel of Education" – TVEI

By the mid-1980's unemployment was approaching the three million mark and rising rapidly. Of these, half a million were school-leavers. So the economic interest was now overwhelming, leaving schools vulnerable to attacks not only from the media and the CBI for turning out unemployable kids, but also from other forms of educational provision . And an alternative form of provision was indeed provided, not by the Education Department but by the Department of Employment, under the entrepreneurial direction of David Young.

Lord Young (1932 –) – the son of a businessman, he trained as a solicitor before entering the world of banking and property development and becoming an executive for Great Universal Store. He later became Chairman of the International Council of Jewish Social and Welfare Services, and a member of Margaret Thatcher's 'think-tank', the Centre of Policy Studies. He was also adviser to Keith Joseph in the Department of Industry. In 1984 he was made a life-peer and entered the Cabinet and where, single-handed and un-elected, he threatened to transform, with his TVEI, the British educational system.

After two and half years in the Department of Industry, Young had been offered the chairmanship of the MSC (the Manpower Services Commission, set up in 1973 as an adjunct of the Department of Employment) by Norman Tebbitt, the new Employment Minister, who saw him as the man for the job - a view the self-confident, dynamic and ambitious David Young would not disagree with:

> "By one of life's better ironies it represented all that I came into government to change...it was the corporate state personified...it assumed that government could better discharge its duties by abrogating them to a series of agencies...The more I looked into it the more I became convinced that nothing less than a wholesale pruning and simplification of the organisation would do." (24)

As one of his first acts and in response to the alarming unemployment figures, Young set about developing a Youth Training Scheme (25). He had previously been impressed, by his fundraising work for the Organisation for Rehabilitation Through Training (ORT) an international network of vocational schools, by the way in which students had responded given an appropriate learning environment:

> "I had seen many similar schools around the world. Young people, not academic by nature, had come alive as soon as their education had changed to technical or vocational subjects...I suggested to Keith that we open a series of technical schools. 'Let them be outside the existing state system if we have to. We could run the programme through the MSC. Let them succeed and we will infect the system. Then they will all want to change" (26)

Keith Joseph, no doubt still mindful of the poor return for the bottom 40% of the school population got from their schooling, agreed. So Young began to look around for buildings that would be suitable for technical schools. But before the development could get off the ground, Young received a request from Joseph that he meet some of his officials.

> "Early next morning three senior officials from the DES came round. I could see that they were utterly shocked and rather fed up. After a while they came to the point of their

visit. Could we run the programme within the existing system and let it be administered by the local education authorities? 'Yes' I replied, 'as long as we make sure that it does happen and it will not be taken over and treated merely as extra money for the present system" (27)

Being the favourite of Margaret Thatcher ("Other ministers bring me problems, David brings me solutions") Young could count on her full support and it was the Prime Minister herself who, in November 1982, announced the ambitious Technical and Vocational Initiative (TVEI) inviting local authorities to submit proposals for projects aimed at equipping 14-18 year-olds in full-time education to better enter the world of employment. They were to be aimed at the 15-85 percentile of the ability range: the top 15% would continue with their traditional courses, whilst the bottom 15% were excluded. Not only was Keith Joseph's education empire being threatened with colonisation but education itself was in danger of being redefined.

Contrary to the general view in the government that LEA's should have their powers considerably reduced, Young was anxious to involve them from the start, inviting them to submit their proposals for implementing the scheme, and promising generous financial support. The momentum of this initiative is well captured by this extract from David Young's memoirs:

> *"At the beginning the local authority associations thought that here was a pot of money merely for the taking. They were quickly disillusioned. We set a tremendous pace; by the end of November we convened the first meeting of the National Steering Group, assembled a national management team and issued public invitations to LEA's to come and take part. Then before Christmas we asked for and received outline proposals, judged them and selected the projects' localities. By mid-February we appointed local chairmen and put project teams in place. By the end of the month they were all up and working. By mid-March we had Exchequer funding agreed for each local project. Then all we had to do was to make local preparations, staff development and in-service training, and open our doors in September. This in the world of education, where progress was usually measured over*

decades! We had stormed the citadel of education and from now on our only problems would be coping with the demand." (28)

In submitting proposals, the local authorities had to provide such details as the target group, course content, provisions for qualifications, and administrative arrangements. In the event 66 proposals were received for this first phase and 14 were accepted.

Given David Young's background in business and his familiarity with hierarchical corporate structures, it would have been understandable if he had picked up the capitalist model of Taylorism, and placed the workforce in straitjackets, constrained by precise measurable objectives. In fact he did no such thing. His approach was so open and the aims so vague that it is impossible to produce a definitive TVEI model - it was to be a catalyst for curriculum change rather than a precise blueprint. Projects were to be characterised by the encouragement of initiative, problem-solving abilities and personal development, including active learning and students taking responsibility for their own learning. There should be a balance between general, technical and vocational elements, suggesting the revival of a practical curriculum, where there was neither a single-minded focus on academic content nor vocational skills. (29)

So by no stretch of the imagination could TVEI be said to be prescriptive. Curricula should be negotiated and for this purpose teachers formed consortia in order to design both the curriculum and assessment procedures. We have here the surreal spectacle of the Employment Department bringing LEA's back to the centre of the stage and promoting teacher autonomy, whilst for the previous decade the Education Department had been doing the precise opposite. And by now the Department of Employment was becoming a serious threat to the autonomy of the Education Department, with its appeal to the same clientele, its more streamlined organisation, and with its considerable financial resources - £46 million was promised over 5 years covering up to 14,000 students in 144 schools and colleges. (Almost before the first round was off the ground, the Employment Secretary, Norman Tebbitt, replying to a Parliamentary question, announced that, encouraged by the enthusiasm and commitment shown by local authorities, he had asked the MSC to extend TVEI by about 40 projects, for which £20 million a year would be available.)

A key feature of TVEI was the emphasis upon evaluation, both at the national and local levels. Some of the outcomes were quite predictable:

the relative autonomy given to teachers generated considerable enthusiasm, but in the absence of the professional expertise characteristic of the Schools Council Projects described earlier, development tended to be lacking in theoretical underpinning;

where consortia of schools were established, there was the possibility of shared experiences; evidence suggests that schools benefited both from these and the resources available;

the "student voice" was heard and there was general approval of both new learning and teaching styles and the practically-oriented curricula. However, results in formal examinations were not as good as had been expected (hardly surprising, given that different models of education were involved)

in the absence of formal dissemination strategies, projects were always vulnerable to decline, a lesson which should have been learned from the experience of the Schools Council.

After four years in operation, TVEI still had the force with it, and a White Paper "Working Together – education and training" (30) announced that the programme was to be extended to all maintained schools and colleges as part of an overall drive to create a coherent British vocational education and training system which would be the envy of world, funded to the tune of £90 million a year, taking the grand total to almost £1 billion. But these confident predictions came to naught and TVEI gradually disappeared, almost without trace. Several explanations have been advanced for this surprising decline. Both David Young and the Employment Secretary Norman Tebbitt had moved on - to be replaced by people with apparently little interest in the scheme. And unemployment had declined, lessening the economic interest in favour of a more traditional academic education, held in higher regard by most parents. But it should be borne in mind that the role of TVEI was essentially catalytic rather than prescriptive and it was always possible that, as in the case of the Schools Council, its alternative conceptualisation of curriculum, evaluation and pedagogy may persist within the system, awaiting a revival when circumstances are more favourable.

The events described in this chapter give the lie to the idea that education stands aloof from material matters and is indifferent to struggles between interest groups. We have seen how central government, in response to orchestrated demands for greater discipline in our schools and for less frills, had taken various powers to itself by a gradualist approach and so legitimated its entry into the "secret garden". But whilst local authorities and teachers were on notice that they must both be accountable to the state and responsible for the standards in their schools, it should be noted that so far such demands had stopped short of dictating the precise nature of the school curriculum. But the next Education Minister, unlike his predecessor, was determined, not only to change all that, but to place the authority of the academic curriculum beyond dispute.

NOTES AND REFERENCES

1. DES (1967) Children and their Primary Schools. HMSO. London
2. R. Lyon, (undated) Black Paper Three. Critical Quarterly Society. London
3. S.H. Froome (undated) Black Paper Two. Critical Quarterly Society. London
4. Szamuely op cit
5. Bennett, N. (1976) Teaching Styles and Pupil Progress. Open Books London. Bennett initially defined "teaching styles" and from this developed questionnaires to 871 primary schools in NW England. By a cluster analysis of their responses he produced a typology of 12 teaching styles. This was subsequently reduced to seven and 37 teachers selected to represent these types. In June 1973 these teachers administered tests in reading, mathematics and English to pupils on exit from third year classes. They were again tested a year later on exit from the fourth year. Bennett collapsed these seven teaching styles into "formal", "informal" and "mixed", and claimed that formal and mixed teaching gave significantly better results than informal, the differences being equivalent to 3- 5 months..
6. Reimer, E (1971) School is Dead. This was one of five "subversive" titles published simultaneously by Penguin Education.
7. The contents of the Yellow Book were leaked to the Times Educational Supplement and published October 15, 1976
8. TES October 22, 1976.
9. op cit
10. Department of Education and Science (1977) Educating Our Children.
11. The conferences followed a predictable pattern, as did the unofficial television and radio 'debates' which went on alongside them. Well-known positions were reiterated by representatives of various interest parties....evidence to support views put forward continued to be scarce and where it conflicted with predetermined positions was generally discounted on some ad hoc grounds which cast doubt on its reliability or enabled it to be explained away". Reid, W.A. (1978) Thinking About the Curriculum. Routledge and Kegan Paul. London.
12. DES (1977) Education in Schools: a Consultative Document.
13. DES (1977) Annual Report

14. See Salter and Tapper op cit for an interesting and detailed account of these developments.

15. DES (1978) Report on Education. Assessing the Performance of Pupils. HMSO. London. Steering groups were set up for the separate subjects to identify those performances which would constitute valid standards. In the case of Science:

using symbolic representation

using observations

using apparatus and measuring instruments

interpretation and application

designing and investigating

performing investigations.

The idea of including aesthetic development, personal and social development and physical development was dropped, presumably because of the impossibility of accommodating any data within the positivist framework necessary to provide the stamp of authority.

16 . DES (1977) Education in Schools: a Consultative Document. HMSO Cmd 5720

17. DES (1977) A New Partnership for our Schools. HMSO London

18 Thatcher, M. (1993) Margaret Thatcher: the Downing Street Years. Harper Collins. London

19.The LAPP project was intended to incorporate a variety of elements:

an emphasis upon equipping pupils with the necessary skills of communication, literacy and numeracy;

the acceptance of a degree of differentiation and negotiation in the curriculum;

a development of profiling in which the student measures progress against mutually-agree objectives;

work experience placements within a continuous programme of work induction.

Some schools used this project to develop "thinking skills". See Holly,P. (1976) The Dilemmas of Low Attainment. Further Education Unit, DES. London.

20. Times Educational Supplement, November 30, 1984.

21. With norm-referenced examinations, examination boards adjusted the grade boundaries so that most examinees were in the middle range. In the case of criterion-referencing the grade is absolute, so that if examination questions are not set at exactly the right level of difficulty, the distribution of examinees' marks can be idiosyncratic,

as we shall see later.

22 "Better Schools" (1985) HMSO Cmd 9469

23 Denham, A. and Garnett, M. (2001) "Keith Joseph". Acumen. Chesham.

24 Young, D. (1990) The Enterprise Years. Headline. London.

25 The Manpower Services Commission, in response to rising youth unemployment, had introduced a Youth Opportunities Programme (YOP) providing work experience for unemployed school-leavers ("Watching, not training" was Young's pithy comment. He introduced the Youth Training Scheme to provide a limited period of training.

26. Young,D. op cit

27. op cit

28. op cit

29. See David Yeomans paper (1986) "Constructing Vocational Education from TVEI to GNVQ. School of Education. Leeds University.

30. DES (1986) White Paper Education and Training. HMSO. London

CHAPTER EIGHT

CONSOLIDATION AND CONTROL: The National Curriculum and Ofsted

> *"I am proud that we let some indestructible genies out of the bottle. We pushed through testing. We secured truly independent inspection. We published league tables of results. And on the basis of proper information we began to give parents a real choice. Basic facts about education will never again be able to be suppressed". (Prime Minister John Major)*

GERBIL : The Great Education Reform Bill
The Politics of Making a Common National Curriculum
     (a) *are school subjects what they seem ?*
     (b) *setting up the framework - territorial disputes*
     (c) *subject working-parties: acrimony and resignation*
     (d) *the problem of external examinations*
The Standards Regime:
     Testing Pupils (SATs)
     Inspecting Teachers (Ofsted)
Marketisation : league tables etc.
The " New" Vocationalism:
     getting it right: NVQ's
     still getting it right: GNVQ's
     and still getting it right: 14-19 Learning
Can "Vocational Education" be Educational?
Mixed Messages

GERBIL - The Great Education Reform Bill

The popularity and growth of TVEI, sponsored by a well-endowed Employment Department, corresponded with a low point in the fortunes of the Education

Department. The monetarist Education Secretary, Keith Joseph, had allowed schools to become run down, there was a long-running teachers' dispute over salaries, industry was repeating its mantra "schools are failing industry"; right-wing pressure groups such as the Hillgate Group ("Save Our Schools") were carrying on where the Black Papers had left off, demanding direct financing of schools from central government, independent school boards and parental choice of schools. In other words, there was the radical demand that the state education system be "marketised". The Institute of Directors made this quite explicit, by calling for the abolition of rate support and the opening of schools to market forces. (Even a junior education minister called for the privatisation of education.) In short, the government was generally unpopular, confirmed consistently by opinion polls - and the education system was once again in crisis, not only identified as a major source of public discontent, but with its whole raison d'etre being questioned.

It was in this climate that Kenneth Baker, recognised for his political and communication skills, was chosen in May 1986, as the new Education Secretary in succession to Keith Joseph. A smooth operator, he was not a man to be assailed by doubts, unlike his predecessor. Writing about his approach to the Education Reform Bill, he had this to say:

> *"To be successful, a politician has to have a clear vision...I knew what I wanted in the package and I knew I would have to drive it through my department, persuade the prime minister and colleagues it should be adopted in the form I wanted and then steer a major piece of legislation through Parliament." (1)*

Kenneth Baker (1934 -) – had a grammar school and Oxford education before joining Royal Dutch Shell. Elected as M.P in 1968, eventually becoming Education Minister where he introduced, without prior consultation or justification, the National Curriculum. He introduced in-service training days for teachers ("Baker Days") and is presently opposing, as Lord Baker, the expansion of faith schools.

Kenneth Baker adopted, with Cabinet approval, an expansionist policy, in contrast to his predecessor. He found an extra £50 million for local authorities and settled the teachers' pay dispute. But in a series of speeches he made it clear that there had to be some fundamental changes including:

- a national curriculum with precise syllabuses and age-related tests
- independent school boards with control over school finances,
- the opportunity for schools to opt out of the system as grant-maintained schools,
- the setting up of city technology colleges subsidised by business, and
- parental choice of school (but, unlike private schools, with tax-payers footing the bill).

To some extent the ground had been prepared for these radical reforms in the previous decade by the continued assault on local authority independence and teacher autonomy. Certain continuities can thus be seen with the initiative launched by the Great Debate:

centralised intervention into teacher practices was extended to precise control over curriculum content ;

teacher accountability was to be made more substantial through regular testing of pupils and inspection of schools;

the position of local authorities within the educational system was weakened by setting up independent school boards and providing schools with "opt-out" opportunities.

"Parental choice" was to be brought about by a series of stages, all designed to make schools independent of local authority control. In the first stage, budgets would be delegated to schools, to be managed by the school governing body. This would be followed by "per capita funding" so that money would follow the pupil, with popular schools being allowed to expand by a policy of open enrolment. And schools could become "grant-maintained" by direct finance from central government. It was envisaged that, apart from managing their own budget, the governors would have the power to appoint the teaching staff, agree a policy on admissions, and own the school and its assets.

Most of these measures found ready agreement among the Tory party (wedded to the slogans of "freedom" and "choice"). But it was the intended structure of the national curriculum which brought Kenneth Baker into repeated conflict with Margaret Thatcher. In a speech to the North of England Conference in January 1987, Kenneth Baker revealed his five objectives for a National Curriculum:

1. set a standard of knowledge which would give a clear incentive for all our schools to catch up with the best and challenge the best to do even better;
2. provide teachers with detailed and precise objectives to support their work;
3. provide parents with clear, accurate information about their child and the school;
4. ensure continuity and avoid duplication;
5. help teachers concentrate on the task of getting the best possible results from each individual child.

As is customary with government pronouncements there was little attempt to define "education" in clear, unambiguous terms or to justify the choice either of particular educational objectives or curriculum content. We get an insight, however, into the Minister's thinking in a later consultation paper, where he refers to a ten-subject curriculum with tests at the age of 7, 11 and 14 leading to the GCSE at 16.

The Prime Minister was not amused by this suggestion:

> "I never envisaged that we would end up with the bureaucracy and the thicket of prescriptive measures which eventually emerged. I wanted the DES to concentrate on establishing a basic syllabus for English, Mathematics and Science, with simple tests to show what pupils knew.....I had no wish to put good teachers in a strait-jacket. Unfortunately, my philosophy turned out to be different from that of those entrusted with the drawing up of the national curriculum and the formulation of the tests alongside it." (2)

But in his memoirs Kenneth Baker claims that he was adamant:

> *"I wanted to ensure that every boy and girl took not just Science but also Technology up the age of sixteen... Furthermore our national record in foreign languages was abysmal since many gave them up at fourteen. I wanted to ensure that not only was the teaching of foreign languages more relevant and more practical but that all children had to continue with them up the age of sixteen. I also wanted to ensure that as regards History, our children would leave school with real knowledge of what has happened in our country over the last thousand years... Geography too was important but was in danger of disappearing into the less rigorous form of environmental studies... I also wanted to include art, music and sport... However a National Curriculum was not sufficient by itself to improve education standards unless progress was measured at regular intervals."* (3)

The Prime Minister continued to demur over details, so that Kenneth Baker was eventually compelled to make it clear that if he were to continue as Education Secretary then the curriculum would have to be as agreed previously with Cabinet colleagues.

As a result, the Education Bill was introduced to Parliament three weeks later, in 1977. Apart from the proposals mentioned above, it provided for the setting up of two separate bodies, the National Curriculum Council (to establish the curriculum and keep it under review) and the Schools Examination and Assessment Council (SEAC). It was greeted with considerable hostility from churches, teacher unions and parent-teacher associations, voluntary organisations and local authorities. A mere two months were allowed for consultation during the summer holidays; even so a large number of submissions were made, to be summarily dismissed as "self-interested". The Education Secretary put the position plainly to the Tory Party Conference:

> *"I have to say that we will not tolerate a moment longer the smug complacency of too many educationists, which has left our national educational performance limping along behind that of our industrial competitors".* (4)

Perhaps in defining educational performance in industrial, instrumental terms, Kenneth Baker was telling the Tory Party what he thought it wanted to hear. But his subsequent legislation on the National Curriculum is not only at odds with this, but suggests he was not only totally indifferent to the achievements of TVEI at the Employment Department, but also uninterested in the work of the Schools Council and also the ideas of curriculum radicals. By and large he had taken a traditionalist stance by ensuring that all children had a similar education to that which he enjoyed at grammar school : that was to be the extent of any discussion of the education interest.

The Education Bill, introduced in November 1987, with minor concessions, received the Royal Assent and passed into law the following July. But not all the provisions of the Bill were to be welcomed. Many industrialists cold-shouldered the idea of city technology colleges, preferring to invest their money in other ways. And comprehensive school parents often remained indifferent to the blandishments of the grant-maintained trust.

The National Curriculum: What Every Pupil Should Learn

But the greatest challenge for the Minister lay ahead: to put flesh on the bones of the National Curriculum. Since this initiative is of historic importance, providing insights into some of the problems facing curriculum development and later arguments against the present curriculum, it is worth looking at it in some detail. It represents an extreme example of a technical curriculum model, with nationally-agreed objectives, made up of precise syllabuses, for all 5-16 year-olds in the state system. There would be attainment targets for all subjects and standard attainment tests (SATS) would be taken at the end of four key stages:

> Key stage 1 (KS1) 5-7year olds;
> Key stage 2 (KS2) 7-11 year-olds;
> Key stage 3 (KS3) 11-14 year-olds;
> Key stage 4 (KS4) 14-16 year-olds.

Programmes of study were also provided for the teacher, setting-out the matter, skills and processes to be taught, incidentally decreasing the scope of the teacher's professional judgment and completing this particular stage of "deskilling the teacher".

The Politics of Making a Common Subject-Based National Curriculum

In response to the Prime Minister saying that "something has to be done about the schools", the Secretary of State had taken upon himself what to most people would be the impossible task of laying down a national framework for what every child in the state system should learn (albeit at different levels), irrespective of needs, interests, social class, culture and race – as though the Schools Council had never existed, apart from its acceptance of an Objectives Model. Doubtless basing this framework upon his own (and most other minister's) school experience he stipulated that what were seen as unproblematic subjects would provide the structure. At least he had the good sense to set up working parties of "experts" to work out the detail within the following foundation subjects:

> Mathematics, English, Science, Technology, History,
> Geography, Art, Music and Physical Education.

(a) *Are school subjects what they seem*?

Perhaps from our own schooling we have come to believe that school subjects are made up of unchanging and uncontentious bodies of knowledge, encapsulating all that is worthwhile in terms of our human heritage. If so, a brief look at the evolution of school subjects and the work of the subject committees described here will disabuse us of that idea .Several subjects have started life as practical activities concerned with solving relatively concrete problems. Whether due to a process of natural development or in the struggle for status and recognition, they have developed abstract conceptual schemes and come to be recognised as academic disciplines.(5) For instance, whilst Biology may have begun as "nature study" (fit only for girls!) based upon observation and classification of living organisms, it has developed into a full-blown scientific discipline dealing with some of the most profound problems with the most complex theories and procedures - and raising some of the most intractable of ethical issues in the process.

There is also a constant struggle for subjects to obtain an ever more respectable position within the school curriculum. For this purpose subject associations are formed to make out the strongest possible case for inclusion in the curriculum – which normally means displaying their academic credentials in the most favourable light. What is already a complex situation is further complicated by the fact that there are divisions within subject associations themselves as to what constitutes appropriate content and procedures (6). Apparently unaware of these complexities the Secretary of State was about to enter a minefield. It is well worth looking at some of the (often angry) exchanges preceding the entry of a subject into the national curriculum, given the profound significance of this particular stage in curriculum development.

(b) Setting Up the Framework: territorial disputes

Kenneth Baker, recognising "the enormous task of creating a National Curriculum for the first time in our history" had ensured that the Education Act made provision for the establishment of two independent bodies. As mentioned above, the National Curriculum Council (NCC) was to establish and review the national curriculum whilst the Schools Examination and Assessment Council (SEAC) had the job of creating a system of testing and assessment.

Duncan Graham, education administrator and former chief education officer for Suffolk, was appointed to the official positions of chairman and chief executive of the NCC, whilst unofficially he became mediator between opposing factions. From the beginning, his position was undermined by Education Department mandarins, who clearly believed the creation of a national curriculum was within their own and no-one else's remit. According to Kenneth Baker (who was suspicious both of left-wing tendencies within the Department and their over- familiarity with teacher unions) the Department of Education spent a lot of their time trying to second-guess the work of the NCC, and Duncan Graham gives a blow-by-blow account of his dealings, as chief executive of the NCC, both with the Department and the working parties (7). The obstructive tactics employed by the bureaucrats included "strangling the budget", controlling publications, interfering at meetings and keeping Graham away from ministers. But Graham's problems did not end there - he also had to deal with disputes both internal and external to the subject working parties. **For a fascinating and enlightening account of the various disputes both within the subject working parties and with officials and ministers, see Appendix 2.**

The Problem of External Examinations

A fundamental problem which had been placed on the backburner until now concerned the articulation of the National Curriculum with external examination requirements. Now the relationship between the NCC and the Minister became even more fractious when attempting to accommodate GCSE's within the Key Stage 4 framework. The NCC wished to give priority to the "broad and balanced" national framework and promoted the "70/30" solution up to the age of 16, which would give the extended core (English, Maths, Science, Technology) 60% of the timetable, History and Geography 10% and the remaining 30% to other subjects. Kenneth Clarke argued that the national curriculum should not become too prescriptive and exclude a variety of options. How dismissive he was of the NCC becomes clear from the account Duncan Graham gives of hearing from him the night before he gave an important speech to the North of England Conference in January 1991:

> "I only knew what he was going to say the night before he said it when he rang to tell me. The gesture was no more than a cold courtesy. I pointed out to him that the NCC had not heard from him since the first week in November despite requests to meet him before important decisions were made. The council was told that he was too busy, that he was angry with it for having made a complete mess of key stage 4, that he was not going to have it...I realised then that if a Secretary of State was prepared to treat a well–disposed advisory council in that way he would be prepared to do anything if it suited him." (19)

In his speech, Clarke announced that children would be required to take only Maths. English and Science at GCSE, all pupils would take Technology and Modern Languages to 16 (i.e. as part of the National Curriculum), History or Geography to 14, Art and Music would be optional but some sort of physical exercise would be expected. We now had official confirmation of the relative standing of the various subjects from top to bottom:

Maths. English and Science;
Technology and Modern Languages;
History and Geography
Art, Music and Physical Education

Whatever Happened to Religious Education?

As this narrative has shown, the Anglican Church had for the past two centuries fought tenaciously to retain both a toehold on the school curriculum

148

and a substantial share of State finances. The absence of RE as a mandatory subject in the National Curriculum is therefore at first sight surprising. It is perhaps less surprising when one realises that the Education Bill placed the onus on LEA's and schools to provide religious education. It was when the Bill reached the Lords that opposition emerged in the shape of a group of Anglican peers, who wanted both compulsory religious education and a (predominantly Christian) daily act of worship. When it was pointed out that in a multi-cultural society all the principal religious traditions would have to be represented, they demanded a separate act of worship. The Prime Minister set her face against this and firmly rejected the idea. Controversy, however, still surrounds the subject, with Church groups proposing a statutory National Syllabus for Religion. The situation remains confused, but it should be borne in mind that voluntary schools, supported wholly or partly by the taxpayer, form a substantial part of the educational system and in these faith schools both the overt and covert curriculum can play a vital part in the Christian development of their pupils.

So the National Curriculum was now made up of officially-recognised subjects which, in the absence of the historical perspective provided above, would come to assume the status of absolute and uncontentious knowledge.

THE EDUCATIONAL AND SOCIAL SIGNIFICANCE OF THE NATIONAL CURRICULUM

A curriculum can of course, be organised in several ways, depending upon underlying principles, theories and values. It will be recalled that the Hadow Committee recommended that the curriculum be conceived in terms of activities and experiences, rather than facts to be stored. The National Curriculum, on the other hand, is organised in terms of fixed bodies of knowledge and structured in terms of measurable objectives, a bureaucratic assumption given the lie with the controversies arising within the working parties. It also represents a departure from the tradition of the curriculum being the sole responsibility of educational professionals. A precedent had been set, with politicians and bureaucrats being prepared to intervene. Admittedly, in the case of the National Curriculum, there had been discussion with subject experts, but only within the framework laid down by the Education Minister. This political interference, rejected out of hand by previous Ministers, can be represented as a move towards totalitarianism, where possible alternatives are ignored - even those of its own intellectuals, the HMI. In fact HM Inspectorate had recently developed a broad, balanced, relevant and coherent curriculum structure with an entirely different conceptual basis, which in the normal course of events would have been the model put forward by the government, but which in this case has been totally ignored. For the purpose of comparison I outline its structure below.

AN ALTERNATIVE NATIONAL CURRICULUM: HMI curriculum 15-16

The structure is made up essentially of two axes: "areas of experience" and "elements of learning".

areas of experience – made up of the following elements

aesthetic and creative ;
human and social;
linguistic and literary;
mathematical;
moral;
physical;
scientific;
spiritual;
technological.

elements of learning include:
knowledge;
concepts;
skills:

communication, observation, study, problem-solving, physical and practical; creative and imaginative; numerical;
personal and social.

The teacher to use his / her professional judgment to ensure that each area of experience and element of learning be given appropriate attention, depending on the needs of the child. Curriculum content could be mediated through topics to bring in cross-curricular aspects such as the environment, and differentiated to take account of pupils' differing abilities. Assessment would be diagnostic to assist the teacher in matching work to abilities and readiness. (20)

In a democratic rather than a totalitarian context, such an alternative would provide the basis for discussion. It could also serve as a framework and checklist for a negotiated democratic curriculum (see "Democratising Education").

But here a Secretary of State has imposed his own ideas unilaterally, based upon his own experiences and opinions. At the same time his own Inspectorate was being marginalized and losing its influence to a new body, the Office for Standards in Education (OFSTED), whose work we shall consider shortly. We will need to discover whether this radical undemocratic departure sets a precedent for further government initiatives.

The Standards Regime

(a) *the testing of pupils (SAT's)*

A major plank in the structure of the National Curriculum was regular testing (either by teacher assessment or written tests) of the entire school population at the ages of 7, 11 and 14. Kenneth Baker had set up the Schools Examination and Assessment Council (SEAC) to devise a suitable system. As he himself explains:

> "The purpose of introducing regular testing to underpin the national curriculum was not to try to fail children but to determine what they had actually been able to absorb and assimilate at a particular time in their education. Only in this way would teachers be able to determine whether their pupils needed special assistance...and what additional teaching could be provided." (21)

Yet almost at once, unaware of the contradiction between formative and summative assessment, he adds:

> "I also wanted the results of the tests to be published so

that parents and the local community would be able to see how well schools were doing. These were the famous 'league tables'. I ensured that the requirement for publication was embedded in the legislation, otherwise, successive Secretaries of State might well have been persuaded to go soft on this". (22)

This legislation for league tables represented another step on the road to marketisation of schools. Parents were to be encouraged to shop around looking for "best value for money" (taxpayer's money). But the ruthless competitive ethos encourages cheating, undermining what validity the tests may have had. Children are also tested to destruction: it is possible to take 46 weeks out from lessons for the purpose of examinations in the course of a school career and to be subjected to 105 tests and examinations. Not surprisingly, students are de-motivated and education suffers as teachers spend more of their time preparing for tests and examinations instead of teaching. And the tests inevitably are superficial, failing to tap the deeper structures of knowledge and understanding. The annual cost to the country of this exercise in pursuit of "standards" and "accountability"? £200 million.

There has been considerable opposition from education professionals to the idea that the character and quality of a school could be captured in the form of tables based upon SAT's, public examination results and truancy rates. The earlier tables were extremely crude, taking no account of the quality or social status of the pupil intake; eventually adjustments were made to give what was claimed to be a "value-added" dimension. But unease about the whole concept has persisted and interestingly the Welsh Assembly has actually abolished them in the Principality, so far with no apparently adverse effects (whilst this government, in the face of logistical disasters has recently expressed its intention to cancel KS 4 tests).

(b) The Inspection of Teachers: the OFSTED cudgel

The last piece of this bureaucratic jigsaw concerned the quality of teaching in state schools. John Major, now the Prime Minister, had launched a Citizen's Charter, with the intention of raising the quality and standing of public service: both the testing of pupils and inspections of teachers came within its orbit:

"Among all the Charter's innovations, the setting publicly of standards of service and reporting of results, together with the publication of league tables, has had the most far-reaching effects...We were right to do so. We were also right to insist on the formal separation of powers between those providing them and those checking on them. The creation or strengthening of independent inspectorates was an important component to lever up standards. When the plan to create a powerful Office of Standards in Education (OFSTED), statutorily independent of the Department of Education, was suggested, it had few friends in government...Yet once more, the received wisdom seemed to be profoundly wrong...I am proud that we let some indestructible genies out of the bottle. We pushed through testing. We secured truly independent inspection. We published league tables of results. And on the basis of proper information we began to give parents real choice. Basic facts about education will never again be able to be suppressed...Under its first chief inspectors, professor Stewart Sutherland and Chris Woodhead, OFSTED was quite fearless in condemning low standards and opening up information long hidden from parents." (23)

Whilst accepting that evaluation is a fundamental part of a school curriculum, the manner of its implementation is a measure of the values, purposes and beliefs underlying the system and hence itself should be open to scrutiny. OFSTED was acclaimed as an independent, privatised body, but the educational assumptions on which its practices were based were never scrutinised. It was pragmatic, rather than philosophical, serving the purposes of reassuring the public that "standards" and "accountability" were being adequately taken care of. Intending inspectors (including failed heads and teachers) were required to respond to advertisements in the press and undergo a brief period of training. Schools were to be inspected every four years, with the pre-announced inspection lasting from 5 to 57 days, depending upon the size of the school. A publicly - available report was to be available within 5 weeks of the end of the inspection, and the school was to produce an action plan no less than 40 days later.

This initiative represents a less-than-creditable episode in the history of state education:

(a) it was political rather than educational: it was intended to demonstrate to the public at large that education was now firmly in the control of the State. This was illustrated by the appointment as Chief Inspector of Chris Woodhead, a "dyed-in-the-wool" traditionalist with a predilection for rote learning, having a low opinion of the teaching profession and revealing a lack of commitment to state education by his later career choices. He could be relied upon to do the government's job of "hammering the teachers" and stamping out any traces of progressivism or educational diversity. His general attitude to the teaching profession and his personal integrity can be gauged by his unsubstantiated claim that there were 15,000 incompetent teachers - this from a person who demanded rigour from others.

(b) it was a punitive rather than a developmental exercise. Most teachers can get better at what they do if for example they can observe other teachers at work or get feedback on their lessons, or alternatively work in teams. But OFSTED is not interested in professional development. Indeed it was made clear to inspectors that they were not to engage in discussions with teachers about their work or stray into giving on-the-spot advice. Few people would disagree with the principle that incompetent, unreformable teachers should not be allowed to continue with the important task of educating children a moment longer than necessary. But a competent head should be able to quickly resolve this problem without any need for intervention by a team of inspectors.

(c) it was crude, because the assumptions underpinning it are knowledge-as-objective-fact and teaching-as-delivery. As far as human relationships and classroom ambience are concerned there is not even an explicit recognition that a classroom with an inspector in it is not the same environment as one without. Whilst the rhetoric is ambitious - "the spiritual, moral, social and cultural development of pupils" - one wonders how accessible these complex, intangible qualities are to brief formal inspection. And the final reports often lacked credibility on account of their incoherence and inconsistency.

But it has to be said that these proposals for mass inspection of schools were welcomed by a large proportion of the electorate. Over the years, the teaching profession had been denigrated by those in power and depicted as left-wing propagandists or incompetent progressives. The previous Prime Minister herself had talked of "anti-racist mathematics" being taught and it was widely believed that children's interests were being betrayed through ill-thought out modern teaching methods. This crude populism, reinforced by the media, undoubtedly prepared the ground for unthinking acceptance of government rhetoric and the assault on the teaching profession in the name of the Citizen's Charter.

And it has to be remembered that these changes were taking place within a dominant culture which by now had absorbed many of the practices and ideas of corporatism: for example, the competitive ethic, leading to league tables, and the hierarchical division of labour personified by the structure of OFSTED. All was now accepted as normal, as the natural order of things. What is missing, though, from John Major's account above - inevitably so for leaders who have no ongoing organic contact with the grass roots - is the punitive context for the inspections, which for the more sensitive teachers was highly threatening and intimidating and led to a mass exodus from teaching. (It has to be said, though, that had local education authorities built up ongoing, productive and cooperative relationships with their own schools through their own inspectors, the case against OFSTED would have been much stronger. This they had largely failed to do.)

By now it would appear that the State was in firm control of both the content and delivery of the school curriculum, as well as the examination system, and was receiving regular information on both the quality of pupils' work (through SAT's) and the efficiency of schools (through OSTED), information which was made available to the public through published reports and league tables. But there was one important area where the State seemed impotent. The concentration in the National Curriculum upon the "academic interest" led to a neglect of vocational education. I will now look at the faltering steps which the state has taken to take control of this sector of education.

VOCATIONAL EDUCATION

The Marketisation of Education

The Education Bill gave succour to different strands of political thought. On the one hand it could be said to satisfy the "Standards" lobby with the presence of academic subjects in the national curriculum together with a rigorous (and rigid) testing regime. On the other hand, it provided support for the marketeers in the Tory Party with its emphasis on the commercial values of competition and "freedom of choice". Parental choice was to be supported by the provision of league tables, whilst the power of local education authorities was diminished by the transfer of responsibility for budgetary affairs to the schools themselves ("local management of schools") and by the setting up of grant-maintained schools. But obsession with such matters led to a continuing neglect of the technical and vocational aspects of education, with an inevitable decline in our industrial competitiveness, a possibility which had not escaped the notice of the industrial lobby. The provision of such an education, however, would bring its own set of problems in train, as we shall see.

The Vocational/Academic Dilemma: Liberalists versus Vocationalists

For decades governments have agonised over the provision of an appropriate vocational education and so far have satisfied nobody. Industrialists have argued that current vocational programmes do not meet their needs, whilst educationalists have argued that school is no place to be training youngsters for work. Yet before the divisions of class and labour accompanying the Industrial Revolution, there did not seem to be a problem. Earlier educational institutions were unashamedly vocational in the sense of pursuing a calling. Medieval universities were to provide a vocational education in law and theology. As regards schools:

> "The first English schools, from the late sixth century, had a primarily vocational character, but this was such that implied a particular social training and a particular definition of a proper general knowledge.....two kinds of school, often in practice connected, were instituted: the grammar school, to teach Latin; and the song school, to teach church singing. Necessarily, in view of their objects, the specialised training of both these schools was part of a general training in Christianity and the particular social character it then carried". (25)

As far as the lower orders were concerned, the dominant mode of entry into the world of skilled work was by means of an apprenticeship, under the auspices of the Ancient Guilds, with subsequent qualifications being obtained through the City and Guilds of London Institute.

In other words, the present academic / vocational dualism has its origins in the mass schooling of the early nineteenth century, which found the sons of the rich following an academic classical curriculum in "public" schools whilst children of the poor had a limited practical training in elementary schools. With children gradually spending longer at school, however, there arose the inevitable question of how usefully they were spending their time. Even by the time the Cross commission met in 1888 to enquire into the workings of the elementary school, "vocational education" was officially on the agenda - although rejected by an aspirational working class which saw this as an inferior form of education. (26) As for the "employers of labour", the perceived qualities of their workforce included habits of discipline, obedience, self-help and pride in workmanship (that is, an emphasis upon the 'affective' rather than the 'cognitive' aspects of the curriculum).

These demands became orchestrated through the setting up in 1916 of the Federation of British Labour FBI (eventually transformed into the Confederation of British Labour CBI representing almost 200 employers and 4 million employees). This official line continued to stress these affective qualities mentioned above, whilst bemoaning the poor levels of literacy and numeracy. More recently "key/core skills" have been added to the desired attributes in school-leavers, including the (non-contextual!) skills of:

> communication;
> application of number;
> information technology:
> working with others;
> problem-solving;
> self-management.

The division of opinion and the heated arguments between the liberalists and the vocationalists came to a head with the raising of the school-leaving age to 16 in 1972 (ROSLA) at a time of increasing unemployment (due, according to employers, to the unemployability of young people as a result of a failed education). The resulting struggle can be quickly summarised:

> the liberalists believed that "slow learners" now had another year in which to continue their general education, and the Schools Council - still with some influence - recommended a new Certificate of Extended Education, based upon the traditional curriculum as an appropriate qualification.

at the same time the Further Education Unit of the Department was commissioned to work on this problem, the result being the launch in 1984 of the Certificate of Pre-vocational Education (CPVE) made up of a common core of what were now seen as the usual key skills together with substantive studies involving business, production, distribution, technical and people services - and work experience.

Significantly, the Education Minister came down on the side of the vocationalists, inviting the relevant validating bodies to make the necessary arrangements, a decision reflecting changing cultural values, and marking the first sortie into formal vocational education by the government. But such was the fundamental nature of disagreement and strength of feeling that the Minister's ruling was initially ignored by the examination boards to the extent that the Certificate of Extended Education remained available to the new sixth formers for some time thereafter.

And all this was happening at a time when the Department of Employment was launching its own highly promising Technical and Vocational Educational Initiative!

Getting it Right: National Vocational Qualifications

The Education Department was now committed to providing vocational education for non-academic pupils, in consultation with employers and other interested organisations. The momentum was maintained by the setting up in 1986 of two working parties: one to consider the criteria for pre-16 pre-vocational courses (just before the National Curriculum became reality) and the other to review the current system of vocational qualifications. The outcome was a White Paper (27), stating the government's intention to bring all existing vocational qualifications within a new national framework to be called the National Vocational Qualification (NVQ) to be administered by a National Council for Vocational Qualifications (NCVQ). The NVQ had certain radical aspects, including the following:

the emphasis was moving from skills (demonstration of a set of functional behaviours) to competences (the combination of understandings and abilities producing a performance in a given setting) in the workplace, involving practical as well as technical knowledge;

these competences took the form of the "application of knowledge and skills" in increasingly complex contexts, at five different levels; from routine to unpredictable, with increasing amounts of autonomy. There was thus a clear built-in progression, so much so that, whilst professional bodies found the first four levels acceptable, they felt that Level 5 infringed their own professional interests. There were to be eleven occupational families, including:

> engineering and manufacturing;
> providing goods and services;
> tending animals, plants and land;
> providing business services;
> communicating; and (oddly)
> developing and extending knowledge and skill.

Assessment was by observation of work practice, interview and product quality.

Whilst the move towards competences is a move in the right direction towards a true cultural location of the work, it nevertheless is very limited. The notion of "application of knowledge and skills", rather than "interpretation", emphases the codified and technical rather than the practical and personal; and analytic rather than intuitive thinking. (28) It therefore fails to capture the full complexity of life in the workplace. Also the attempt to "decompose" competencies into different levels in the name of "standards" weakens the emphasis upon social and cultural roles and dehumanises the activity. Grugalis, drawing on in-depth studies of the implementation of NVQ's in three private sector organisations expresses similar reservations:

> *"Candidates are required to work towards criteria that may not match their roles and responsibilities; developmental work is systematically discouraged and work becomes routine". (29)*

Still Getting It Right: the General National Vocational Qualification

With education rising up the political agenda and more students and parents demanding a first -class education, the pressure was on the government to provide real alternatives to the A-level curriculum, alternatives which had "parity of esteem". In April, 1993, the Secretary of State announced the introduction of the General National Vocational Qualification (GNVQ) aimed primarily at 16-19 year olds but available in some form to 14-16 year olds, to provide a genuine alternative to A-levels. All GNVQ's consisted of vocational and core skills.

> the mandatory core skills included communication, information technology and application of number, whilst there were non-mandatory personal skills;
> the initial vocation areas were Art and Design, Business Health and Social Care, Leisure and Tourism, Manufacturing, Built Environment, Hospitality and Catering and Science and included both mandatory and optional units;
> GNVQ's could be Foundation, Intermediate and Advanced, the latter being equivalent to A-levels. Assessment would be by projects, assignments and external tests.

The National Advisory Council for Education and Training Targets was subsequently set up and announced its targets for 2000. For example, by the age of 19:

> 85% of young people should either achieve 5 GCSE's at Grade C or above; an Intermediate GNVQ; or an NVQ level;
> 60% of the workforce to be qualified to NVQ level 3, Advanced GNVQ or 2 GCE A levels;
> 30 % to have qualifications at NVQ level 4 or above.

In the event, less than 20% reached NVQ level 3 whilst only 3% reached level 4 or 5. Official disappointment was expressed at the lack of coherence in the system, whilst Peter Robinson of the Centre for Economic Performance claimed that there was no evidence that NVQ's had led to an increase in competitiveness: they had merely displaced such traditional qualifications as "hairdressing" and "secretarial". And of the 794 NVQ's on offer, 364 had not been awarded to anyone! As far as GNVQ's were concerned, they were due to be phased out by 2007, to make way for yet another bout of bureaucratic engineering.

And Still Getting It Right: 14-19 Learning

Difficult problems still remained, then. The performance of young people generally left much to be desired: the proportion with level 2 or 3 NVQ's was below that of our continental neighbours and far fewer poor students gained entry to university. Whilst A-levels were still considered the educational gold standard, "parity of esteem" between academic and vocational was a chimera. Foolish claims that there was "no difference between academic and vocational learning " would cut no ice with a public that only had to look at the hierarchical occupational structure (with "academic" at the top and "vocational" at the bottom) to see how deluded such claims were.

In the event, matters were taken temporarily out of the hands of the government. There had been growing scepticism about the standards of A-level as the number of passes increased year on year; and now anger was expressed about the quality of marking, with both heads and parents expressing doubts about the reliability. Once the credibility of A-levels was destroyed, talk of gold standards would be empty. What was the government's response? It immediately set up a 14-19 working group which quickly produced the following recommendations:

an overarching diploma for all students at entry, foundation, intermediate and advanced levels,

with a basic structure of core, main learning and common skills,

to strike a balance between generic skills for further development and specific subject knowledge.

In other words, academic A-levels would rub shoulders with vocational subjects and be submerged within the overall diploma. In the words of the working party report, "there is no absolute distinction between vocational and academic learning", although no examples or justifications were given for this ambitious assertion.

But the implied threat to free-standing A-levels was too much for the government to swallow and the main thrust of the working party report was ignored. In February 2005, the White Paper "Education and Skills" was published, which included the following key points:

offer of high quality vocational routes,

improvement of vocational education with the introduction of 14 specialised diplomas covering all occupational areas, to replace NVQ's,

retaining GCSE's and A-levels as cornerstones,

stretching the most able students to help universities differentiate between the best candidates;

ensuring that all young people master functional mathematics and English before leaving school.(30)

DfES WHITE PAPER 14-19 LEARNING Education and Skills

Young people from the age of 14 onwards will be able to choose between a:
(1) "General Diploma", awarded to those with the equivalent of 5 A*-C grade GCSE's including English and Maths, and a
(2) new employer-designed "Specialised Diplomas" at three levels up to advanced level covering the occupational sectors of the economy. Though employer-led they are not intended as a direct preparation for an occupation - they require young people to develop good basic skills and develop the broader skills employers want. The specialised diploma balances theoretical and practical understanding with three components:
principal learning, focussing in particular on developing and applying the knowledge and skills that are relevant to that line of learning;
generic learning, including

functional skills in English, Maths and ICT
personal learning and thinking skills
work experience

a project offering a chance to show potential
experiential learning, attained through observation, simulation and participation, engaging

mind and body in a process of activity, review and application.

Assessment will meet the requirements of validity, reliability and comparability and include external assessment with a variety of approaches. Internal assessment will be supported by moderation and verification.
At level 1 and 2, units may be either 30 or 60 GLH (guided learning hours)
At level 3, units may be 30, 60 or 90 GLH.

On December 14 2005, an Implementation Plan was announced with the following milestones:

2006: subject-by-subject coursework review;

2008: five specialised diplomas to be introduced:
ICT,
engineering,
health and social care,
creative and media industries,
construction and the built environment.

2009: five more specialised diplomas;
land-based and environmental

manufacturing
health and beauty
business administration and finance
hospitality and catering

2010: remaining specialised diplomas;
public services
sport and leisure
retail
travel and tourism

2013: all aspects of 14-19 reform to be in place;

2015: nine out of ten young people opting to stay on after 14.

A Critique:-

(1) The Implementation Plans are currently being developed at such a frantic rate that they bode ill for the emergence of coherent, well - thought schemes. (To keep in touch with developments see QCA/ DfES "14-19 Learning".) For example, whilst it is claimed that each Diploma reflects the needs and demands of the sector it represents, what can this mean with something as amorphous as "Public Services" - teaching assistant, community worker, nurse, garbage collector?

(2) The General Diploma marks off academic students (5 A*-C GCSE's) from the rest, who will in theory be developing the broader skills employers want. These "specialised diplomas" then are in reality vocational courses. And they need to be judged on this basis.

(3) The emphasis is on skills rather than competences, and on application rather than interpretation, suggesting the possibility that these courses will once again lead to rigid rule-following and the application of codified technical knowledge, rather than practical and intuitive judgment.

(4) The hierarchical nature of the occupational structure and the differentiation of mental and manual labour does not seem to figure in these schemes. What educational purchase could be obtained, for instance, from those jobs at the bottom of the hierarchy? (When I ask this question of those engaged in the development of vocational educational programmes, answer comes there none.) Those working on vocational education ignore issues of political economy and fail to recognise the political nature of vocational courses.

(5) Doubtless linked to this is the manner of conceptualisation of specialised diplomas. Running alongside these will be vocational GCSE's, including Applied Science, Applied Art and Design, Applied Business and Applied ICT - a reminder that the academic/vocational distinction is as much a matter of social status as of the epistemological underpinnings.

Can "Vocational Education" be Educational ?

The developments described above could be classified under the heading "Occupational Training". By sleight of hand and without apparent demur they are now categorised as "vocational education". What definition of "education" might justify such a shift? It has been customary to see vocational activities in instrumental terms (that is, as a passport to something else) as opposed to the claimed intrinsic nature of academic activities. But this will not do. It is quite possible for instrumental activities to provide intrinsic satisfaction, whilst an academic in his intrinsic search for truth may have instrumental matters in mind.

So what counts as "education"? The liberal philosopher R.S Peters (31) when considering the attributes of the "educated man" makes the following points:

> *"We do not call a person educated who has simply mastered a skill even though the skill may be very highly prized such as pottery. For a man to be educated it is insufficient that he should possess a mere knowhow or knack. He must have also some body of knowledge and some kind of conceptual scheme to raise this above the level of a collection of disjointed facts…yet we might (still) refuse to call him an educated man. What then is lacking?…it is surely a lack of what might be called "cognitive perspective"… an educated man could be trained in one sphere and yet be sufficiently cognisant of other ways of looking at the world, so that he can grasp the historical perspective, social significance or aesthetic merit of his work and of much besides."*

The Marxist philosopher, Antonio Gramsci, approaches the problem from a different perspective but comes to similar conclusions. According to

Gramsci it was essential for workers to learn not just the basic skills and competencies to do their particular job but to widen their knowledge both of the whole productive enterprise, and then of the whole social, historical and cultural context of capitalism itself. (32)

Judged by these criteria the vocational education courses on offer are not educational at all. And neither are academic courses! For vocational training to develop an educational perspective requires that the training, apart from having a strong cognitive component, be set in a political, socio-economic, historical, as well as a technical context. But the problem facing the teacher is not so much philosophical as pragmatic - how to engage alienated youngsters, with a history of school failure, with such issues and arouse their enthusiasm and interest and develop their critical thinking.

Mixed Messages

This chapter has shown the Education Department generally tightening its grip on general and vocational education by exerting centralised control over the curriculum and its agencies. But, as we shall see later, this control is weakened by the many contradictions in its implementation, with the left hand not knowing what the right hand is doing - and by an overall lack of vision. The number of attempts at getting vocational education right suggests something faulty at the roots, whilst in the field of general education, the Department is either speaking with a forked tongue or attempting to present a more human face, particularly in the areas of curriculum, inspection and pedagogy, as the following examples suggest:

(a) *the National Curriculum*

> *"It is widely accepted that the National Curriculum has been too congested. Since 1998 there has been a succession of measures to thin out the content of the National Curriculum......we welcome attempts to reduce the amount of detailed prescription in the National Curriculum and suggest these should continue." (33)*

(b) *Inspection*

Even Ofsted is taking a lighter approach, first with briefer inspections and now with an emphasis on "self –evaluation". It is without apparent irony that a recent report contains the following heart-warming passage:

> *"Ofsted believes that schools are best placed to recognise their own strengths and weaknesses. This is why we are introducing a new inspection system which puts more onus on a school to be pro-active and demonstrate to inspectors that it can not only diagnose where its strengths and weaknesses are but, more crucially, do something about improving and developing them." (34)*

A framework has been developed for this purpose and is available to teachers to provide them with a "helpful template" against which they can carry out their self-evaluation.

(c) Pedagogy

There are also signs of the Education Department bringing a more humane and less dogmatic rule-following approach to teaching, with a move away from a technical "delivery" model to a more hypothetical cooperative model. For instance, a "national conversation" has been established in the case of personalised learning:

> *"We would like you to join in a national conversation about how personalisation can be used to drive success in every school" (35)*

And, indicating a move from the "strength-through-suffering" model of education:

> *"Enjoyment is the birthright of every child……children learn better when they are excited and engaged …… When there is joy in what they are doing, they learn to love learning." (36)*

Something the rest of us have known for a long time.

The apparent readiness to engage teachers in consultation is evident in the Secondary Curriculum Review:

"The Qualifications and Curriculum Authority has been commissioned to lead on the Review and will be running a national consultation on the revised secondary curriculum between 5 February and 30 April 2007. The consultation is open to anyone with an interest in what is taught in schools." (37)

There are differing possible interpretations of these initiatives:

that it is a cynical exercise designed to reassure an increasingly disenchanted teaching profession that "we're all in this together";

that there is a genuine conflict of values in the Department;

that there is a fundamental ideological shift .

Teachers with long memories will be sceptical about mention of consultations - and their scepticism will be more than justified by events to be described later. And whilst SAT's and league tables remain in place, talk about flexibility, opportunities and personalisation is just empty rhetoric.

Meanwhile, another element of control has entered the state education system, as we shall see in the next chapter.......

NOTES AND REFERENCES

1. Baker, K. (1993) The Turbulent Years. Faber and Faber. London
2. Thatcher, M. (1993) The Downing Street Years. Harper Collins. London
3. Baker, K. (1993) The Turbulent Years. Faber and Faber. London
4. Baker, K. op cit
5. David Layton from his analysis of the evolution of science since the nineteenth century suggests a three-stage process of evolution. See Goodson, I.
    Becoming an Academic Subject Br. J. Soc. Educ. 2.2
6. For fascinating accounts of the development of school subjects see McCulloch, G. et al (1985) Technological Revolution? Falmer Press. London and Goodson, I.F. (ed) (1985) Social Histories of the Secondary Curriculum Falmer Press.
7. Graham, D. (1993) A Lesson for us All. Routledge. London
8. Baker, K. op cit
9. Graham, D. op cit
10. Baker, K. op cit
11. op cit
12. Graham, D. op cit
13. www.aqa.org.uk
14. Graham, D. op cit
15. op cit
16. Thatcher, M. op cit
17. Baker, K. op cit
18. Thatcher, M. op cit
19. Graham, D. op cit
20. op cit.
21. op cit.
22. DES (1985) The Curriculum from 5-16. HMSO
23. Baker, K. op cit
24. op cit
25. Major, J. (1999) John Major. Harper Collins. London
26. R. Williams op cit
27. Brian Simon (Education and the Labour Movement 1870-1918) describes the evidence given to the Cross Commission by Thomas Smyth, representative of the London Trades Council, when questioned on the desirability of vocational education: the working class "do not desire it at all......they feel that it is a waste of time

and that it will interfere largely and prejudicially with the general school work if it is introduced."

28. DfES (1986) Working Together – Education and Training
29. See M. Eraut op cit for a detailed exposition of the development of professional knowledge and competence.
30. Grugulis, I. (2000) "The Management NVQ: a Critique of the Myth of Relevance" in J. Voc. Education and Training vol.52 no 1.
31. DfES (2005) White Paper Education and Skills
32. R.S. Peters op cit
33. www.arisite.org/ngn2.htm
34. NACCE Report www.dfes.gov.uk/nacce/072_100pdf
35. www.ofsted.gov.uk/ofsteddirect/
36. DfES (2004) A National Conversation about Personalised Learning. DfES Publications. Nottingham.
37. DfES (2003) Excellence and Enjoyment – a Strategy for Primary Schools. DfES Publications. Nottingham.
38. www.qca.org.uk/secondarycurriculumreview/

PART THREE:

THE NEO-ACTIVE STATE SELLING OUT: "EDUBUSINESS"

The combination of neoliberalism and a corporate hegemony led to a change in the educational power structure with marketeers now on the offensive, regarding education as a commodity to be traded in the market place in a culture of instrumental consumerism. Businesses were actively encouraged to penetrate schools, regarding them as sources of future customers and potential employees.

The organisation of state education was also fundamentally changed with public services being denigrated and schools subjected to Public Management procedures. Outside businesses were also encouraged to take over the running of what were now called academies.

CHAPTER 9

A POISONED CHALICE : ALIEN VALUES

"The tragedy was fourfold: that educational questions were subordinated to business considerations; that administrators were produced who were not in any true sense educators; that a scientific label was put on some very unscientific and dubious methods and practices; and that an anti-intellectual climate, already prevalent, was strengthened." (R. Callaher. Education and the Cult of Efficiency)

The Rise of Neoliberalism

The Attack on Public Services: New Public Services Management
Edubusiness:
    (1)the commercialisation of education
    (2)the privatisation of Education:
        Education Action Zones
        City Academies: "The schools of the future!".
        Trust schools: the 2005 White Paper
        Comprehensive Education

The Rise of Neoliberalism and the Impact on Education

Arising out of the ashes of the Great Depression and the Second World War came a new social and economic philosophy: social democracy. In this new order, the emphasis was both upon welfare provision, with public services generously funded by the State, full employment and collective action through a unionised workforce. For a couple of decades, Britain prospered both socially and economically, so that opposing ideologies received little publicity. But in the 70's came a crisis in capital accumulation, accompanied by negative hostility from powerful union barons to any government attempts to deal with the crisis, such as an incomes policy. By 1975 inflation was running at 25% and unemployment rose above 1 million.

It was in this situation that an alternative ideology, neoliberalism, began to achieve much more recognition and support (including the evangelical and intellectual support of academics such as US graduates at the "Chicago School"). Its central tenet was the threat to civilisation through the disappearance of freedoms and human dignity, along with private property and competitive markets. It was thus given the moral authority and the appeal to "common sense" which successful ideologies need. The basic neoliberal theory included the protection of individual property rights, free trade and the rule of law under the protection of the state. More specifically, it was essential for the state to:

> liberate private and entrepreneurial enterprise;
> eliminate workers' and union rights;
> reduce public expenditure;
> deregulate;
> replace the concept of "community" by "individual responsibility".

In 1979, at a time of industrial unrest, the Tory Party was returned to power under Margaret Thatcher, with a mandate for radical change. Despite this, it was necessary, given the embedded nature of social democracy, to win the battle of ideas and manufacture public consent. Much was made of "freedom", "choice" and "wealth" with the enthusiastic support of the right-wing press. But in order to consolidate her position, she was still anxious to emasculate any opposition. Thus, when she undertook a mass programme of privatisation of key utilities such as communications, energy, transport, she was careful to offer them at bargain prices - and to include the populist measure of selling-off council houses cheaply.

Although it is doubtful if she was following a coherent neoliberal strategy, she had quickly set about attacking those icons of social democracy: public services and collective action. For instance, she castrated the power of trade unions by reducing their legal rights and by substantially raising interest rates, with a resultant massive loss of jobs as Britain's industrial base was crippled. She also cut back public expenditure, especially the funding of local government. But it was a different matter when she tried to dismantle the welfare service, since she now came up against middle-class, as well as working-class, interests; and she had to be content with such strictures as financial control and changes in working practices. And it is the change in educational working practices that we turn to now.

The Attack on Public Service: New Public Service Management

As the state came increasingly under the sway of neoliberalism and a corporate hegemony, it was natural that the public sector would come under close scrutiny. In order to provide legitimation for what would be revolutionary changes in working practices, public services were presented, with strong media support, as being bloated, overbureaucratic, lacking in enterprise and accountability – and generally unproductive. They were seen as lacking the drive coming from competition and also as denying genuine public choice. It therefore became possible to bring into the system, over time, an increasing absorption of private business practices and principles into the public sector. Collectively they have come to be known as new public management (NPM) with the following general characteristics and emphases:

- a change from maintenance administration to entrepreneurial management;
- increasing provision of services through contracting out and competitive markets ;
- performance targets and comparative tables of performance;
- use of consultants ;
- customer-orientation with feedback;
- maximisation of profits (unless not-for-profit trusts)
- staff appraisal and performance-related pay

These new management practices have fundamentally changed school structures and relationships. For example, whereas the school head would have been seen as a colleague and fellow-teacher he/she was now a manager, in a hierarchical relationship with regard to the rest of the staff. Along with greater powers such as budgeting, resource allocation and monitoring, there was now a greater degree of accountability to the governing body and parents. With these structural changes and power relationships comes an inevitable change in the school culture, from what has been described as traditional collegiality to one of power relationships, with the head having a measure of control over a teacher's career prospects. Indeed, these changes at the micro-level reflect a major ideological shift from a collective public service ethos to one of individualistic self-interest in the context of market forces and profit, the significance of which should not be lost sight of.

EDUBUSINESS:

There is no objection in this book to business per se, which over the years has made a large contribution to material prosperity and human happiness. But we are now dealing with a predatory corporate capitalism which exploits both nature and human and has no respect for either. Apart from the obvious exploitation of the education system by using it as a market-place for the generation of business, there is the more concealed use of business methods; for example, to allegedly improve the educational process, as a way of presenting a more attractive face to young people, or even to use schools as recruiting agencies or as initiation into a consumerist culture. I shall explore these various possibilities in the following pages.

(1) The commercialisation of state education

In 1983, the European Round Table (ERT) was set up, made up of employers' organisations from 7 European Union countries. It has issued a series of reports increasingly critical of European education, referring constantly to the widening gap between the skills required by employers and those developed by schools. As a remedy, they significantly recommended a partnership between schools and business:

> *"European business clearly requires an accelerated reform of educational programmes. European industry has responded to globalisation but the world of education has been slow to respond. As a remedy, partnerships should be formed between school and local business"*
> *(1)*

The term "edubusiness" has been coined to refer to this partnership of business and state education. I will give a few examples of this partnership in this country in recent years, in the context of the prevailing mantra "private enterprise good; public services bad":

(a) *at the national level :"failure breeds success"*

In 2000, Capita Group plc (whose chairman Ron Aldridge had loaned the Labour Party £1 million) were awarded a £55 million contract by the Education Department (after competitive tendering) to take responsibility for the Individual Learning Account, a scheme whereby 2.5 million adult learners were each given £200 in credits towards the cost of their course. Three years later the Individual Learning Account was abandoned because of financial irregularities – an estimated £67 million in fraud and £19 million in irregular payments. (2)

Unabashed, the Department a year later awarded Capita a £177 million contract "to provide educational and operational support services for the National Strategy", including improving numeracy and literacy in primary schools. Capita in 2005 made a profit of £190 million on a £1.4 billion turnover – much of it from edubusiness.

(b) *at the local authority level :"targets are there to be missed"*

A critical Ofsted Report on Islington LEA led to a seven-year contract worth over £10 million being awarded in 2000 to Cambridge Education Associates (CEA) to implement the privatisation of Islington LEA and take full responsibility for matters ranging from special educational needs to school improvement. A year later it had to pay back £300,000 for performance failures. And in 2002 CEA faced allegations of examination malpractice in one of its primary schools, with the result that the exam results were squashed. More recently it has been fined £518,645 for failing to meet seven out of eleven strategic targets and five out of 29 operational objectives. (3)

(c) *at the level of pupils: "children are the commercial future"*

The examples above involve contractual arrangements between the government and private business in the expectation of the generation of profit. Other firms have a different approach to a partnership with schools, seeing pupils as future (as well as present) customers and also possible members of the workforce. They thus set out to gain their loyalty by wooing them in various ways. I will just give a few brief examples to provide a flavour of the changing culture.

1) Walkers Crisps were pioneers in this "partnership" by offering schools free books in exchange for vast numbers of crisp packets.

(2) Tesco have targeted mothers by offering computers (and education software) in exchange for a large number of vouchers (1 voucher for every £10 spent). This "computers for schools" project is claimed to be "a good example of cause-related marketing where companies and causes come together to benefit the community".

(3) McDonalds have made a more direct approach to the penetration of the school curriculum by providing schools with teaching packs, artfully advertising in the guise of educational knowledge such puzzles as:

Maths: add a collection of "Fries"

Geography: where in England would you find McDonald's restaurants?

English : identify the words "Chicken McNuggets", "Happy Meals" etc in the Wordsearch.

Music: complete the jingle "Old McDonald had a Store"

The McDonald's staff operations manual is revealing:

"schools offer excellent opportunities. Not only are they a high sales generator but schools are some of the best customers you could have". (4)

(4) Pizza Express add a touch of sophistication to the exercise. Primary school children are given a "food technology lesson" in the Pizza kitchen by a chef who takes them through the various stages, before the cooked pizzas are boxed so that they can be taken home. Legitimation is provided by the handing out of worksheets at level KS 2 and 3. The project is justified on the grounds that it is an "original initiative which brings together Education and Business in a mutually beneficial partnership."

There is clearly a fundamental cultural shift here. With global liberalisation and NPM comes a redefinition of education from a public good to a marketable commodity, with markets ostensibly open to parents and with the goods on display carrying league table guarantees. This cultural shift is clearly authenticated and underlined by the following remarkable government Education document:

> *"We want all young people to experience the world of work throughout their school life. Companies today are discovering that partnership with schools can help bring real business benefits. They can acquire better market knowledge, tap into local creativity to develop new products and gain new and more loyal customers. Working in the community aids networking and recruitment. You can help us raise standards in education, prepare*

young people for adult and working life and improve our
competitiveness in the international arena." (5)

In other words, the various initiatives described above carry the government seal of approval. Education – and the curriculum - can be expected to be redefined in the interests of business. And the structures of schools will echo those of business: as mentioned above, "managerialism" in schools has resulted in an extended hierarchy of staff relations, with the headteacher as chief executive with both budgetary autonomy and responsibility for teacher performance, as well as accountability to its customers.

(2) The privatisation of State Education

Ever since the inception of mass schooling, there has been opposition to the idea of state intervention, initially from an ideology of laissez-faire, but more recently on the grounds that public services are less efficient than private enterprise, in accordance with neoliberal philosophy. The most authoritative advocate of complete privatisation of educational services in recent years has been the economist E.G. West who, from his historical researches into state education, pursued the policy to its logical conclusion by advocating for-profit privatisation. He made the following assertions:

- non-profit monopolistic organisations, run by administrators rather than entrepreneurs, are sluggish in their response to change;
- only a very small minority of parents cannot be trusted to choose the education for their children;
- voucher schemes are both desirable and feasible and are of the greatest benefit to the poor;
- a genuine market in education would lead to the development of new ways of providing education that we cannot, at the present time, even envisage (6)

In short, West believed that the provision of education by profit-making organisations would lead to greater dynamism and innovation in our schools. His ideas are being kept alive and developed at the E.G. West Centre at Newcastle University, where the chief mission is "to develop knowledge and understanding of the role of non-state education in achieving Education for All" (7).

The radical 1988 Education Bill ("Gerbil") travelled part of the way down the E.G. West route, loosening local authority control by giving heads responsibility for their own financial affairs (local management of schools) and by putting on the agenda the use of vouchers to increase parental choice. And perhaps most importantly, in view of subsequent events, by inviting business to sponsor city technology colleges, an initiative which - whilst it failed to gain momentum when potential sponsors preferred to invest their money elsewhere - provided a model for future politicians. And it is a model which was enthusiastically taken up by New Labour.

(a) *Education Action Zones*

The New Labour government, after its election in 1997, developed the idea of bringing business into the running of schools, this time on extremely favourable financial terms. Such a fundamental reform, going to the very heart of the principle of state education, would inevitably attract considerable opposition and so a policy of "gradualism" and legitimation was in order. The first "test-bed" took the form of education action zones, legitimated as a means of driving up standards in areas of social disadvantage and legalised through statutory orders. These zones were typically made up of two or three secondary schools and its feeder primaries, in partnership with local business. Each zone was to receive an annual grant of £1million, £750,000 from the government and £250,000 from private sources. Six years later, in 2003, the report of an evaluative study funded by Economic and Social Research was published which came to the overall conclusion that there had been a limited and inconsistent effect on national test results:

> "Many of those working in the Zones felt the pressure of having to meet narrow short-term exam, exclusion and truancy targets, making it much harder to be innovative in ways that could challenge educational disadvantage" (8).

In other words, any innovation was expected to take place within the prevailing educational culture of targets. More specifically, curriculum innovation, instead of being based upon student's actual experiences was often found to be peripheral to them. And although Education Action Zones were run by partnership forums, they reflected existing power structures and were not representative of the local community. The researchers (using regression modelling on exam results) came to the conclusion that the Zone schools studied may even have done rather worse than non-zone schools.

So where precisely was the dynamic innovation, expected from the introduction of business into the educational process?

> *"The private sector was expected to play a significant role in investing and running zones. But the researchers found that businesses were not able to invest the resources, energy and knowhow to transform education"* (9)

On the other hand, there was no evidence of far-reaching commercialisation. So what had been the precise contribution of business? This is a question we shall need to keep asking when we look at other examples of corporate involvement in our schools. Whilst economists may talk of "dynamism" and "innovation", educationists will ask what differences in pupils' learning and attitudes are being brought about. And political commentators may wonder if these initiatives have more to do with politics than education. In this particular piece of research, a complex relationship was indeed found between "spin" and "substance", evidence that Education Action Zones were a political as well as an educational initiative. In any case, the experiment provides a salutary reminder of the problems facing cultural transplantation.

(b) *City Academies: " THE SCHOOLS OF THE FUTURE "*

Education action zones - despite their dubious educational benefits - were followed up by the much more ambitious plan of City Academies. It was in 2000 that the intention to launch a massive programme for the building of City Academies was announced in the Learning and Skills Act. These Academies were to be underpinned by a similar rationale to the ill-fated City Technology Colleges, that is, they were to be run as independent charitable trusts headed by private sponsors. **Thus did a Labour Prime Minister, by means fair and foul, undermine two centuries of working-class struggle for a democratic, comprehensive education.**

True to his conviction that the future lay with a partnership between education and business, Blair had invested considerable political capital in the venture to make it a success and was determined to use every effort in that direction. For example, sponsors of academies, unlike those for City Technology Colleges, would only be required to provide up to £2million (on favourable terms if necessary), in return for which they would have control of the curriculum, governing body and staffing - the rest of the building costs (over £25 million) and running costs were to be funded by the taxpayer. With regard to local authorities, the Prime Minister made it clear that funding would be dependent upon cooperation:

> *"That is why the prospectus published today invites every local authority to consider the scope for academies in their area. Why it encourages them to engage directly with potential sponsors. And why it stipulates that funding approval will be dependent on the role they proposed to play" (10),*

an invitation regarded by some as nothing short of blackmail. True to form, the whole City Academy programme was bathed in the glare of publicity and razzamatazz, with the use of top architects contracted to design expensive flamboyant buildings.

But the idea of the penetration of state schools by private organisations represented a fundamental ideological reversal of original Labour Party policies and could therefore be expected to be subjected to considerable opposition and hostility. The most hostile reaction came from the National Union of Teachers:

academies put schools in the hands of an unaccountable sponsoring body;
academies can threaten fair admissions procedures;
academies threaten teachers' job security and conditions of service;
academies have a damaging effect on other local schools;
academies threaten children's entitlement to a broad and balanced curriculum;
academies undermine the independent role of school governors.

So the government was faced with a massive legitimation campaign and the Prime Minister missed no opportunity of selling the idea. For example: when opening the first City Academy:

> *" This £31 million pound project symbolises so much that we are seeking to achieve across our education system nationwide through investment and reform – not just better facilities but a wholly new and better way of delivering education, developing the potential and aspirations of each individual child. All the radical*

things about this academy - the independent sponsor; the business and enterprise specialism; the state-of-the art facilities and the use of IT; the reformed curriculum and ways of teaching and learning ……..it's about a fresh way of doing things. It's about keeping the ideal of equality of opportunity that gave rise to comprehensive schooling, but changing radically the traditional comprehensive model to achieve that ideal." (11)

But instead of dealing with specific points raised by its critics, the government waged a propaganda war featuring political spin and hyperbole: "the future of education", "parent power" etc. An important Education Department (12) document is more sober in its tone, and will be invaluable for future reference in the case of developments which threaten this basic philosophy. It tells us that Academies:

- are all-ability schools located in areas of disadvantage,
- are sponsored by business, and faith or voluntary groups, with
- a key part to play in the regeneration of communities, and will
- provide a broad and balanced curriculum, focussing especially on one or more subject specialisms and will offer local solutions for local needs .

What the document does not tell us is that city academies are not accountable to the taxpayer, claiming "commercial confidentiality" for their coyness. They do not have to employ qualified teachers, they do not recognise trade unions and they can opt out of agreements – a further step on the way to an Edubusiness paradise. And they are not subject to the Freedom of Information Act, so that what morsels come our way depend upon the largesse of the Education Department. One such morsel obtained by a persistent enquirer was that the percentage of Academy pupils obtaining A*-C grades in 2005 were as follows:

- English and Maths 17%,
- English, Maths and Science 11%;
- English, Maths, Science and a Modern Language 5%

(the national overall average for all schools - which the Department refused to divulge for academy schools - is 53%). As the writer wryly observes "Any comprehensive school with results like these would be at risk of being replaced by an academy." (13)

The programme was to be delivered by the Specialist Schools and Academies Trust. From the start, it was marked by flamboyance and publicity. The first purpose-built academy, Bexley Business Academy, was designed at a cost of £31 million by Sir Norman Foster and Partners, with a business court, a mini-stock exchange and trading floor (hardly the stuff for regenerating a deprived community). It was soon recognised as not being "fit for purpose", having far too much glass in its construction, classrooms with 3 walls and an open side and tempting balconies. As Sir Cyril Taylor, chairman of the Specialist Schools and academies Trust, puts is:

> *"The whole building side has been a nightmare…I would never have built that building. You can't teach in that, so we're filling (the open sides) in. We're not going to have any more glass palaces. We're going to have functional buildings built of brick. Glass is hot in the summer, freezing in the winter. People can look through it and nasties throw bricks through it. And you don't have balconies on schools, anybody can tell you that" (14)*

THE FIRST CITY ACADEMY: BEXLEY COLLEGE

Opened September 2002. Designed as hitec purpose-built academy by Foster and Partners at a cost of £31 million.

Sponsored by property investor David Garrard
Intake: nursery to sixth form. Applicants chosen from bands based on non-verbal tests.
"Centre of excellence for entrepreneurial skills and knowledge, business and industrial development, with links to business and commerce. Broad, balanced, innovative academic and vocational curriculum."

In 2005 47 Academies were open - of these 24 have Business and Enterprise and 15 Sport as their subject specialisms (some academies offer both).By September 2010 the number was expected to rise to 230.

Evaluation

As part of the legitimation exercise it would be necessary to carry out regular evaluation using such material as examination results in an attempt to rebuff opponents in a war of selective interpretation. The government, instead of requesting Ofsted to carry out the necessary early inspections, appointed a team of consultants to carry out a five-year evaluation. The first annual reports on the earliest academies by Price Waterhouse Cooper have already been published There is something in these reports for everyone, allowing Ministers to express satisfaction in the progress being made and confidence in the overall project. But the waters have been muddied from the start by the ideological nature of the City Academies programme, ensuring that it would become an arena for contestation, with selective use of data – or no data at all! Whilst, for example, the Prime Minister, has claimed that academies teach the poorest children, there is evidence of "cherry-picking". By 2005, the number of children having free school meals (a clear indicator of poverty) had fallen from 45% in the original schools to 31% in the academies (15).

Independent academic studies are therefore extremely important if we are to get anywhere near an accurate and comprehensive evaluation. Terry Wrigley (of Edinburgh University and editor of "Improving Schools") concludes from his own research that so far Academies have failed to improve examination results compared with the comprehensive schools they have replaced - a mere 0.2% for A*-C grades in English and Maths. The response from the Education Department is that, if English and Maths are excluded, the improvement is 8%! (Wrigley also points out that there has been a marked diversion of students in academies from GCSE's to what are seen as less demanding GNVQ's (13% in the comprehensives to 52% in the academies) in order to boost rankings in the league tables. But the Prime Minister, in a speech to the City of London Academy used the misleading figure of an 8% improvement in GCSE's, without any qualification or reference to less flattering evidence - such as some Academies failing Ofsted inspection – in order to justify both a target of 200 City Academies by 2010 and the removal of local authorities as providers of education. (16)

But comparison of examination results alone just will not do. It is important to remind the government that academies are supposed to regenerate the local community, so a different kind of research and type of data will be needed to explore this aspect (including the effect on neighbouring schools) and to consider the issues raised. Given that City Academies have been introduced only recently and that data is relatively sparse, I will take just one or two examples in order to see how far academies challenge educational orthodoxy.

POLITICS AND CITY ACADEMIES

Over the years, although there has been some differences in the agencies of control, state education has settled into a broad consensus in terms of curriculum content and its articulation with the examination system. So it has come to be assumed that it is neutral and non-political, an idea which is challenged by the following example.

Skulduggery at Islington Green School – and elsewhere

The recent history of Islington Green School is worth recounting at this point in the context of claim and counterclaim. This was the school that the Prime Minister declined to send his own children to. Indeed Francis Beckett in his book "The Great City Academies Fraud" suggests that subsequent developments involving this school are partly due to the embarrassment caused to him and hence the need to "prove" that it was in fact a failing school:

> "Islington Green School has had enemies in high places ever since it embarrassed the Blairs by being the local school to which they did not wish to send their children. It would be politically convenient for them if it were a failing school. It would make their decision look less like mere snobbery." (17)

Islington Green was clearly a challenging rundown school in 1997, with a

184

genuine comprehensive intake, with one-third of the pupils learning English as a second language. Despite this, the GCSE results were reasonably good (38% with 5 or more passes at A*-C in 2005, ten times the average rate of increase for city academies) the second best in the borough and named in a list of the 100 top improving schools. Ofsted inspectors were unanimous in their judgment that the school was not failing. But Woodhead, the Chief Inspector at the time, overturned this decision, sent in a second team of inspectors, but refused to publish the results of this second inspection. (A memo released in 2005 under the Freedom of Information Act reveals that these inspectors were also of the view that the school was not failing).

Irrespective of any possible fraud - and given the financial inducements - it was clearly the intention of the Liberal Democratic council that Islington Green comprehensive school should be merged with Moreland School to provide a new city academy. This plan has been so strenuously resisted by parents, pupils and teachers organising public meetings, raising petitions and protesting on the town hall steps that the would-be sponsor ARK (a group of bankers and speculators) has withdrawn and the Moreland School governors have rejected the plans. Ken Muller, NUT representative at Islington Green, has been unrelenting in his opposition to an academy:

> "What persuaded ARK to pull out was the imaginative and increasingly effective campaign we waged to defend comprehensive education in Islington...We have won a battle but the war goes on. Already there are suggestions that a new sponsor, the City of London Corporation, is being lined up for a new academy on the Islington Green site...If the Corporation does decide it wants to sponsor an Islington Green academy, we will have to take up where we left off with ARK. After all if we were opposed to a charity set up by fat cat bankers running our schools, why should we want an undemocratic oligarchy chosen by fat cat bankers controlling them instead" (18).

The Council has now issued a closure notice with the intention of opening as an academy in 2008. But this decision is being challenged. (At the time of writing, the challenge was ongoing - but see later).

[Before leaving this account, the implications of Woodhead's unpublished decision for the future of the school must be noted. The majority of the

185

staff (which had voted 89 to 3 against an academy) have resigned from the school and many parents have withdrawn their children, making the school less representative of the community, in terms of class and race, than before. The effect on the children left there can only be imagined. It is a salutary reminder of how a school can be easily damaged - and recovery made more difficult - by well-publicised destructive comments from "authority", whether that is the intention or whether it is the inevitable result of government-by-the-ignorant. It is worth mentioning in this connection that the events described above were shortly followed by a policy of "naming and shaming" of schools.]

A similarly dubious situation occurred, in the north-east, with Brackenhoe School, which was replaced by the Kings Academy, and was described by Ofsted inspectors as " a rapidly improving school that has identified its main weaknesses and is making inroads into resolving them". The deputy head of another school replaced by an academy had this to say:

> *"We had six times the national average of special needs pupils and 35 per cent of pupils eligible for free school meals....We had the best Key Stage 3 results in Middlesbrough in 2002"*

and the Ofsted inspection in the same year reported that the "school provided a good quality of education, a good climate for learning and good management and efficiency" (19) Yet it was replaced by an academy !

So much for "failing"schools. The question of intake has also proved controversial. Whilst the rhetoric is of all-ability mixed intake, there is plenty of evidence that a policy of covert selection is being operated. One academy has expelled ten times the national average and the impression of parents and one ex-teacher is of a totalitarian oppressive regime, with 148 students being suspended in the first six months for such offences as walking the wrong way down the corridor or not carrying a Bible. According to the official spokesman, such measures are necessary in order to provide a calm, stable environment. It certainly is not to provide the supportive environment necessary for disadvantaged children. The intention is clearly to obtain the best possible examination results, a policy which seems to be working, given the improvement in GCSE pass rates and the rapturous comments from Ofsted inspectors.

A further indication that the Foundation is not meeting its social obligations is provided by the fact that the number of children eligible for free school meals in one academy has dropped by more than 100 compared with the school it replaced. And the democratic deficit is striking: in one academy, of 7 seats available on the governing body 5 are nominees of the sponsor whilst some academies have no parent representatives at all.

THE CURRICULUM AND ACADEMIES

In line with the points made above, the school curriculum had settled into a generally accepted "broad and balanced" pattern, congruent with the conception of education as concerned with the development of intellectual, physical and emotional capacities. This view of the broad, balanced curriculum was reinforced by its accommodation with a well-established examination system. But the Academies programme disturbs this equilibrium by the intervention of powerful businessmen, as we shall see now.

Totalitarianism in the Curriculum

Sir Peter Vardy, with his Emmanuel Schools Foundation, is so far the leading figure in the City Academies programme, sponsoring three academies in the north-east (Emmanuel, Kings and Trinity) and promising to be the local education commissar with his intention of investing £12 million in the Academy programme. He is a practising Christian with fundamentalist beliefs, dismissive of evolution ("I don't believe my ancestors were monkeys"). The official aim for the Emmanuel Schools Foundation "curriculum-as-theory" is at first sight unexceptional:

> "to promote the highest possible standards within comprehensive secondary education through provision based upon Christian principles, valuing every individual and welcoming those of all faiths and of none". (20)

But this claim looks rather hollow when set against the reality of a collective daily act of Christian worship.

But it is the curriculum-in-practice which has caused most consternation among educationists and scientists. Again the rhetoric does not accord with reality. The education is not based upon Christian principles: rather it is based upon Judae-Christian fundamentalism. So Creationism and the Genesis story are taught as literal truth, with the same credibility as if they were scientific theories. Indeed, both religion and science are regarded as faith positions ("science is …a glimpse into the rational and powerful hand of the almighty".) Whilst it has been denied that fundamentalism suffuses the curriculum, the evidence is otherwise. Thus history students are presented with two basic alternatives: that history is a haphazard collision of individual moments, or the unfolding of a story overseen by a greater power and moving towards the creation of a new Heaven and Earth (more specifically, did Hitler pause at the English Channel because God was calling a halt to this march of evil ?) Mathematics is a " disciplined thought-structure which is used to describe the numerical and spatial attributes of God's creation".(21) And Religion and Art are linked together by a common goal: to serve the glory of God and celebrate the complex beauty of His Creation. Admittedly, teachers claim that they present alternative points of view, but as past students pointed out, the teachers made it clear which was the official version, confirmed by the impressions of another teacher:

> *"It's the one-sidedness and absolutisms that I found so troubling……There was an authoritarian atmosphere. I've never experienced one like it anywhere in the world. It was totalitarian in that you did not speak – say what you think – (but) accepted what you are told to do and teach. It did not tie in with how I see Christianity." (22)*

Fundamental issues arise from these brief accounts:

(a) the nature and workings of our education system; for example, who is accountable to whom?
(b) the need both for a detailed justification of a school curriculum and the subjection of it to critical scrutiny.
(c) the importance of presenting alternatives, where possible, when developing personal autonomy and of providing a curriculum particularly suited to the needs of poor children in deprived areas .

It is worth reminding ourselves at this point that the rationale for City Academies included the following:

local solution to local needs
regenerating communities
in areas of disadvantage.

And yet the government has set out plans for independent schools to become self-governing city academies (although there is a theoretical requirement for "open access": no fees or selection.) Already one Girls' Days Schools Trust, the Belvedere School in Liverpool, has made the transition and others are preparing to follow. One could ask the question: in whose interests is this initiative? Capital will certainly be available for building improvements and there is scope for philanthropy in a city like Liverpool. But the specialism at Belvedere is modern languages and 10% of the pupils are selected by aptitude. If the original intention of city academies was to meet the needs of poor children in disadvantaged areas, there is as yet no suggestion that these needs will be met by this initiative. One is left with the impression that the city academies' rationale was merely a piece of rhetoric to help legitimate the radical proposal to allow private interests into state education - and that this was merely the beginning of a campaign to universalise the initiative, a campaign which was about to be launched through Trust Schools.

(c) Trust Schools - The 2005 Education White Paper

We are here witnessing a continuing development of the initiatives announced in the 1988 White Paper, the quasi-privatisation of the education system, weakening the link with local authority, as private interests are allowed into the educational enterprise, funded largely by the tax-payer. Both the powers given to trust schools, as well as the attenuation of LEA control is illustrated clearly in the 2006 Education and Inspections Bill, from which the following extracts are taken:

THE EDUCATION AND INSPECTION BILL 2006

Trust Schools
"This Bill will enable all schools to become Trust Schools by forming links with external partners who will be able, should the school choose, to appoint the majority of the Governing Body. Trust Schools will:

> own their own assets
> employ their own staff
> set their admission arrangements.

Local Authorities
  will take on a new strategic role including
  duties to promote choice, diversity and high standards for every child
  a duty to respond to parental concerns about the quality of local schools
  acting as decision-maker on school organisation matters

Fair Access
  reaffirming the ban on selection by ability
  a ban on inter viewing
  an extended duty to provide free transport for the most disadvantaged families

---

According to the Education Secretary, this Bill is all about:

> *"using their ideas, energy and talents. The flexibilities and freedoms that trust status provides will allow school leaders to better respond to the needs of their communities, work in partnership to tackle challenges and to work with parents to shape the direction and ethos of their school" (23)*

All good, ministerial rhetoric. But teaching unions are clearly unconvinced by it . For example, the Association of Teachers and Lecturers (ATL) fears that governing bodies could be dominated by a single group, whilst the National Union of Teachers (NUT) claims that legislation rejecting parental ballots will take power away from parents and give control to sponsors. And the fact that the Schools Commissioner for Trust Schools is at present an unaccountable departmental bureaucrat does not provide much optimism that we are on the verge of a democratic revolution in our schools. Indeed the love affair between government and big business suggests that Trust Schools will go the same way as Academies.

However, it needs to be pointed out that, as well as business foundations, Trusts can now include educational charities, universities, and community groups. Of the first batch of Trust Schools, seven are sponsored by religious organisations, chiefly the United Learning Trust (a subsidiary of the not-for-profit United Church Schools Trust). This trust promises high-quality education based upon Christian principles of service and tolerance. The possibility that these principles might lead to the development of a broad and democratic curriculum is extinguished, however, on discovering that all their specialisms are "Business and Enterprise", confirming the impression that education is now seen as an economic, rather than a humane enterprise.

Already the Trust School initiative has been branded an exercise in "creeping privatisation" (in a rapidly-changing situation 47 trust schools were set up in the period July-September 2009.) When it is remembered that throughout the entire history of mass schooling, there have been articulate, persuasive and influential opponents advocating the complete withdrawal of state support in favour of private education, it is imperative that Trust Schools, using taxpayers' money, be put to the test of full accountability, that their educational programmes be justified in terms of basic educational criteria - and that information be provided not only by government bodies but by independent educational researchers.

In the face of continuing public unease and hostility (as social democratic policies are being steadily replaced by those of neoliberalism) it is still necessary for the government to continue to provide legitimation for its new policies in order to carry the country with it. And this legitimation process requires the continued denigration of comprehensive schools. I will therefore now look briefly at what appears to be the present state of comprehensive education in this country to see how far this denigration is justified.

Comprehensive education

This historical account has traced the struggle of the working-class first for elementary, then secondary and finally comprehensive schooling (although most "comprehensives" were not truly comprehensive and they had no overall coherent rationale.) We have now reached a stage where the government, supported by the opposition, has revealed a clear intent, in the name of marketisation and partial privatisation of state education, to destroy both local education authorities and comprehensive schools (described elegantly by the prime minister's cultured press adviser as "bog standard," a term which has become firmly attached to the word "comprehensive", confirming the public prejudice.) But the story of comprehensive education is actually one of remarkable success against, in this country at least, fierce opposition from the Establishment, whose support for comprehensives has been at best half-hearted. Comprehensive schools have seldom been genuine all-ability, but have had to compete for talent with local grammar schools. Bearing this qualification in mind, it is time to provide some evidence to indicate that true comprehensive schools, with dedicated staff committed to the comprehensive ideal, have nothing to fear from alternative institutions.

At the international level, there is plenty of evidence to suggest that well-resourced, all-ability comprehensive schools, with good teaching and strong leadership are highly successful educational institutions, judged by conventional standards. For example, Finland's comprehensive schools (all-ability intake from nursery to 16 years) have come out top of the latest PISA (Programme for International Study Assessment) tests for 15-year olds in maths, reading and science. The Director of the Finnish General Education Division attributes this success to a "culture of trust", whereby national inspection and tests for basic education have been abolished in favour of self evaluation and municipal and teacher autonomy (24).

Since the government and the media lose no opportunity in publicising the "failings" of comprehensive schools, omitting to mention difficult social circumstances and the unrepresentative intake, it is worth mentioning the experience of Lady Manners Comprehensive in Derbyshire, in more propitious circumstances. Its latest Ofsted Report states that it consistently "provides its students with an excellent education" and that "no significant areas for improvement were identified". 74% of pupils gained five or more GCSE/GNVQ A*-C grades in 2005 compared with 53% national average. The breadth of activities is illustrated by the variety of sports on offer and by the number of music groups: the senior orchestra has won the area symphony orchestra competition and is performing in the national Schools Prom. Perhaps the finest accolade is provided by the parents who decide against private education in favour of the local comprehensive. There are several reasons advanced for the success of Lady Manners:

(1) the staff are totally committed to comprehensive education, resisting all selection procedures and the lure of specialist school status;
(2) every subject is taught by a specialist;
(3) its buildings are on a single site;
(4) it was built around an existing grammar school and inherited its ethos;
(5) it has an all-ability intake.

The situation at Lady Manners reflects the situation generally in rural areas. An existing grammar school is absorbed into the comprehensive and there is a genuine all-ability intake. The position in urban areas is quite different - there is competition from a variety of institutions: faith schools, single-sex schools, specialist schools, grammar schools, city technology colleges and now city academies and trust schools. In a complex situation like this, selection procedures, both academic and social, are the order of the day. The most successful urban comprehensives attract the children of wealthier discerning parents (often the parent of an "achieving" child) and thus go from strength to strength (some even outperforming public schools). The least successful comprehensive schools, on the other hand, attract fewer and fewer able pupils, enter a cycle of falling standards and eventually become failing schools in "special measures". As Benn and Miller put it:

> *"A significant minority of children are in schools which struggle with a wide range of social problems and not enough funding to deal with them. They suffer from a polarised system which 'creams off' many of the more motivated and wealthy families in their locality to the private, selective or faith sector. The existence of these struggling schools has led to the perception that the comprehensive ideal itself has failed when, in fact, the existence of so many 'escape routes' from the local school has meant it has never been given a chance to establish itself properly." (25)*

Because many of these failing schools, with their mass truanting and poor performance, are located in London, under the gaze of the national media, they have provided easy headlines for the press and reinforced the general impression of "bog-standard comprehensives". In other words, sufficient attention has not been drawn to the various problems these particular schools face, or to the possible solutions that could be provided by a government really believing in the comprehensive principle and committed to the provision of resources comparable to those of city academies.

Apart from the problems outlined above, comprehensive education has been bedevilled by an inappropriate curriculum. From the start it was expected by some to take the shape of the grammar school; it was, in fact, sold to parents on the slogan "grammar schools for all" by some members of the government. An academic - and latterly a national - curriculum therefore formed the basis of comprehensive education. Apart from an inappropriate curriculum, teachers are not generally trained to use their subject disciplines to exploit and build upon pupils' own experiences. But, despite this, the overall picture is not just one of success but of improving standards. As Clyde Chitty explains: (26)

"Both Conservative and New Labour governments have been very keen to stress that all secondary schools should be judged by the percentage of their Year 11 students gaining 5 or more GCSE passes at Grades A*-C. So whatever reservations one might have about this national obsession with the five A* to C benchmark, it seems fair to point out that there has, in fact, been a pretty remarkable increase in the proportion of entries achieving these 'top' grades or their equivalent since comprehensive schooling became national policy in the mid-1960's. In 1962/3, the proportion was just 16 per cent; by the year 2001, this had risen to around 50 per cent. In 1970, 47 per cent of students left secondary school at sixteen with no qualifications whatsoever; by 2001, this figure had fallen to just 5 per cent. As far as GCSE Advanced Levels are concerned (again a narrow criterion of 'success') the percentage of eighteen-year olds passing in at least two subjects has risen since the early 1980's from 14 to around 30 per cent; and this year (2002) the proportion of A-level entries achieving at least an E grade or higher has risen by 4.5 percentage points to 94.3 per cent, the steepest rise in the exam's 51-year history".

NOTES AND REFERENCES

1. Monbiot op cit
2. DfES (2005) Individual Learning Accounts
3. The Business of Education (2005) Unison Bargaining Support. London
4. Guardian April 1 2000
5. http://www.dfes.gov.uk/ebnet/business/
6. E.G. West op cit
7. http://www.ncl.ac.uk/egwest/about.html
8. S. Power (2003) "Paving a Third Way? A Policy Trajectory Analysis of Education Action Zones" ESRC. Swindon.
9. op cit
10. Speech by the Prime Minister "Building Schools for the Future" at the opening of Capital City Academy, September 2003.
11. opcit
12. Dfes: the standards site
13. Roger Titcombe, letter to Guardian June 16 2006
14. Education Guardian February 7 2006
15. Guardian October 31, 2005
16. Guardian, May 22, 2006
17. Guardian, Sept 12, 2005
18. See, for example, the Socialist Worker February 19 2005
19. www.emmanuel-schools.org.uk/-
20. www.politicalog.co.uk/?m=200509
21. all these examples are taken from Burn,J. and McQuoid,N. (1995) "Christianity and
    the Curriculum ". The Christian Institute.
22. S. Robertson "Religious Schools Come under TV Fire" Sunday Sun. Mar 5, 2006
23. www.politics.co.uk
24. Ms. Irmeli Halinen "The Finnish Curriculum Development Processes" PISA 8.12.2005
25. M. Benn and F. Millar (2005) A Comprehensive Future. www.compassonline.org.uk 26. C. Chitty (2002) Caroline Memorial Lecture http:// www.socialisteducation.org.uk/benn02.htm

CHAPTER TEN

REFLECTIONS: CONFLICTS OF INTEREST

That comprehensive education should be in crisis, with success stories like the ones above, is a clear indication that it is not without its enemies. Indeed, this book has been concerned to illustrate how, in the course of the past two centuries, developments in mass education have represented the outcome of struggles between competing interest groups. It is time, therefore, as we conclude this section of the book, to look back and examine the effects on the educational system of the major vested interests. But "interest" has proved to be more complex than appeared at first sight. Leaving aside the psychological interpretation of "interesting", we have seen, in the course of this narrative, how assumed consensual interests - such as those of the teaching profession or of the early industrialists - have turned out to be anything but consensual. And what was believed to be in the best interests of a group, such as attaining a grammar school education for all working-class children, proved in the event to be illusory. There is the further complication of addressing the "public interest", a term which seldom rises above the rhetorical. Given these caveats, let us reflect upon the vested interests of powerful groups as revealed in this narrative and consider the possible implications of conflicts arising between them.

The Religious Interest

I have shown earlier how it was the Christian faith which was first to provide the initial impetus for mass schooling and in 1833, to obtain financial support from the state for its monitorial school (support which has continued to this day in the forms of its "Aided" and "Controlled" schools). Apart from instilling Christian virtues, through both its formal and hidden curricula, in children of the poor, its legacy is far-reaching in other respects. For instance, the emphasis has been upon the written word, initially with biblical texts and the catechism ("In the beginning was the Word…..and the Word was God") leading to one of the most persistent elements in schooling: rote learning. Children thus learned that both the written word (reinforced by the emergence of text-books) and certain forms of knowledge were the most important.

When New Labour came to power in 1997 there were almost 7000 state faith schools in existence, about a third of the total number of state schools. Over 4700 of these were Church of England, 2100 Roman Catholic and over 30 Jewish. The government was committed to a policy of multi-culturalism and the expansion of state-aided faith schools, with a Government Paper "Schools – Achieving Success" proposing that there be a large increase in the number of schools run by religious organisations. Given that the principle of state aid for Christian organisations had been established in 1833, it would have been difficult in any case to refuse financial aid for other religious organisations. Be that as it may, the government, in the shape of the Prime Minister, showed marked enthusiasm for religious diversity in our schools, claiming that not only are faith schools popular with parents but they also provide a distinctive ethos and character. Ten Muslim faith schools alone have come into existence in the past decade and it is claimed by the National Secular Society that the government has plans to include 150 new state Muslim schools.

Objections to State-aided Faith Schools:

(a) Selection

Who will go to these schools? It is noteworthy that an amendment to the 2006 Education Act compelling faith schools to take a quarter of pupils from other religions or none was heavily defeated. The Education Minister made the following comments:

> "I have listened carefully to colleagues on this issue and recognise that we all share the same goal for a more cohesive society where faith schools play an important part in building understanding and tolerance of other faiths and communities." (1)

In other words, the government was quite relaxed about the matter, sending a green light to faith schools to operate their own admission procedures. Christian schools generally require pupils to belong to that particular faith, leading to many ambitious parents suddenly acquiring religious convictions and becoming regular attenders at Church in the belief that a better education is on offer in Church schools. And any hopes that minority faith schools will operate a more open policy are absurdly unrealistic, as indicated by the recent notorious case of the Jewish boy refused admission to the Jewish Free School, because although his mother was Jewish she was not the right kind of Jew ! The fact must be faced that minority faith schools generally operate a rigid exclusion policy, with the sole purpose of reproducing that particular faith and culture - a purpose which becomes more emphatic with the requirement (approved by government legislation) that all employees also share that faith and culture.

(b) Segregation

Although governments might persist in the belief that faith schools foster cohesion, available evidence points in the opposite direction. The European Union Monitoring Commission in a lengthy report based upon a mass of evidence, has pointed to the dangers of segregation:

> *"The EUMC stresses the crucial importance of education and training measures in combating racism, xenophobia, anti-Semitism, Islamophobia and related intolerances. Equal access to quality education for all is a critical foundation for integration and community cohesion. Segregated forms of education should be either completely abolished or reduced to short-term preparatory classes leading to the integration of minority children into regular schooling". (2)*

(c) Curricular

It is true that faith schools are nominally obliged to follow the national curriculum (although it is steadily being eroded), but to be reassured by this obligation is to ignore the hidden curriculum. Not that it is all that hidden. We are variously told in Muslim schools that the national curriculum can be taught from an:

- Islamic perspective, with a meeting of the Qur'an and secular knowledge,
- in an Islamic environment inculcated with the ethos of Islam,

- and that there can be a "conceptual transformation of knowledge" providing inoculation against a secular curriculum.

So far the large majority of Muslim schools are independent, although the government is currently encouraging them to enter the state sector and has provided a £100,000 grant to the Association of Muslim Schools to ease the transition. As mentioned above, 10 Muslim state-aided schools alone have come into existence in the past decade, with possibly another 150 to follow.

So it is worth looking briefly at one such independent Muslim school curriculum: (3)

Aims:
    To provide a sound Islamic Education to children from 5 to 12 yrs old and to help them develop a sense of belonging to the Muslim Community.
    To enable students to fulfil their obligation to worship Allah in the manner that the Qur'an and Allah's messenger have described.

Objectives:
    To be able to read, write and understand commonly used Arabic terms and phrases including Quranic reading;
    To be able to understand and perform the rituals that are practised in Islam;
    To have a full understanding of basic Islamic beliefs;
    To acquire the necessary knowledge and skills for practicing Islamic etiquettes and morals.

Content:
    1. Arabic / Quran;
    2. Sirah of the Prophet Muhammad
    3. Stories of other Prophets
    4. Morals / Manners based on the teaching of Prophet Mohammad.

We are not given any indication of how this curriculum will be taught, but even with the most sympathetic dialogic teacher respectful of the student voice, it is difficult to see how this could be anything other than indoctrinatory and undemocratic, with little opportunity to develop personal autonomy. It is a stark reminder that an educational institution should be a place for enquiry, not worship and that a democratic curriculum involves the critical study of the major belief systems of the world rather than the worshipping of one.

The fear of segregation, insularity and secrecy is further compounded by the recent decision to give private Muslim schools the power to appoint their own Ofsted - style Inspectors. The chief inspector recently expressed his concern about such developments in a speech on Citizenship, a speech for which he was subsequently demonised by the Muslim community:

> *"As my annual report will show there has been a significant growth in the number of independent faith schools.... the growth in faith schools needs to be carefully and sensitively monitored by government to ensure that all pupils at all schools receive an understanding not only of their own faiths but of other faiths and the wider tenets of society...I worry that many young people are being educated in faith-based schools with little appreciation of their wider responsibilities and obligations to British society....As my annual report will say about Muslim schools - many schools must adapt their curriculum to ensure that it provides pupils with a broad general knowledge of public institutions and services in England and helps them acquire an appreciation of and respect for other cultures in a way that promotes tolerance and harmony". (4)*

We see in these developments how a democratically-elected government is ignoring the wishes and perceived interests of the majority of the electorate (a Guardian / ICM poll, for example, finds that two-thirds of those questioned oppose state faith schools) and is sustaining, through its moral and financial support, a system which is incompatible, through its authoritarian nature, with the values of western democracy (although it is claimed by some Muslims that there is no inevitable incompatibility with democracy, provided it is imbued with Islamic values).

Be that as it may, there is clearly a potential conflict of interests. A similar tension exists between Islam and corporate capitalism, although, here again, there are attempts by some Islamic states to redefine capitalism in Islamic terms, consistent with its values. But before we examine the current state of the business interest here, we shall first look at the academic interest.

200

The Aristocratic (Academic) Interest

At the start of this narrative, the aristocracy, made up of titled nobles and landed gentry, were, through wealth, status and power in an unrivalled position as the governing elite of the country. They saw their interest in terms of ensuring their inheritance passed directly through the male line, with boys educated at public schools and Oxbridge, in appropriate attitudes and knowledge, totally independent of common utilitarian considerations. This was theoretically education for its own sake, "pure" and "intrinsic" in the sense of being free from contamination by the material world. Indeed, the Establishment in the nineteenth century, in the face of increasing pressure to broaden the curriculum, made the position of public schools clear:

> *"The classical languages and literature should continue to hold the principal place in the course of study (since) they supply some of the noblest poetry, the finest eloquence, the deepest philosophy, the wisest historical writing" (1864 Clarendon Report)*

[Contamination from the material world there was, however. Landlords were not averse to profiting from mineral resources found on their estate, for example. But with the collapse of the agricultural base to the economy in the late nineteenth century, the landed gentry were obliged to take a more serious interest in the commercial world and to turn to investments in the City.]

This "pure" education had been confined to the ruling elite, with the lower orders being trained in routine menial tasks by means of rote learning. It was the National Curriculum, described earlier, which made academic subjects theoretically available to all children. But at the same time, arguments were increasingly being made for vocational education, arguments generally found unacceptable to parents on the grounds of it lacking "parity of esteem". In an attempt to overcome these objections, one recent government report has suggested the creating of an overarching diploma, within which academic and vocational courses are granted equal status. But so far, the government has supported the academic interest by rejecting this proposal, believing A-levels provide the "gold standard" against which all other subjects can be compared, a position which it will find increasingly difficult to sustain.

The Business (Bourgeois) Interest

The instrumental values representing the business interest are in inevitable tension with intrinsic "education for its own sake". Not that this tension was particularly noticeable at the start of this narrative. Initially, the interest of businessmen in the role of formal education was slight: the emphasis was upon the self-made "practical man" – and mill-owners generally believed that children should be in their factories rather than at school. Even the restructuring of industrial practice along capitalist lines did not fully awaken employers to the possibilities of education, apart from believing it to be utilitarian in nature. So, for their own offspring, new schools were established to provide a "useful" secondary education, an appropriate model for this development being described in an earlier chapter. As far as the education of the workforce was concerned, concerns were unimaginative and parochial, even when businessmen organised themselves into pressure groups. Indeed, the education interest of the CBI (Confederation of British Industries) has been consistently expressed in negative terms, blaming schools for their failure to produce employable school-leavers, without making constructive suggestions or getting involved itself. It was in the absence of an overarching rationale that over the years a plethora of confusing vocational initiatives emerged, such that eventually the Education Department took vocational education "in-house" with the New Vocationalism described earlier. With vocational education in schools now vying for attention with academic subjects, the tensions mentioned above came out into the opening, with the results described earlier.

But a developing corporate hegemony has reinforced the instrumentalist approach to education. And as the Business and State interest have moved closer together, the CBI has taken a more positive interest in the vocational education of early leavers. In its "Response to the Leitch Review on Skills", it makes the following recommendations:

> the content of vocational GCSE's to be improved;
> employers to be involved and encouraged to provide resources and work placements;
> career guidance to be improved.

It should also be noted that the new 14-19 diplomas are being developed by an employer-led Sector Skills Council with the aim of ensuring that desirable key knowledge, skills and attitudes and addressed. The question remains: "How much autonomy will the student have, and will his voice be listened to and taken seriously ?" Hitherto, the student has been placed in an a-cultural straitjacket.

The Working Class Interest

So much for the educational interests of upper and middle classes. What of the lower orders? The early part of this narrative shows how the Church and State together attempted to define their interest for them: to become conforming, law-abiding members of the workforce, with some notion of the Christian way of life. Working-class Radicals saw this as indoctrination into capitalist and paternalistic notions of utility and demanded for working-class children an education which was practical, relevant and critical - that is, "Really Useful Knowledge". But these attempts by the working-class to define its own educational interests met with no support from the State. So whilst there were some isolated contributions from travelling lecturers and other activists, in the absence of a political base, these alternatives never took root.

Indeed, working-class educational interests have always met with continued resistance from the governing class. We have seen here how the State, faced with an increasingly powerful Labour movement and a more strident voice demanding "Equality of Educational Opportunity" staged a series of tactical retreats in order to maintain the sanctity of the social order. Even when comprehensivisation finally arrived, it was half-hearted and partial, omitting public schools and most grammar schools. Comprehensivisation also threw new light on the concept of the "educational interest", revealing dramatically that the holy grail of a grammar-school education for all was certainly not in the interests of all children. One response of the State to this potentially disruptive situation has been to provide a series of not-very-successful vocational training courses, mentioned above, with the latest attempt being 14-19 diplomas, which are currently in the stage of being developed or implemented. Since the ultimate objective serves the instrumental purpose of acquiring the necessary skills and attitudes to perform a particular series of tasks in the manufacturing or service sectors, these diplomas can be expected to revive the controversy between "liberalists" and "vocationalists" dealt with earlier, and serve as a reminder of the inevitable tensions and conflicts to be expected between competing interests in a democratic society. It has been assumed hitherto that a major role for the state was to act in the public interest by reconciling and accommodating such "conflicts of interest". Let us see how well it performs this role at the present time.

The State Interest : The Reproduction of the Socio - Economic Order

This narrative has revealed opposing views on the role of the State in the provision of education. The political right's slogan is "Roll Back the State" so that free markets can flourish and individual enterprise be rewarded. The political left, on the other hand, looks to the State to protect the weak and vulnerable and to introduce a measure of fairness and equality into society. There can be further confusion over the precise meaning of "nation-state". The term "nation" has conventionally referred to a loose body of peoples held together and gaining their identity through common language and traditions. In other words the "glue" for a nation was essentially cultural. The state, on the other hand is a political and territorial entity, with clear boundaries and very conscious of its need to protect them. Hence it requires a series of structures both for defensive, administrative and ideological purposes. Whilst there was a collective approach to such problems in the simpler forms of nation, in what is now a dominant and rapidly expanding state, these tasks are now performed by trained employees in governmental "departments of state". But the state is more than this. Its various appendages, for example, include what have been characterised as the "oppressive state apparatus" (prisons, army, police) and the "ideological state apparatus" (church, schools etc). But it is when considering the source of power in the state that confusion sets in. The answer to the question: "Who runs the country?" may well now be "the media barons" or "quangos", whilst some decades earlier it would have been "the union barons". Even two centuries ago, the perceptive William Cobbett was exercised by this question and expressed his unease about the system in terms of what he labelled the "Thing":

> *"What name to give such a government it is difficult to say. It is like nothing that was ever heard of before. It is neither a monarchy, an aristocracy, not a democracy; it is a band of great nobles who, by sham elections, and by means of all sorts of bribery and corruption, have obtained an absolute sway in this country. Such is the government, such is the Thing."* (5 Political Register 33.[1818])

He would now probably use the term "Establishment", a term invented by the journalist Henry Fairlie in the Spectator of September 1955:

> *"By the "Establishment" I do not only mean the centres of official power - though they are certainly part of it - but rather the whole matrix of official and social relations within which power is exercised."*

So far as explanations can provide us with any clues as to how the "Thing" operates, the two more influential of the theories of the state are : the liberal-pluralist and the Marxist. Let us see how they stand up to the events described in this narrative. The liberal-pluralist theory acknowledges the existence of valid competing interests in society, and it is for the state to act as "honest broker", accommodating and reconciling all the various interests. Thus it has responded to the religious interest by financing the Church and, more recently, by supporting the expansion of faith schools. It can also be claimed that working-class education has benefited through the state acting as honest broker by its gaining access to secondary schooling in accordance with the principle of "equality of opportunity". As for the business interest, the State has been concerned to provide vocational education for early school-leavers in order to meet the needs of industry and, more significantly, has encouraged the entry of business interests into the education system.

But the Marxist theory would regard all such explanations as superficial and simple-minded. According to this theory, the state acts as the instrument of what might be termed the ruling class. It would be odd if it were otherwise, since the most powerful members of society share a common heritage of a privileged upbringing and a public school education – with all the shared values implied by this. They can thus be expected to have a prejudice - consciously or not - in favour of the ruling elite. But with the growth of the bourgeoisie and the increasing power of the business interest and corporate capitalism, there has necessarily been some - if uneasy - accommodation of aristocratic values with those of the commercial world. This accommodation has taken the form of an increasing absorption of business values and acceptance of the corporate interest to provide the basis of what is now more accurately described as the dominant class. [That this basis is in a state of tension is indicated by the fact that whilst the bourgeoisie may be subordinate politically, it is dominant economically.] And so vital has the economic interest been to the welfare of the modern state, that governments, of whatever political complexion, invariably favour the employer at the expense of the worker. This bias in favour of the business interest is made more potent by the growth in the lobbying and "advising" of government departments (often assisted by ex-ministers and former civil servants) to the extent that it is now such a prime and respectable business activity that politicians can look forward to a comfortable and lucrative second career on stepping down from politics. (A factor doubtless influencing their attitude towards privatisation). With business interests also coordinated through such organisations as the CBI, the pressure of business upon the state, to the exclusion of other interests, has become progressively more intense.

Indeed, we have seen in this section, how the state, apart from encouraging the commercial penetration both of schools and the education system generally, has provided financial inducements to business men to run academies, introducing in the process the values of corporate capitalism, and redefining education in economic rather than developmental terms. So the idea of the state as honest broker has finally been laid to rest: the historical reality is presently more of the state acting, not as broker, but as the agent of the business interest in educational and other matters. In short, according to this theory, the State acts as the educational agent for corporate capitalism.

But whilst focussing upon vested interests in this way may give some explanatory purchase, it ignores another important societal dimension, that of the social order. We have seen in the course of this book, how the state has staged a series of sequential tactical retreats in response to the Labour movement's continuing demands for "Equality of Educational Opportunity". These controlled concessions, which subsequently led to no fundamental social changes included the following:

the entry of a controlled number of "bright" children into grammar schools on passing selection tests based upon spurious "scientific" criteria;
the legislation of "Secondary Education For All" in its 1944 Education Act, but favouring a tripartite selection system;
half-hearted comprehensivisation, allowing grammar schools to remain separate from the system and assuring public schools both of their continuing future and their favourable charitable status.

In other words, at the end of all these apparently radical changes, the social order has remained largely unchanged, with the upper class (admittedly now in tension with capitalist forces) still dominating the structures of power and influence. Whilst these structural and organisational matters are highly visible - and hence open to contestation - there have been more subtle processes at work, in the shape of the school curriculum. The conventional curriculum is based upon "pure" subjects, having their origins in the public school system and hence bringing with them high status and public acceptability. Furthermore, these subjects are perceived to be made up of largely objective (reified) subject matter, which, being largely factual (in a positivist mode) and hence readily assessed, enables the public examination boards to parade a certain legitimacy in terms of reliability and validity and thus to attract the confidence of the general public. What is of even greater significance is that the apparent objectivity and authenticity of the examination system leads to the examinee accepting all too readily this external evaluation of his / her present ability - and hence future prospects.

Furthermore, the subject matter being examined, being largely inert and external to the learner, can also be guaranteed to provide little of intrinsic interest to the student. Motivation is therefore external and instrumental, confined to the successful who can exhibit deferred gratification, in the knowledge that rewards will certainly follow in the form of a successful career. Since this curriculum is delivered in middle-class mode, the working-class student is further denied ready access and hence is more likely to fail the system. These school failures will have little motivation in taking the curriculum seriously and be more likely to be turned off, thus compounding his / her deprivation. Worse than this, they make up the "bottom 20%" which has proved to be a constant irritant to mass education. As Paul Willis has demonstrated (P.Willis op cit) certain working-class lads, showing unsuspected creativity and enterprise, have set up counter-cultures which, while possibly providing some self-gratification in the short term, ensure in the longer term that they join the dole queue or enter the lowest rungs of the occupational structure, thus unwittingly helping to maintain the socio-economic order. The education system, then, together with the public examination, provides a virtually pre-destined entry into the occupational hierarchy, with its associated social status, from the dominant (executive) class down to the underclass of casual labour.

But there is more to this in terms of a cultural dimension than the nature of school knowledge and its examination system . The culture and the values of the public school, for example, reflect those of Oxbridge, so that these students (let us call them "scholars") have been inducted into a serious learning milieu (with few disruptive students) in a residential situation, enabling prolonged close contact with Oxbridge-trained tutors, who are able to prepare them both for examinations and interviews.

In other words young people from the upper classes have acquired, both at home and school, the appropriate "cultural capital", in contrast to the sad situation of those living in poverty, described earlier. Even those working-class students who buck the system by obtaining good examination results often find themselves not being called for interview for university admission or not having sufficient cultural capital (or "soft skills") to impress the interviewers - or compete on equal terms with applicants from public schools. Many do not even apply, feeling uncomfortable and socially inadequate at the prospect of mixing with members of the upper class, even to the extent of being alienated from the system. (An earlier chapter details the great injustice being dealt to those "failed" students with higher potential than those public school students who are successful in gaining admission.) We thus have an apparently fair, legitimate and equitable system which serves to maintain and reproduce the socio-economic order. It provides further an illustration of the school acting as "ideological state apparatus" reproducing not only the conditions of economic production but also the rules of submission to the socio-economic order.

This analysis, then, allows us to draw the following important conclusions:

the State educational interest serves to reproduce a socio-economic order reflecting the hierarchical class and occupational structures in society in order to support a corporate and consumerist culture, with education redefined in economic rather than developmental terms. In the process students are denied formal, educated access to real problems facing them in the outside world, such as environmental, political and social challenges.

It is worth remembering at this point that, according to the Sutton Trust, 70% of judges were educated at top public schools (78% at Oxbridge) 68% of barristers (82% at Oxbridge) as well as 54% of medics. Whilst politicians of a particular caste talk from time to time of somehow limiting the influence of public schools, the reality is that the State actively supports them to the tune of £100 million of tax breaks per year in the process of maintaining the social order. Talk of "social mobility" in such a context verges on the lunatic.

It is also worth bearing in mind that, in this context, education policy changes, as in the recent Academies Bill, accompanied by heart-warming talk of "freedom" and "choice" etc, are fated to be subordinated to the overall State educational interest summarised above .

Thus is an unfair, divided and unequal society perpetuated. It was just such a combination of economic injustice and social and economic inequality which contributed to the decline of the Roman Empire:

> *"From the time of Augustus, the leading economic development in the Roman Empire was the steady concentration of land in fewer and fewer hands, with the gradual disappearance of small, independent peasant landowners. The economic system was frail, it could support only a tiny minority, whose prosperity rested on intensive exploitation of the masses living on a bare subsistence level ....the pattern was for the richest noblemen to become dramatically richer.... The taxes levied to maintain the army were massive and they fell largely on the poor; but the Roman rulers also managed to ruin the middle class, which had been the backbone of the Empire... It was this class which had held the culture of the ancient world together and by the fifth century it had gone and it did not reappear in Italy until the rise of the mercantile families of the High Middle Ages"* (6)

And the challenge to our way of life involves more than the system described above. Challenges to our civilisation from environmental and cultural degradation are far more daunting than anything dreamt of by previous civilisations. The growing gap between rich and poor, both locally and globally, ensures a world of conflict as well as a demoralised population, compounded by a materialistic and dehumanising instrumental culture, denying the human satisfaction of intrinsic needs in a world of diminishing resources.

It would seem from all of this that we are involved in inevitable and irreversible processes, reinforced by state support for hegemonic corporate capitalist practices. But the resultant "commodification" of education has led to some counter - resistance and to the seemingly impossible task of challenging the status quo. Some of these bold and enterprising attempts to provide a more meaningful education for young people in various social and political contexts will be recounted in the next and final section.

NOTES AND REFERENCES

1.Mail OnLine 26 Oct 2006

2.EU Monitoring Commission on Racism and Xenophobia

3. Such extreme examples of the Islamization of the school curriculum are increasingly the subject of political and academic scrutiny.
See for example Dr. Shiraz Thobani "The Dilemma of Islam as School Knowledge in Muslim schools" iis.ac.uk/ContentLink. asp?type=cont&id=110192

4.BBC 17 Jan 2005 "Citizenship in Muslim Schools"

5.Cobbett, W. (1818) Political Register 33

6. Berman,M. op cit

PART FOUR:

COUNTERACTIVE

CHALLENGES TO THE STATUS QUO

Despite the powerful forces acting in support of the status quo, attempts are made to mount various challenges by presenting alternatives. These can include challenging the notions of fixed intelligence, institutionalised education, fixed-term schooling through life-long learning, as well as the conventional wisdom sustaining school knowledge, a "delivery" curriculum and objective examination.

CHAPTER ELEVEN

TAKING STOCK: THE EDUCATION INTEREST

"There is no wealth but life. Life, including all its powers of love, joy and admiration. That country is the richest which nourishes the greatest number of noble and happy human beings; that man is the richest who, having perfected the functions of his own life to the utmost, has also the widest helpful influence, both personal and by means of his possessions, over the lives of others.

(John Ruskin "Unto This Last"
1862 Hendon Publishing)

Two Speeches on Education
The aristocratic curriculum (intrinsic):
*   education for its own sake: subjects as bodies of knowledge*
The bourgeois curriculum (instrumental)
Utilitarianism: education for survival
A person-centred approach: educating interests
What is Education For?
The Material World:
*   reproduction of the workforce: the examination system*
*   changing needs of the economy*
*   material deprivation*
*   the classroom as a target-meeting production line*
consumerism and the search for happiness
the therapeutic school

Two Speeches on Education

(1) Enoch Powell, Tory Cabinet Minister and Classics Professor, speaking in 1985:

"There could be no place more suitable than this hall to unburden myself of an anxiety about an educational heresy which all recent governments....have busily and powerfully promoted. It is the heresy that education is useful. The heresy has been promulgated by Ministers, including some whose own educational record makes their action especially surprising, in order to justify not only the expenditure of public money upon the provision of education, but a bias towards branches of education which they are pleased to regard as signally useful and economically advantageous......All this is the sound of barbarism. Education is a Good Thing because man has an insatiable appetite to learn and to understand and ....communicating to others. Education is self-justified. It not only needs no secondary justification. It actually shrivels at the touch of secondary justification........Spending money on education is a work of charity. It consists of giving what is inherently good for the sake of doing good. All true learning and all true teaching are to the glory of God." (1)

(2) Tony Blair, New Labour Prime Minister and barrister, speaking in 2006:

"Every employer knows that without basic competence in literacy and numeracy, few people are employable in the modern economy. But now vocational skills are also vital, and so are what used to be called 'soft skills' – the ability to communicate effectively, to work in teams, to recognise responsibilities. That is why we need to take further the change in Britain's schools. Trust schools and city academies build on the success of specialist schools, modernising the old-style comprehensive model and by engaging business partners and others, open up the system to diversity, greater parental choice and greater school freedom. Together with a modernised curriculum, including new specialised vocational diplomas being developed in close collaboration with employers, these are critical reforms to equip our young people for the future .....We need to push harder and further with the changes to our education system to align it better with the demands of the modern workforce". (2)

These two extracts, one worshipping God, the other glorifying Mammon, give the lie to the notion, fostered in totalitarian states and in the brainwashing provided by educational institutions, that Education is absolute and God-given. These two opposing views give a sharp reminder that education is a social and political construct meeting the perceived interests of states and other powerful groupings, and often in sharp tension with each other.

I shall therefore provide examples of alternative educational conceptions, which have been influential at various times, before looking critically at the principles and assumptions upon which they are based.

An Aristocratic (Intrinsic) Curriculum

(a) "Education for its Own sake"

This particular conception of education (whilst disclaiming any connection with "utility") has served the immensely useful purpose, by its very mystique, of maintaining the social distance of upper and lower classes. It has been used to great effect to justify the classical "academic" education of public school boys in the past. And by its apparently pure intrinsic nature and hence its ostensible uselessness it has presented itself as a morally superior form of education, ideal for the ruling elite. That it maintained its distance from any sort of overt instrumental activity can be seen from the inquiry by the Clarendon Commission into the nine great public schools in 1861 where it reaffirmed the Establishment view that "the classical languages and literature should continue to hold the principal place in the course of study".

Utility then was certainly not to be a justification for inclusion in this curriculum. As Dean Farrar, public school science teacher, put it when giving evidence in his appeal for Science to be included in the curriculum:

> *"And no sooner have I uttered the word "useful" than I imagine the hideous noise which will environ me, and amid the hubbub I faintly distinguish the words vulgar, utilitarian, mechanical......when it is over, I meekly repeat that it would be more useful - more rich in practical advantages, more directly available for health, for happiness, for success in the great battle of life. I for one am tired of this "worship of inutility". One would*

*really think it is a crime to aim at the material happiness
of the human race". (3)*

The extent to which the idea of a superior "education for its own sake" for
the privileged permeated the consciousness of various governments has
been referred to already – for example,

by Robert Morant, following the 1902 Education Act, in devising
the curriculum for the new secondary schools along the academic lines of
the orthodox grammar school ;

and with the 1944 Education Act, with the provision of an
unproblematic high-status academic curriculum for the "brighter" pupils
and a low-status practical curriculum for the others.

Thus, the academic curriculum, underpinned by a philosophy of proclaimed
intrinsic "education for its own sake" or "an end in itself" has been
used to maintain a social division between the high-status theoretically-
minded student, and his/her practically-orientated contemporary. And this
conception has been strengthened by its opposition to "instrumental" - or
education as a means to some other end. [Though, as discussed elsewhere,
there is no necessary separation between the two: it is quite possible in the
real world for a person to obtain intrinsic job satisfaction, whilst working
instrumentally also for a bonus.]

But the idea of an "end in itself" might itself prove to be a dead-end. P.S.
Wilson meets this challenge by introducing the concept of " instrumentally
intrinsic ":

> *"Perhaps I educationally value knowledge when I
> value it "for its own sake" or an "end in itself". But
> this won't do. My knowledge has to be instrumental
> to something or my reason for valuing it ceases to be
> intelligible at all. The question is: what educational
> ends is its functioning instrumental to? ...If knowledge
> is distinctive of education....the more you have of that
> form of knowledge the more you can therefore get."*
> *(4)*

In other words, engaging in this instrumentally intrinsic worthwhile activity,
rather than leading to a dead end, gives rise to a growing commitment
to learn more and to an increased understanding. The reference is now to

the engagement of the person rather than to knowledge itself, unwittingly confirmed by Jill Parkin, when responding to the Education Minister's claim that there is no place in university for such esoteric subjects as medieval history:

> *"Education for its own sake is easily sneered at but it gives some of the keenest enjoyment mankind knows"* (5).

In other words, it appears that here "education for its own sake" is referring to the disciplined engagement with academic knowledge, giving rise to a host of possible intrinsic human states of mind, such as enjoyment, fulfilment and satisfaction ("education for enjoyment"). And this knowledge represents the fruits of the ongoing endeavour of generations of committed intellectual workers, searching for truth and seeking to extend the boundaries of understanding . These disciplines are thus "alive" in the sense of constant growth, refinement - and in the face of sufficient counter-evidence - redefinition. They are instrumentally intrinsic and provide a major resource for the teacher with their infinite potential for growth and development. The crucial question though is: how are they to be presented to the student in the curriculum?

(b) A Subject-based Curriculum; bodies of knowledge

Corresponding to these disciplines in the curriculum are school subjects. Whilst the former can involve exciting and controversial activities in a constantly-changing and dynamic context, subjects often come across to pupils following this traditional curriculum as boring, unchanging and God-given. There is indeed a godly origin to subjects, according to John White (6), through the endeavours of the English Old Dissenters and Scottish Presbyterians in the 18th century and beyond. Believing that personal salvation depended on a comprehensive grasp of the nature of God's world, they classified and organised this world into discrete subjects. But - as we have seen in a previous chapter - over the years, in more secular and competitive times, subject associations have been formed to promote their separate interests. In order to enhance their claims for inclusion in the academic curriculum, they have developed and emphasised their modes of enquiry and conceptual schemes, coming to resemble academic subjects in the process.

A philosophy of "ends in themselves" and the demands of examinations can all too easily lead to living academic disciplines being transformed into inert bodies of knowledge - commodities - of no apparent relevance to the unmotivated student, particularly if no explanation of the purpose of the activity is provided. The limitations of school subjects as vehicles for emancipatory learning have been shown by M.F.D. Young (7) to lie in the underlying organising principles of literacy (written rather than oral work) individualism (rather than cooperative group work) abstractness (rather than the concrete, here-and-now) and unrelatedness. With regard to the latter, if the school knowledge is unrelated to the student's life experiences, it will be external to the learner and unproductive. The emphasis then will be upon memorisation rather than comprehension and will reinforce the "cult of the fact" (celebrated in mainstream culture in such high status TV programmes as University Challenge and Mastermind). Furthermore, as we saw before, the above principles accord with the culture of the educated middle classes, so that children coming from such a background will have an immense educational advantage over those from the lower classes, where there is often a relative absence of literature in the home, communication is largely oral in a linguistically limited code, and family discussions are at a premium.

A Bourgeois (Instrumental) Curriculum - Utilitarianism: Education for Survival

It has historically been the rich and privileged, whose material needs were satisfied, who have talked of "education for its own sake" to justify a superior classical education. Working class radicals, as we saw earlier, talked instead of "really useful knowledge" as a means of improving their lot in life. The burgeoning middle classes also demanded an education which was useful. Whilst this led to a cluster of private schools and colleges opening in the mid nineteenth to meet their proclaimed needs, it was no more than tinkering, adding a few "useful" subjects to the existing curriculum. It was left to a group of middle-class intellectuals, the Philosophic Radicals, to bring fresh philosophical ideas and new approaches to the problems of society. They were often called Benthamites after their leading light Jeremy Bentham (1748-1832) a child prodigy from a Tory family who trained as a lawyer but became radicalised through his disenchantment with the legal and administrative system of the day and decided to reform the law rather than practice it.

The basic guiding principle of Bentham was that the sole purpose of reform was the promotion of happiness, of pleasure over pain. This principle of "the greatest happiness of the greatest number " has become inextricably linked with Utilitarianism and served to influence the development of a more humane climate in this country, leading to the introduction of State education and the reduction of child labour. It needs to be stressed, however, that Bentham was in the bourgeois tradition, being in favour of a laissez-faire economy and the maintenance of the class system . Education of the working-class was to be sufficient only for them to be able to make some educational decisions for themselves.

The basic premise of Utilitarianism, then, was that pain and pleasure were the "sovereign masters" of man, and it was for them alone to guide our actions. The "principle of utility" following from this was that every action should be judged right or wrong according to how far it tends to promote or diminish the happiness of the community. Whilst utility was now a valid educational aim, little work seems to have been done at this stage in designing a coherent utilitarian curriculum. It was left to Herbert Spencer (1820-1903) later in the century, to put his mind to this task.

Herbert Spencer: Which Knowledge is of Most Worth?

In 1859 Charles Darwin had launched the scientific theory of evolution with his "Origin of Species", giving the concept of evolution scientific credibility as a subject for empirical enquiry. Two years later Spencer had coined the expression "survival of the fittest" and used the concept of "survival" as the basis for his utilitarian curriculum. In his essays on Education he posed the question "Which knowledge is of most worth" before proceeding to consider the relative values of knowledge: (8)

HERBERT SPENCER (1820 – 1903)

Born in Derby in 1820 into a family of teachers. Obtained a job as a civil engineer in 1836, where he first experienced the exploitation of workers by bosses. Became sub-editor of the Economist before turning to full-time writing, in such fields as social evolution and psychology. His health began to decline when he was in his sixties but before his death he was nominated for the Nobel Prize for Literature.

HERBERT'S SPENCER'S ULITARIAN CURRICULUM

"WHAT KNOWLEDGE IS OF MOST WORTH?"

"Our first step must obviously be to classify, in order of their importance, the leading kinds of activity which constitute human life:

1. those activities directly ministering to self preservation, demanding a knowledge of physiology;
2. those activities indirectly ministering to self-preservation, requiring a knowledge of mechanics, biology, geology, chemistry and physics;
3. those activities having for their end the rearing and disciplining of offspring, requiring some acquaintance with physiology and the elementary truths of psychology;
4. those activities involved in the maintenance of proper social and political relations, needing an education in descriptive and comparative sociology, interpreted in the light of biology and physiology;
5. miscellaneous activities making up the leisure part of life, best appreciated through knowledge." (8)

Principles of learning
experiential, rather than rote;
sensory interaction with environment;
acquisition of knowledge naturally through exploration
        content to be arranged in terms of increasing complexity, from concrete to abstract.

Spencer's curriculum can in its contemporary context be regarded as progressive, even in today's world. It offered a promising bourgeois alternative to the inert gentry classical curriculum, in terms of its direct relevance both to the life of the individual and society. It was therefore a threat to the status quo, and could be expected to attract serious criticism from the Establishment. And so it proved. His contradictory attitudes made him an easy target: for example, it is difficult to reconcile his individualist concept of "survival of the fittest" with the altruistic "greatest happiness of the greatest number". His obsession with the educational potential of science and his reduction of all human activities to a scientific basis was also absurd (in anticipation perhaps of neuroscience – see later). For instance, he believed that poetry was good insofar as it paid attention to those laws of nervous action which speech obeyed. In the end – not least because it was fundamentally opposed to the ideas and interests of the ruling class – Spencer's "worthwhile" curriculum never took root. The same fate has awaited other more recent attempts to construct a curriculum based upon similar utilitarian ideas (9) and at odds with the prevailing academic tradition.

A Person-centred Approach - "Educating Interests"

The curricula described above may, in their various ways, be said to serve the "two cultures", the academic and the business interest. More recently the emphasis has shifted to the student interest. This shift is illustrated nicely by Paul Hirst, who, as we have seen, had earlier constructed an influential, rational model of the "forms of knowledge" to provide the base for an intrinsic approach to education. He now sees the forms of knowledge, not as intrinsic, but as instrumental in servicing a person's wants and satisfactions:

> *"We must shift from seeing education as primarily concerned with knowledge and see it as primarily concerned with social practices…….. Reason, knowledge and understanding (now) have the instrumental functions of helping us to discern, develop and order coherently those basically given elements of wants and satisfactions from which the good life is to be composed……what constitutes the good life for an individual can in detail be determined only by that particular person. The content of education must therefore be conceived as primarily initiation into certain substantive social practices" (10)*

This shift in the conception of education by Hirst hints at a totally different approach to educating children. Instead of a curriculum being imposed from above on the learner (justified, of course, by its being "in the pupil's interest") the curriculum, if such it can still be called, is built around the pupil's own interests, what he / she finds relevant to the good life. This person-centred approach requires, of course, a fundamentally different pedagogy. Instead of the teacher delivering bodies of knowledge, he / she now has the considerable problem of responding productively to the student "voice" (using the intellectual and rational resources mentioned above by Hirst) so that the process is genuinely educative.

It is not, however, a case of "anything goes". As well as it being an interest "owned" by the pupil, it must also be serious in the sense of it being moral and capable of being educated. According to P.S. Wilson (11) an interest is an inclination to pay attention to something, enter into an appropriate active relationship with it and submit to the discipline of trying to understand what is appropriate to that interest. The interest can be maintained by providing an enabling environment; that is enabling the learner to appreciate and understand his / her interest more fully. In short, the person-centred teacher helps the learner to structure experience and activity in ways which enable him / her to see more of their intrinsic point and value – an extremely difficult and challenging role for the teacher, involving a reconceptualisation of "teaching" and requiring a sufficient injection of resources by the state.

One person-centred approach has developed its own vocabulary and teaching strategies. The basic underlying assumption for this approach is "constructivist"; that is learners construct their own meanings in solving problems of their own choosing by active, experiential learning. It has its roots in psychotherapy and requires the acquisition of new competencies on the part of the teacher. For example, the teacher, apart from being an instructor, has to:

> be a facilitator of learning, creating an environment for engagement;
> establish trusting, non-threatening and empathetic relationships with the learner;
> be a good listener, knowing when to intervene and when to withdraw;
> ensure that the learner owns both the process and the product.

A highly significant aspect of authentic person-centred education is that it shifts the curriculum mode from "delivery" towards the "emancipatory" (qv). It is the student who makes the running, with the teacher responding appropriately. It is clearly a pedagogy making extreme demands upon the competence of the teacher and needs to be reflected in teacher training courses, which currently are moving in the opposite direction towards tight uncreative control of the pupil-teacher relationship.

Many ambitious claims are made for this sort of learning. For example, that it:

> aims to develop each individual's true potential, including intellect, feelings, and creativity;
> helps children to exercise power with responsibility;
> stresses the centrality of human relationships;
> helps children become reflective, resourceful and discriminating. (12)

The Education Department has recently introduced the concept of "personalised learning" into its advice to teachers. (13) Information so far is sparse but a consultant Stephen Heppell (Heppell.net) throws some light on it. According to him personalised learning "looks at where you want to go, the result you want to achieve and asks for collaboration from the student in order to get there". The "you" refers to the teacher, not the learner, so personalised learning, according to this, represents another way of getting the learner to meet someone else's objectives. There is therefore no logical connection between the Department's idea of personalised learning and the person-centred education described above.

What is Education For?

Whilst there have been several attempts, detailed in this narrative, to outline educational aims in official reports, these have been largely ignored by governments. It will not have gone unnoticed that in recent years there has been a marked absence of attempts by the State to reach any sort of consensus on the purpose of schooling. Any attempt will surely prove highly contentious, given the cultural nature of the education, but this is no excuse for shirking the attempt to seek some compromise and arrive at an accommodation in the form of a working hypothesis. In the absence of such a framework, and with the inexorable progress of a predatory corporate hegemony, education has come to be identified – not with desirable, fulfilling personal qualities – but with servicing a capitalist economy. As has been suggested this development can only lead to stunted, diminished individuals, ironically incapable of producing the creative, entrepreneurial, well-balanced people which the economy so desperately needs. It is clear that such an approach will certainly fail to deal with the problems addressed by this book : the development of personal and moral autonomy both for the good of the individual and society. What other responses might there be, then to the question " What is education for ?"

It is a question which would be treated with disdain by those purists who are wedded to the first model above (Education for its Own Sake). They would claim, indeed, that its supreme value lay in its having no extrinsic utility whatsoever (although we have shown that in reality it has the greatest possible utility in preserving social stratification.) But for a book concerned with the education of future generations to live fulfilling and responsible lives, this model, in its pure form, has little to offer.

The second model is based upon a utilitarian philosophy and promises, on the surface, to maximise human happiness. But its application in practice has not only proved to be biased, favouring the privileged, but its promise of "happiness" is hardly the holy grail of human fulfilment. It can also be said to violate the principle of individual human rights in denying personal autonomy.

The third model, of person-centred education, on the other hand, is free from this objection, but suffers from the absence of a safeguard to ensure that these rights are exercised in the common, rather than selfish interest.

It is "Education for the Good Society" based upon equality, freedom, solidarity, justice which would seem to meet the limitations of those models above - and underpinned by such abstract moral principles as virtue, integrity, empathy and respect for the truth. But - while admirable in themselves - these principles will be subject to differing interpretations and provide ambiguous guidance for action. It is **education for empowerment**, set in a more concrete context, which can provide more positive guidance for the alleviation of a social malaise characterised by the following features:

> political apathy;
> economic illiteracy;
> individualist materialism;
> environmental ignorance.
> cultural "dumbing-down".

Such education will clearly involve the relevant base of knowledge and critical understanding . But it will also involve the right attitudes, born of confidence in and love of learning and a determination to take appropriate action where necessary. It is, in other words, the development of personal and moral autonomy in a democratic context, which I took as the primary educational focus, concerned to produce the active citizen rather than the passive consumer, with the understanding and confidence to take on those challenges, environmental, political and social, waiting in the future. For example, our future citizen will need :

> to be equipped with the necessary environmental awareness and understanding in order to appreciate the significance of ecological and climatic change;

> to be able to fully appreciate the political context in which these challenges take place, and to critically evaluate evidence being adduced to support a particular position;

and to be aware of the social impact of technical and political developments, both locally, nationally and globally.

All this, of course, is a counsel of perfection. The implications for education, in terms of both its matter and manner, are daunting, and some of these will be taken up in more detail in the next chapter. But in the absence of support from a political party offering democratic alternatives to our present way of life and its accompanying social malaise, public impact will be limited. Teachers will be compelled, once again, to swim against the tide and make what headway they can in leading students towards the "Good Life".

The Material World

The examples described above indicate that education models and theories such as those described above tend to be idealist in nature, ignoring the constraints imposed by the material world. Nevertheless, these models are available as resources for the teacher in the classroom. For example, an education for personal autonomy - the enabling of a fulfilled, moral and informed journey through life - implies a productive engagement with the disciplined forms of knowledge, the acquisition of competences for survival, and the development of significant personal interests, all features of the above educational models. But the material world places severe constraints upon such an education, some of which I consider below.

Reproduction of the workforce - the examination system

One of the more obvious tensions arises from the demand by the state for schools to sort out their pupils into future career paths through public examinations. As we have seen, the competitive ethos underpinning examinations arose out of a burgeoning capitalist culture of the early 1900's, leading to the emergence of private examination boards. These boards have recently been in crisis for a variety of reasons:

the rising cost, exacerbated by the recent extravagant offer of the right of examinees to appeal and have their exam paper remarked;
the increase in both the number and complexity of examinations;
the shortage of examiners;
the increase in plagiarism, aided by the Internet (but easily resolved by competent tutoring and a short viva);

public disquiet, for example, at both the structure of the examinations (position of A-level etc), complaints of inadequate marking and charges of falling standards. This disquiet has been exacerbated by a continuing number of fiascos resulting from government incompetence. (14)

If, of course, examinations come to lack credibility with a public now more than ever attuned to the idea of "fair competition", there will be a subsequent loss of confidence in the system, with the whole edifice in danger of collapse. In the face of this impending catastrophe, examination boards have gone to considerable lengths in attempting to solve such technical problems as:

validity (the test should be assessing those attributes it claims to be testing);

reliability (different markers would award the same mark / grade for the same piece of submitted work) and

comparability (for example between different examination boards and for different years).

But in the end, one has to accept that it is impossible to produce, apart from computer-marked multiple choice tests, a wholly objective examination, free from subjective elements. There is always the possibility, then, that - instead of sophisticated examinations, projects and course-work testing a variety of higher-level attributes - objective multiple-choice questions marked by computer will become the norm, further reducing the educational process to a technical exercise and illustrating the constraints material considerations place upon ideal situations.

However, my main concern here is pedagogical rather than technical. Formal examinations affect classroom relationships and practices in several ways. Apart from examinations inevitably leading and constraining the curriculum and defining what is to count as valid knowledge, they reveal the teacher as a representative of the prevailing power structure and thus as a dispenser of life chances in a competitive environment, highlighting the successes and failures in the process and encouraging the development of a delinquent sub-culture. It is also the individual student, rather than the group, who is the focus of the examination, reinforcing the perception of society as individualistic. But perhaps the most significant distortion of the educational process lies in the nature of the engagement of student with curriculum content. Instead of this engagement being intrinsic, knowledge is seen instrumentally as a commodity to be exchanged in the market place for certain rewards. In short, there is a contradiction between education as involving intrinsically worthwhile activities and schooling as being instrumental in advancing career prospects.

Examinations do violence, then, to the nature of knowledge, as well as to the quality of teacher-pupil relationships. Although attempts have been made to introduce project work into examination syllabuses, it is doubtful whether the authentic quality of disinterested disciplined enquiry can ever be captured under examination conditions. HM Inspectorate in the past has had cause to complain, for example, for overloading the modern world history syllabuses with factual material that the "intrinsic interest and the essential flavour of history were being squeezed out". (15) A more subtle objection is raised by Lawrence Stenhouse when he quotes the literary critic Northrop Frye:

> *"From this point of view (the analysis of a poem in terms of knowledge and understanding) poetry is something to be explained, and the notion that any kind of commentary will ever explain any kind of poetry is of course vulgar. Even if there is a hidden meaning, a poem which contains no more than what an explanation of that meaning can translate should have been written in the form of the explanation in the first place." (16)*

For similar reasons, writers complain bitterly about their creative work being used for examination purposes; for example, the playwright and poet Adrian Mitchell. (17) All of which points up the inevitable and apparently irreconcilable tensions between the demands of education and the demands of the socio-economic order. As well as the need to ensure that examinations follow and do not lead the curriculum.

The Changing Needs of the Economy

With the growing dominance of a corporate culture has come a shift in curriculum demands towards the instrumental, from the liberal to the vocational. The growing preference for applied over pure subjects as students seek to enhance their career prospects is clearly revealed in a ten-year comparison of A-level subject choices:

Subject	1996	2006	% change
Business Studies	29100	30648	+5.3
Chemistry	40455	40064	- 1.0
Classical Studies	7345	6168	- 16.2
English	86627	86640	+ 0.2
French	27490	14650	- 46.7
Geography	42876	32522	- 24.1
Law	11982	15241	+27.2
Maths	67442	55982	- 17
Physics	32801	27368	-16.6
Technology	11061	18684	+68.9 (see note 18)

And as far as university entrance is concerned, English was the only non-vocational subject among the top ten choices (19) It would be simplistic to draw too firm a conclusion about these trends (the media, for example, claim that students are simply opting for easier subjects). Some of these subjects start from a low baseline and there are also several apparent anomalies. Nonetheless there are serious implications for the future of the "hard" sciences in higher education, with some universities closing down science departments, whilst extending the number of vocational subjects on offer.

This may be highly significant for the future of liberal education: a drop in the number of good science graduates will lead to a fall in the supply of competent science teachers in schools and the beginning of a downward spiral. But how important is it for our future economic prosperity? There is little empirical support for a direct cause-effect relationship between the economy and education. However, economic experts assure us that we have now entered the knowledge economy. A Work Foundation Report (20) claims that Europe has a knowledge economy at least as big as the United States, employing 40% of the workforce (rising by 24% in the past decade compared with 6% overall employment growth), but lagging behind in productivity because of a lack of investment in the knowledge base. That, then, is the clear message of the above Report. But we are not told by these experts what kind of political economy or knowledge they have in mind - whether technical or practical, analytic or intuitive etc. And the categories they supply are so unexceptional that we are more or less left where we were, and it is difficult to see what are the implications for schools and colleges. (21)

Recently the Treasury commissioned the report "Prosperity for all in the

Global Economy: World Class Skills" from the businessman Lord Leitch. (22) This talks of:

> low-level skills level 2 (5 GCSE's (A*-C) or the vocational equivalent),
> intermediate skills level 3 (2 or more A-levels)
> and high skills level 4 (foundation degree level).

Out of 30 OECD countries, the UK comes 17th on low skills, 20th on intermediate skills and 11th on high skills. Unsurprisingly, the Leitch Report recommends increased skill attainments at all levels. More interestingly it recommends both a strengthening of the employer voice and an increase in employer investment, together with a much-awaited pledge to voluntarily train more employees at work. There is thus a possibility at last of employees being initiated into the culture of work and the development of practical knowledge. Otherwise, we remain at the level of technical skills, the limitations of which have been discussed earlier.

Material deprivation

When dealing with the interaction of the material world and education, mention must also be made of the major constraints placed upon what might be considered the ideal teaching-learning situation, by problems of deprivation in the wider society, such as widespread poverty (i.e. below 60% median net disposable income). It is a truism that in our present society the rich get richer as the poor get comparatively poorer. What is not as well known is that over the last two decades of the twentieth century, the relative poverty among Britain's children tripled, so that, according to Oxfam (23), almost 1 in 3 children (almost 4 million) now live in relative poverty. This can vary dramatically according to location: it is claimed, for instance, that 50% of children in Inner London are in poverty.

It is difficult to overestimate the damaging educational impact of low wages and unemployment on the life chances of children belonging to poor families. We have already dealt with the interaction of home and school. The story of the material determinants of educational opportunity continues with higher education. According to the Sutton Trust, whilst students from independent schools make up only 7% of the school population, they account for 39% of entrants to top universities. And whilst those from less affluent social classes make up 50% of the school population, they account for only 13% of entrants. The situation is even worse for those living in really poor areas: 33% of the population but only 6% of entrants. The Trust report goes on to claim that there are "300 missing students":

> *"Every year there are some 300 well-qualified young people attending state schools and colleges who are not among the 30,000 who are admitted to our dozen or so leading universities, despite achieving grades as good as or better than entry requirements". (24)*

The overall result is that the rich are still able to buy privilege and top jobs for their offspring through the public school system, reproducing social divisions in the process.

Common sense alone tells us that factors associated with poverty such as ill-health, malnutrition, and poor, overcrowded accommodation, redolent of the early nineteenth century, make a mockery of the idea of "equality of educational opportunity". As we saw earlier, the situation is compounded by the fact that middle class parents tend to move out of deprived areas to get their children into "better" schools higher in the league table, leaving the poor to be concentrated in "sink" schools which consequently continue sinking. When one also considers that in our multi-ethnic country, a school can encounter as many as 53 different languages, not only are the idealist notions of education outlined above put into perspective but one can only admire teachers who cope with such situations and achieve, according to Ofsted, "outstanding results". (25)

The Classroom as a Target-meeting Production Line

As we have already seen, New Public Management, in direct line from the capitalist mode of production, has now been applied to the public services in a culture of target - setting. For example:

> *"In 1997, the government set ambitious national literacy and numeracy targets that by 2002, 80% 11-year olds (Key Stage 2) will reach level 4 in English and 75% in Maths."(26)*

Since then, more and more ambitious targets have been set amid official claims that targets are raising the level of performance across the board.

There are, however, many objections to these claims and to the whole concept of target setting:

Targets are arbitrary and non-contextual

Consider the following example taken at random from the National Curriculum levels for Science:

> Level 2
>> Pupils respond to suggestions about how to find things out and with help make their own suggestions about how to collect data to answer questions.
>> They use simple texts to find information.
>
> Level 3
>> Pupils respond to suggestions and put forward their own ideas about how to find the answer to a question. They use simple texts to find information. (27)

There is no significant difference between these two levels: they could be interchanged in different contexts without affecting the overall logic. Yet they could be the basis for government claims for improvements in performance. Such is the result of targets being expressed in general terms, indifferent to specific context.

Targets are not research-based

The targets devised by the Education Department would have been regarded as invalid even by the proponents of Taylorism's "command and control". The work involved has not been adequately analysed to provide a basis for subsequent judgments. Jonathan Solity, of Early Reading Research, is particularly critical:

> *"The government has shown time and time again that its solutions to perceived problems in education are extremely expensive and invariably flawed... This is particularly true of the Numeracy and Literacy Strategy. I suspect matters will only change for the better when the teaching profession takes the lead in demanding that whatever they are advised to teach, from whatever source, is supported by research which they can evaluate and where they have a degree of autonomy in determining what and how they teach." (28)*

Targets are aspirational rather than developmental

The constant search for increased "productivity" leads to targets being introduced for ever younger children and to levels being raised irrespective of child development, with the result that many children do not reach them. The literacy specialist Sue Palmer formulates the problem in this way:

> *"The Department for Education and Skills has taken the targets agenda down to the cradle….whilst developmental milestones come naturally to human infants, writing and punctuation do not, and this conflation of child development and educational objectives is very dangerous…..Many children are now required to reach "literacy objectives" which are developmentally way beyond them…Nursery nurses and childminders could be drawn into the same target-driven insanity now rife in the education system."* (29)

And recent research commissioned by the Institute of Education shows that teaching young children to use basic phonics and write simple sentences does not improve their chances of success later, although encouraging them to talk does!

Targets are fundamentally misconceived

Perhaps the most telling criticism comes from John Seddon who worked in the car industry with systems other than "Command Control". Seddon has translated his ideas to the public sector, replacing targets – plucked from the air - with what he calls "capability measures", derived from the work itself:

> *"Targets focus people on the wrong thing, the things they must do in order to survive, not improvement. Capability measures encourage people to focus their ingenuity on how the work works. Targets have no value in understanding and improving performance; capability measures help both understand and improve the work…. because they put understanding in the right place: in the heads of the people who do the work…. In the name of modernisation Government has created ever-poorer*

performing public sector organisations and created within them demoralised and disaffected people. Our public sector organisations live in a dark age. It is time Ministers got out of management." (30)

John Seddon thus provides an answer to those bureaucrats who argue that without targets "anything goes", with classrooms descending into anarchy.

"Happiness" and the Therapeutic School

Despite the arguments above, the Education Department repeatedly assures us "targets are here to stay". So much, then, for the educative influence of producer capitalism. The other side of the coin is, of course, consumerism. In accordance with the principle of capital accumulation, it is necessary, not only to maintain one's share of the market, but for this market to constantly expand. To this end, sophisticated and expensive marketing and branding strategies – often based upon psychological theories - are brought into play to seduce the vulnerable customer. Even one's worth comes to be defined in terms, not of human values, but of buying power. We are witnessing in fact a general debasing of those cultural values which have served to inspire, integrate and give meaning to civilisation, by a general process of "dumbing down", providing instant gratification and appealing to the baser instincts of mankind. (In the process, what may have been formerly seen in intrinsic terms - nobody would have asked what a great painting was for - is now likely to be considered in instrumental terms for its monetary value – 'Flog it!'.) In short, values in a consumerist culture are seen in terms of marketability.

Commercial culture also holds out a false promise of happiness. Cultural production has now become an industry where audiences are cynically manipulated and left with no choice but to be passive, unthinking and docile recipients. For Adorno (31) consumerism so saturates cultural sensibility that happiness lacks any imaginative dimension beyond the "contemptible fulfilment of commodity desire and its retail therapy" through an "identity-rotting blandishment of kitsch, saccharine films, TV and above all advertising".

Perhaps in this bleak "identity-rotting" environment, it is not surprising that clinical depression is on the increase and happiness is in short supply, so much so that the economist Richard Layard has been anointed "happiness czar". Happiness may be thought to be a highly subjective experience, but Layard claims objectivity for it by combining personal statements he has obtained with neuroscience. One result of this approach is the belief that the sum total of happiness has not increased with personal wealth:

> *"Over the last fifty years, we in the West have enjoyed unparalleled economic growth. We have better homes, cars, holidays, jobs, education and above all health. According to standard economic theory, this should have made us happier. But surveys show otherwise. When Britons or Americans are asked how happy they are, they report no improvement over the last 50 years. More people suffer from depression, and crime – another indicator of dissatisfaction – is also much higher…….When material discomfort has been banished, extra income becomes much less important than our relationships with each other: with family, with friends and in the community. The danger is that we sacrifice relationships too much in pursuit of higher income." (32)*

Layard approaches happiness from an economic perspective. The psychologist Oliver James (33) on the other hand extends this analysis by concluding that the basic cause of mental illness is the materialism accompanying "selfish capitalism" with the following characteristics:

>business success judged by share price;
>privatisation of public utilities;
>suppression of trade unions;
>minimal regulation of business;
>low taxation of the rich.

James talks of infection by the "affluenza" virus, spread particularly effectively in our schools, to explain the emphasis on instrumental rather than intrinsic values leading to an increase in the modern world of depression, anxiety, substance abuse and personality disorder. And it is the Anglo-Saxon countries which seem to have been particularly susceptible to the affluenza virus. According to James, the English-speaking nations are twice as likely to suffer from mental illness as those in mainland Western Europe, whilst the most mentally - ill nation is the USA. R.G. Wilkinson, through extensive epidemiological researches into the major sources of mental ill-health concludes that the main causes are the psychosocial effects of income inequality. With Kate Pickett (34) these researches were extended to other aspects of personal dysfunction, through which they were able to come to the remarkable conclusion that living in a more equal society generally means - not just for the poor - better mental health, longer life, less violence, less obesity, better educational performance and a richer community life - in short, a much healthier, better functioning society.

It is among young people where clinical depression (manifested by a combination of symptoms such as lack of interest, loss of energy, suicidal thoughts, loss of appetite, sleeplessness and behavioural changes) is growing fastest and is estimated currently to amount to 10% of the school population. In response to this growing crisis, the Prime Minister's Strategy Unit has explored the potential for the introduction of "happiness" policies (more accurately termed positive psychology) and recommends that happiness lessons be taught in schools. (35) These lessons would be based upon the theories of Martin Seligman, aimed at enabling people to live healthier lives with a greater sense of well-being, through attention to :

pleasure;

engagement;

meaning,

where "meaning" is defined as something larger and more permanent than oneself. (36). Trials began in 2007 for 11-year-olds in state schools of "happiness / antidepression" lessons to counteract the increase in depression, anti-social behaviour and self-harm. Cognitive behavioural techniques based upon role play will be employed to build up self-esteem and challenge negative thoughts. Martin Seligman himself has been drafted in to train teachers and develop programmes which will be evaluated by the Education Department.

The government clearly believes that both a decrease in anti-social behaviour and an improvement in learning are dependent on increasing the pupil's emotional literacy (what we would have once called emotional maturity). It experimented with the SEBS Strategy, for the teaching of Social, Behavioural and Emotional Skills, before investing £20 million in an "emotional literacy initiative", where emotional literacy is defined by such qualities as:

knowing our emotions: self-awareness - recognising a feeling at it happens;

managing our emotions: handling those feelings of which we aware;

harnessing our emotions in identifying and reaching goals;

recognising emotions in others;
handling relationships,
often summarised as "solving emotional problems".

Schools will now have a responsibility for improving children's emotional and psychological well-being and will be expected to combat factors that are likely to lead to poor mental health or mental disorders. NICE (National Institute for Health and Clinical Excellence) has drawn up "well-being scales" measuring attributes such as attentiveness, the ability to form good relationships and confidence. They involve putting 14 statements to the pupil (from the age of 4) followed by ticking the appropriate box. For example:

"I've been feeling good about myself"……. Always; often; sometimes; rarely; never
"I've been dealing with problems well" ….. etc

The measure of a school's success in making pupils happy and developing a sense of well-being will then be assessed by these scales.

Psychometricians have been quick to move into this field and to question the validity of self-reports, emphasising the need to replace them with the "reading" of emotions. For example, the replacing of "How good are you at perceiving emotions" by the interpretation of the emotions represented in a picture. To satisfy the urge for measurement, they have also developed an "Emotional intelligence quotient" (EIQ) so that emotions may be quantified. For instance, EIQ 16 deals with 16 emotional competencies in four areas:

perceiving emotions,
facilitating thought,
understanding emotions and
managing emotions,

leading to the production of numerical scales.

Many schools seem to be taking up these ideas enthusiastically, but Professor Kathryn Ecclestone adds a cautionary note:

> "There is no robust, independent evidence that making children and young people talk about their feelings in formal rituals at schools will develop lifelong emotional literacy and well-being. Inserting a vocabulary of emotional vulnerability, where children are encouraged to feel different or told they have low self-esteem, is

likely to encourage the very feelings of depression and hopelessness it is supposed to eradicate. Although ideas about well - being seem benign, they are based on judgemental assumptions about 'appropriate' feelings and how to deal with them. But if you try to challenge their educational bandwagon, you are accused of being in "emotional denial". (36)

To which, whilst accepting that schools should indeed help pupils become more emotionally mature, I would add the following points:

(1) having largely removed from the curriculum opportunities for real holistic emotional development through the performing and expressive arts, the government is now incorporating, in its lurch towards technicism, a reduced and fragmented technical alternative . And the sum of these fragments is less than the whole.

(2) talk of emotional "skills" is both vulgar and dehumanising .

(3) a classroom with a ruthlessly competitive ethos is not the place to be talking of developing (let alone measuring) emotional literacy. Once again the gap between rhetoric and reality becomes glaringly apparent. Whilst the rhetoric of government educational documents stresses "intellectual, physical, moral, social, spiritual and emotional development" the reality is of repeated tests of the former only, in a highly public arena.

(4) the initiative is embedded in a dominant business culture, where competition is the order of the day and Emotional Intelligence Quotients (like other psychometric constructs) are significantly used - not to further emotional development - but to select for employment and promotion.

(5) if happiness and emotional maturity depend partly on having meaning and belief in something larger than one's-self, then a largely meaningless curriculum is hardly likely to do the trick.

I have dealt with several different conceptions of education in this chapter, each in a different context. It is worth repeating what I take to be the fundamental educational focus for the purpose of this book: the development of personal and moral autonomy in a democratic context to which all other aims are secondary. Briefly, this would involve the continuing development of basic competences and concepts, as well as an initiation into the major modes of enquiry. On the other hand, it would necessitate creative engagement with the arts and humanities. In other words this education is designed to lead to the development of what is commonly called the "whole person", able to exercise informed choice and take on the role of active citizen, rather than passive consumer. Putting this more formally, the curriculum would for the most part be practical in form and the pedagogy dialogic.

I can imagine several objections to the above proposal:

(1) to those who complain about the instrumental emphasis of this suggestion, I would point out that I have previously rejected the idealistic separation of the intrinsic and the instrumental in the material world. The important question to ask is: "What are these activities instrumental in bringing about?" Unless we educate all our children as fully as possible along the lines indicated here (and developed more in the next chapter) future generations will have neither the awareness, will, understanding nor the competences to face up to the awesome challenges lying ahead, threatening to destroy our civilised way of life.

(2) to those who would argue that not all children are capable of being educated in the ways suggested, I would oppose the ruling elite's propagation of the dogma that human capabilities are differentiated in terms of the social hierarchy with Jerome Bruner's hypothesis that any child can be taught any subject in an intellectually honest way. I would also refer the reader to the exciting and inspiring musical developments which have recently taken place in Venezuela, which are rich in educational implications - and which I briefly summarise below .

EL SISTEMA: "SOCIAL ACTION FOR MUSIC " (FESOJIV)

It was in 1975 that the Venezuelan economist and musician Jose Abreu founded "Social Action for Music" as part of his vision of the orchestra representing the ideal form of society, helping
"the fight of a poor and abandoned child against everything that opposes his full realisation as a human being. Music produces an irreversible transformation in a child. What music gives him remains an indelible part of who he is forever."
Abreu began his project in a ramshackle room with a few instruments and 11 poor children. Such was the enthusiasm generated amongst these deprived children that the project rapidly expanded so that there are now said to be 300,000 children in the system in over 170 orchestras for children and over 200 for young people. Students are given free instruments and training both by trained musicians and by other more gifted children. Instruments are of course very valued commodities, so they are usually taken home for safe keeping, whilst some children are trained to make and repair their instruments. It is claimed that almost a million children, 90% from deprived backgrounds, have so far passed through the system in 270 learning centres ("nucleos"), starting with such basics as

learning rhythms at the age of 2, progressing to an instrument at the age of 4 and playing in an orchestra at 6! Indeed, arising out of what was conceived as primarily a social experiment has emerged the Simon Bolivar orchestra, of top-rank quality, playing not just Latin American music but - what might be considered to be culturally alien - European classical music. The estimated annual budget for such an ambitious scheme varies wildly, but is clearly in the region of $50 million. Largely provided by the government but also with some loans provided by the banking system - a measure of confidence from commercial interests.

It is difficult to overestimate the educational and social significance of these exciting developments. Children, who would otherwise have remained in the gutter, forming part of a criminal underclass, have found a new sense of purpose and interest, acquiring, apart from musical competences, social habits of cooperation, trust and respect. They have revealed startling levels of potential, hitherto untapped in Venezuela and remaining dormant in most Western countries. And they have also questioned the notion that "high" culture is reserved for an elite class. With the Simon Bolivar Orchestra, a new classless exuberance has entered the concert hall. Only time will tell whether this is a permanent and seminal development or whether, like so many social innovations before, it will be lost without trace. [It should be added that in this country, following El Sistema, the government has established an "In Harmony Project", with an initial funding of £3 million, in three trial schools, aimed at using music to transform the lives of children in deprived areas. The children are provided with free musical instruments and tuition from professional musicians and encouraged to play in full-scale orchestras before live audiences. It will be interesting to see if such a project, in a different ideological context, can survive and flourish.]

NOTES AND REFERENCES

1. Speech to the Merchant Taylor's Company. TES Feb 6 1985
2. Speech at CBI annual dinner 16 May 2006. www.directgov.uk
3. Cited in M.J. Wiener op cit
4. P.S. Wilson op cit
5. Times Educational Supplement Oct. 7 2005
6. www. qca.org.uk/11212.html
7. M.F.D. Young op cit
8. D. McCrae, op cit
9. Robin Barrow op cit
10. Paul H. Hirst in Barrow and White op cit
11. P.S.Wilson op cit
12. C. Rogers et al op cit
13. The DfES, presenting a more ostensibly human face than hitherto, has introduced a booklet "A National Conversation about Personalised Learning" inviting all schools to join a conversation about how to develop personalised learning in the classroom. In the language of political rhetoric it will involve "high expectation of every child, given practical form by high quality teaching based on a sound knowledge and understanding of each child's needs". Perhaps we should not expect too much detail until the "conversation" is well under way. But the DfES has put forward an (incoherent) framework within which personalised learning should take place:
    assessment for learning
    effective teaching and learning
    curriculum entitlement and choice
    organising the school
    beyond the classroom.
Beware bureaucrats and consultants!
14. In 2002 AS-levels were hurriedly introduced without adequate training or resourcing of the teachers. The resultant pedagogic shambles was compounded by the fact many of the criteria-referenced maths.questions were set at an inappropriate level so that even teachers could not answer them. The result? A nicely inverted distribution curve of results, with most students failing. The knock-on effect? Hundreds of "failing" maths students withdrew their applications to study maths.at university.
15. Times Educational Supplement November 11 1983.
16. L.Stenhouse in Paedagogica Europaea 1970/71

17. Adrian Mitchell, playwright and poet, requested that none of his poems be used for examination purposes. When he discovered that his poem "Castaway" was to be used by the Northern Examination Association, he sat the exam with a group of O-level students. Marked blind by an independent examiner, he came next to bottom with 14 marks out of 40. Make of that what you will. Cited in the Guardian January 7 1986

18. Buckingham University centre for education and employment research, in Education Guardian

19. The top ten university choices were as follows: See UCAS.com

Law;

Design studies;

Psychology;

Management studies;

Business studies;

Computer Science;

English;

Medicine;

Sports Science;

Social Work. (See UCAS.com)

20. Work Foundation Oct.12 2006 "The Knowledge Economy in Europe"

21. The occupational categories were:

high/medium manufacturing

finance

business services

education and health

    whilst the recommended human skills are

        expert thinking

        complex communication skills

        routine cognitive

        routine manual

        non-routine

22. HM Treasury 5Dec. 2006 Lord Leitch publishes review of long term skills needs.

23. Oxfam (2003) UK Poverty Programme. Oxfam House, Cowley, OX4 2JY

24. www.suttontrust.com/reports/missing - 3000- Report-2.pdf

25. According to The Independent, 26 July 2006, Uphall Primary School, Ilford has pupils speaking 52 languages, with three out of

ten pupils refugee asylum-seekers. Ofsted report that "the school responds to pupils' needs. Standards are rising and pupils achieve well in spite of the fact that almost all have English as an additional language."

26. DfES Numeracy and Literacy Targets
27. QCA National Curriculum levels in Science
28. J. Solity (2003) Teaching Phonics in Context DfES Seminar
29. Ros Bayley. Bring our Two Worlds into One . TES May 2006
30. J. Seddon op cit
31. Adorno and Horkheimer op cit
32. R. Layard op cit
33. James op cit
34. R.J.Wilkinson (2005) "The Impact of Inequality". Routledge. London; and with Kate Pickett (2009) "The Spirit Level":Why More Equal Societies Almost Always Do Better" (2009) Allen Lane.London
35.Martin Seligman op cit
36.http://nannyknowsbest.blogspot.com/2007/06/madness.html

Sampson op cit described the changing composition of the boards of banks and corporations from aristocrats and Tory peers to hard-nosed businessmen, accountants and lawyers.

CHAPTER TWELVE

DEMOCRATISING EDUCATION

A democracy is more than a form of government; it is primarily a mode of associated living, of conjoint communicated experience. Upon the educational side, we note firstthe realisation of a social life in which interests are mutually penetrating."

(John Dewey "Democracy and Education.")

The Democratic Deficit

This chapter marks a point of departure. Whereas up to now I have been concerned to describe and analyse events past and present, I now take on a future orientation by considering what is essentially a prerequisite for the development of personal autonomy. Lest I stand accused of utopianism, I shall be at pains to draw attention to the obstacles lying in the way of such an approach.

It is a truism that the development of autonomy requires a democratic context for its full expression. It is therefore necessary to examine the present state of health of our democracy, beginning with our representative democratic government. Whilst in theory a representative democracy has a 100% turn-out at national elections, in practice the actual situation is rather different. At the 2005 election, only 61% bothered to vote and the New Labour government claimed a mandate to rule the country with the support of a mere 21% of the electorate - the most glaring example of our democratic malaise. There are several possible explanations for this disturbing lack of interest in the democratic process:

the dismissal of the wishes and interests of the electorate in favour of big business, with press barons dictating government policy;

a perceived lack of integrity in career politicians, who increasingly trace a direct route from university to political party and act in self-interest in furthering their career. This lack of integrity manifests itself in several ways: by a cynical indifference to truth, characterised by the phenomenon of mendacious "spinning" and even outright dishonesty. The latter quality is being increasingly revealed, as I write this, by the continuing exposure of some of their unjustified expenses claims, under a Freedom of Information Act, which MP's of all parties fought bitterly to be exempt from. It is clear from these recent revelations that Parliament itself, instead of providing us with ethical examples of behaviour, is itself short on moral autonomy.

Peter Oborne anticipates this current crisis over expense claims when he argues that the high moral standing of the Establishment has been subverted by the emergence of a new Political Class, across party divisions, and acting in its own special interests, and taking care to conceal any corruption by grooming favoured journalists to accept its version of the truth in exchange for newsworthy morsels:

> *"The Political Class has won its battle to control Britain. The civil service, Parliament, the political parties, the judiciary, the intelligence services and the media have all been captured or compromised.........It has debased the language of public discourse....the preferred method of communication involves marketing techniques drawn from the modern advertising industry....To discover the views of voters, politicians have given up canvassing them directly. Instead, political machines make use of so-called focus groups of "representative" members of the general public." (1)*

One of the alarming revelations from the above expenses row was the lack of any expression of guilt or remorse. Politicians could see nothing untoward in their behaviour, a sign that we now live in a time of "moral relativism" where absolute notions of right and wrong are meaningless. One of the root causes of such corruptions of the democratic process can at least partially be traced to the pervasive influence of neoliberalism, which is clearly no friend of democracy or traditional morality. Not only does it redefine citizens as consumers, and persons as commodities, but its favouring of deregulated market forces has led to massive inequalities and a growth in both personal greed in the upper echelons and poverty in the lower. Indeed I write in the midst of a dramatic collapse in the global financial system with an inevitable rise in unemployment. In keeping with the prevailing moral climate, whilst bankers award themselves unbelievable bonuses at the same time as people lose their jobs, the country carries on under the illusion of TINA ("there is no alternative").

The resultant emphasis upon sheer survival in a neoliberal society has thus undermined the conditions for effective political participation and has led to a society of instrumental individualism. This redefinition of citizens as consumers leads, as we have seen elsewhere, to a denial of personal autonomy and a general "dumbing down", together with what can only be described as bureaucratic manipulation.

Several consequences flow from this neoliberal hegemony. Technical processes are emphasised at the expense of values ("technical rationality") and social problems are reconceptualised in psychological terms - to be dealt with by behaviour management, as with the "therapeutic school" described earlier. What would previously have been regarded as autonomous engagement by people, now gives rise to a policy of "support" and "counselling", demanding conformity to state norms. And the principle of behaviour management gives rise to such concepts as "emotional correctness" with all its implications for social control. As Vanessa Pupavac argues:

> *"The redrawing of the citizen and state relationship has been accompanied by the erosion of the social contract conceptualisation of the citizen as an autonomous rational subject". (2)*

In short, neoliberalism is profoundly undemocratic in its social effects, nowhere better illustrated than in our schools, characterised by increasing state control with "new public management" (see elsewhere) penetrating progressively more educational niches. The school itself, for example, now has a clear hierarchical structure and is run by a head who is more of a bureaucratic manager than a collegiate member. Teachers are nowadays taught to transmit prescribed packaged knowledge for subsequent recall for the purposes of "summative" assessment; that is in order to grade pupils rather than to discover how learning might be improved. In other words, the school curriculum is technically rational in form, serving the capitalist economy by sorting pupils into future occupational categories and generally acting as an agent of social control.

These, then, are some of the obstacles standing in the way of a democratic education and the development of personal and moral autonomy. These obstacles take on greater significance at the present time of flux, when schools are being invited to become academies in the context of "parental choice" and "freedom from bureaucracy". In the absence of the detailed spelling-out of their implications, these political utterances are no more than empty slogans. These serve the interests of corporate capitalism for the foreseeable future. ("These little systems have their day; they have their day and cease to be", wrote Tennyson)

Despite this fluid and unsatisfactory state of affairs, I will attempt to operationalise some of the implications of providing a democratic learning context for the development of personal and moral autonomy. At the same time, I will resist some of the fashions beloved of politicians and continue, for the present, to call a school "a school".

The School Context

Many organisational features follow logically from a democratic conception of schooling:

> *transparency:*
> an explicit transparent constitution detailing rights and responsibilities and allowing for representation at all levels of authority as well as for shared decision-making;
> open non-authoritarian management, prepared to listen seriously to views of staff, parents and pupils;
> governors to be elected and representative of the community.

porosity:

the school to be open to members of the community and significant others, and for students to go out into the community and use it as a learning resource as community members, sharing in both community problems and activities. With such electronic aids as video-conferencing now available, the school can now be open to, for example, other schools in different parts of the world in order to establish fruitful contacts and shared experiences.

flexibility:

it is important to move away from the conventional picture of the teacher teaching the entire class behind closed doors. The democratic school demands flexibility of internal structures to meet the varying needs of pupils, so that teaching and pupil groups will fluctuate in both size and membership, with teachers working in teams when this seems appropriate. Pupils will thus be free to follow different routes of enquiry at different times enabling them to be rescued from a labelling procedure permanently condemning some of them to an inferior educational route with low status;

the increasing popularity of alternatives to school, such as home education, are persuading some heads to adopt an even more radical approach to school organisation, such as "flexi-schooling", where students spend part, rather than all, of their time within the formal school programme. It is, of course, necessary for a responsible negotiating process to be in place and for the student to maintain detailed and authentic records of all that s/he does outside the school curriculum – in itself a valuable learning process.

Curriculum Context: "negotiation" not "prescription"

The traditional prescriptive classroom has been described as a place where an adult hones his / her language skills. In what is admittedly a gross simplification of classroom reality, the "Two Thirds Rule" tells us that the teacher talks for two-thirds of the time and two thirds of this talk is concerned with instructing or questioning. This "didactic" or "monologic" teaching, concerned with the transmission of knowledge rather than the negotiation of meaning, is the classic method of classroom control. The teacher exercises his / her control by means of closed questioning of the class (questions to which the teacher knows the answers) and on receiving the required answer from a "bright" member moves on. This "IRF recitation" (initiation, response, feedback) has the result that pupils, insofar as they succeed within the terms of the lesson, take over both the teacher's meaning and frame of reference. (4) This approach supports the delivery model of the technical curriculum, where knowledge is seen as objective and unproblematic ("positivism").

The key element in a negotiated curriculum, on the other hand, is the student voice, both individual and collective. Instead of being heard only in the "recitation" described above, students are now actively encouraged to articulate their concerns and interests as the basis for further learning, concerns which could include school matters, such as general policies, the curriculum and personal concerns - as well as community issues. The teacher has previously vested his authority in specialised subject knowledge which has been transmitted to the learner. He / she must now acquire totally new and demanding competences in this new situation, competences which verge on the psychotherapeutic, where specialised subject knowledge serves the secondary purpose of a resource for learning. As mentioned earlier, these competences will include the following :

be a good listener, knowing when to be silent and when to intervene;
establish trusting and empathetic relationships in what should be seen as a joint endeavour between teacher and student;
be a facilitator of learning, establishing an "enabling environment".

Many features of democratic teaching are already being taken up in varying degrees by enterprising and dedicated teachers, prepared to resist the governments's demands for social control and a delivery curriculum. But, unlike the latter, there are no hard and fast rules to guide the teacher. It is a matter of learning from experience, from in-course training and through action research. As far as broad outlines are concerned - and with the emphasis on enquiry learning - students could be introduced to the broader types of questions, which may both be relevant and serve to make the project manageable. Fundamental questions, for example, which the teacher could draw attention to, particularly when there is a political dimension to the enquiry include:

what do you mean?
how do you know?
in whose interests is this?
why are things like this ?

248

Reporting back by the student is also important, with subsequent discussions allowing both a sharpening of focus and new directions. A new teacher also quickly comes to realise that teaching is an excellent way of learning. Pupils must not be denied this opportunity, but should be encouraged to teach each other

Although much of curriculum negotiation will lie within the practical / emancipatory mode there may well be times when the teacher has to revert to a technical mode - when, for example, giving instruction in basic skills. And for the enquiry to be other than fact-gathering, the student must begin to acquire both the necessary competences and knowledge foundations. For example:

Enabling competences:

critical literacy, functional mathematics (and "functional" everything else !);

such processes as analysis, synthesis and evaluation, within specific contexts;

social competences, to be "caught" rather than "taught" in a democratic context.

Substantive foundations:

basic concepts and structures of major disciplines;

knowledge of local and national politics, coordinated with Active Citizenship;

media studies, to bring a critical perspective to contested topics.

[The Internet, used critically, will be of immense value here, for exploring ideas and pursuing investigative paths. It will also enable students to work collaboratively, to make contact with relevant experts and link up with parents and the outside community, including children with different cultures in other countries. With students gaining in confidence and deriving positive experiences from their enquiries, the basis for life-long education will be established. And with activities being taken outside the school, both to involve and share with adults, it is possible for the elements of a genuine democratic learning community to be established - an important point I return to later, under "the Learning Society"].

A Cautionary Note

Since teachers will probably have had little or no formal training in this mode of learning, initial attempts to introduce a negotiated curriculum will have a very experimental quality and teachers will need all the support possible, perhaps by working in teams and on an apprenticeship basis. A further difficulty arises if the students have been exposed to the prescriptive delivery curriculum long enough to come to firm conclusions about what counts as valid schooling. The consequent culture - shock may lead to a refusal to take matters seriously.

But the serious nature of the negotiated curriculum can be emphasised by insistence on the need to keep written records of all activities and thoughts. These records can then be used for formative ongoing evaluation - both self-evaluation and with the teacher. This evaluation is clearly an important part of the learning process, providing valuable feedback and help with future planning. These records can then provide a basis for a portfolio of work, as both tangible evidence of learning and also for future reference. The eventual totality can then be a pupil profile of attainments, interests and activities, giving a tangible quality to what might otherwise be nebulous in character, the whole available to significant others. In this way the negotiated curriculum can be clearly seen to be a serious part of school and community life and not merely as a soft option .

This democratic approach has served many purposes: it has given children confidence in their learning abilities, developed cooperative attitudes and introduced pupils to a wide range of human activities and disciplines. At some point, however, the school will have to consider the demands of the State in preparing children for future economic roles, by formal learning in a structured situation. But now one can expect students to make informed choices and, with their newly-acquired confidence and abilities in learning, to make relatively rapid progress through their chosen formal curriculum.

Common Core Concerns for a Negotiated Counter-Curriculum

It is perhaps in the selection of curriculum content that tensions between progressives and traditionalists become particularly acute. As Apple and Beane put it:

> *"Democratic educators live with a constant tension of seeking a more significant education for young people whilst still attending to the knowledge and skills expected by powerful education forces whose interests are anything but democratic" (4)*

The "knowledge" referred to here involves a package of academic subjects and has acquired over time a hegemonic quality. According to Connell, school knowledge has the following characteristics:

it marginalizes other ways of organising knowledge;

it is integrated with the structure of power in educational institutions;

it occupies the high cultural ground. (5)

Questions surrounding this particular organisation of knowledge include its accessibility: whether it should be available in its entirety to all students and on what basis. One clear example of a "common curriculum" is provided by the government's National Curriculum. An obvious objection to such an all-embracing curriculum is that it leads to an over crowded curriculum, so that a "core "of what is claimed to be really essential knowledge is generally recommended. In the case of the National Curriculum a core has now emerged of STEM (Science, Technology, English, Maths) – that is, knowledge which is both subject-based and a-cultural, although directly relevant to the economic interest.

Such bodies of knowledge provide, as have seen, a certain objectivity and a basis for controlled teaching and assessment. But we are not here exercised by the concerns of state and examination board, but with the concerns of young people shortly to enter adult life, with all the demands that implies. When considering negotiation, however, as opposed to prescription, it is essential that there should be mutual respect, and that the teacher voice, as well as the student voice, should be heard and respected. It is also important to bear in mind the need for a broad, relevant curriculum, with appropriate frameworks within which content can be negotiated. (see, for example, the HMI Curriculum shown in a previous chapter in opposition to the National Curriculum) So, with this in mind, I am here tentatively proposing as the basis for negotiation an alternative core curriculum with clear concerns for both student and teacher – but concerns which are seen as peripheral by the Education Department. It has the following features:

it exposes the guidelines coming out of the Education Department for the bland out-of-touch recommendations that they offer;

unlike much educational discourse, it does not remain in the realm of the abstract but is based on the concrete and the tangible, providing the substance for sensible criticism and negotiation;

it is culturally located and hence of some likely interest to students, revealing various tensions between competing interests;

251

it provides the basis for group enquiry and discussion, the development of political awareness and work in the community.

But it must be emphasised that this is merely the core of what must be a broad, balanced curriculum, the details of which will be found elsewhere.

A COUNTER CORE CURRICULUM

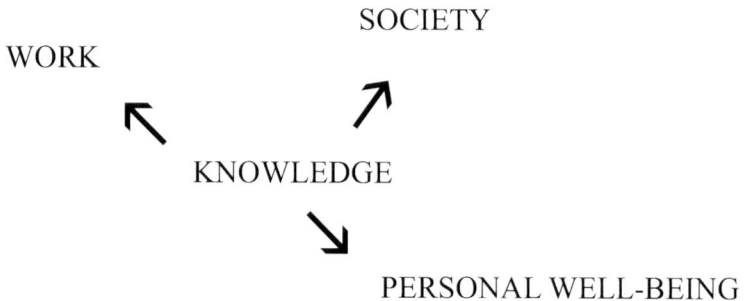

SOCIETY

WORK

↖   ↗

KNOWLEDGE

↘

PERSONAL WELL-BEING

(1) *THE NATURE AND ORGANISATION OF WORK*

Over the years the Education Department has produced a series of government initiatives in the field of vocational training. The latest is "Work-related Learning" for Key Stage 4, made up of three strands:

1. learning through work:
    opportunities to learn from direct experience of work (work experience, part-time working or learning through vocational contexts in subjects);
2. learning about work:
    opportunities for students to develop knowledge and understanding of work and enterprise (through, for example, vocational courses and careers education);
3. learning for work:
    developing skills for enterprise and employability. (6)

This document reveals the thinking of the Education Department on "Work-related learning". It is also worth bearing in mind that for the student on work experience, work-related learning may mean something rather different. It offers a totally-different learning milieu, with different conceptions of knowledge, learning and evaluation, where an academic "failure" may find a more congenial environment and prosper, regaining at the same time lost self-esteem.

But what of the role of tutors? The document has little to say on this subject and it may be thought they are redundant. But it is important for them to stress that an enquiry approach to work experience is desirable, and that workplaces should be regarded as socially-constituted (and thus open to question) rather than God-given and absolute. Students should also be encouraged to report back in order to compare experiences and generate critical discussion. In the absence of any overt reference to critical thought and enquiry learning, the official documentation may be thought to be more concerned with domestication than the development of personal autonomy. That this initiative from the education department lies within the technical, rather than the practical mode, is further confirmed by its use in GCSE and other examinations.

It is difficult to see how "learning about work" can exclude an introduction to political economy. Even though work experience is now occupying a larger part of the 14-19 diploma, it would be unrealistic to expect students to get into the heart of a particular organisation. But perhaps an opportunity now presents itself for students to be presented with a generalised picture of the modern world of work; for example, the hierarchical organisation of industrial capitalism and its division of mental and manual labour, with highly waged executives and managers at the top of the hierarchy, with relatively high job security; whilst at the bottom are the poorly trained and low-skilled operatives, with low job security ("hire and fire") performing routinised repetitive tasks. Financial capital is raised from shareholders and banks, with the incentive of dividends from shares and interest on bank loans. Capitalist firms are thus in thrall to shareholders and desperate to offer the highest dividend, leading to a short-term approach to profit-making, with mergers, takeovers and asset-stripping the order of the day, and job insecurity and worker exploitation the price to be paid..

It is a model, with its advantages and injustices, against which students can measure their own work experience when reporting back. But it is not the only model which could provide a basis for work experience. A clear alternative to the above, involving "worker control" is provided by the Cooperative Movement, which as we have seen, originated with Robert Owen at the beginning of the nineteenth century. The distinguishing feature of mainstream profit-sharing cooperatives is that they are owned, not by shareholders expecting dividends, but by the workers themselves. The workers also exercise control over decision-making, the precise extent of their control being decided democratically and depending upon the structure of the particular Cooperative. They are, in short, the essence of democratic production and consequently demand some attention in a democratic curriculum.

Within this overall framework various types exist, for example, industrial cooperatives, consumer cooperatives and agricultural cooperatives. Although in terms of industrial manufacturing industries, worker cooperatives are not yet major players on the world economic stage, it is estimated that there are about 100 million workers in some form of cooperative (over 100,000 in this country). The largest worker cooperative is the Mondragon Cooperative of Northern Spain, containing 120 worker-owned cooperatives and 40,000 owner-workers. With an annual turnover of $5 billion, it is twice as profitable as other Spanish firms, with a much higher productivity! Given that the cooperative idea has been around for a couple of centuries and with such a track record, students might be interested in speculating why this particular form of production has not become more widespread. [There are also several other approaches to employee ownership; see, for example, Job Ownership Limited .]

Nor should work-related learning exclude possible new forms of organisation. It is a commonplace that – for better or worse - the manufacturing sector has been declining in the developed world, to be replaced by a service, and latterly a knowledge economy in a learning / high skills / modernising society. Students should recognise that in such a society, ambitious "knowledge" claims are advanced from time to time, often aimed at political parties in the hope of preferment. One such includes the prediction that the knowledge economy will signal the end of class and capitalism, with a new moral and political order taking their place in a participative democracy. Instead of a hierarchical separation of mental and manual labour, there will be networks of cellular self-managed teams giving "communities of competition" collaborating within the global knowledge economy. Leadbeater puts it like this:

*"Knowhow companies should be cellular. (they)....
need to be networked and integrated to respond to an
increasingly fluid, complex competitive environment...
The cellular company practises self-management and
self-organisation of motivated, educated ambitious
workers......Leadership in this organisation is a constant
search for creative collaboration, promoting a culture of
curiosity, attacking complacency ....The new economy
requires a new mixed economy of competition and
collaboration. Competitive open markets are the sharpest
spur to innovation ....but collaboration is essential to
creativity and knowledge-creation...There is a large
potential for us to harvest the power of the knowledge
economy to extend equality of opportunity, reinvigorate
public services and open up politics". (7)*

Lest we get carried away with Leadbeater's visions of the New Jerusalem, Jon Cruddas provides statistics showing that so far there has been no withering away of the working class and that the number of manual workers has remained fairly constant in the past fifteen years, with a marked increase in carers:

*"In short, throughout the last fifteen years there has been
no revolution in the demand for labour - rather the key
growth areas have been in traditional often low-paid
jobs, many of which are carried out by women." (12)*

An earlier chapter has shown how the government has made repeated efforts to get its vocational education "right", but with limited success. Now at a time of high youth unemployment (2009) attention has once again focussed upon its shortcomings, and the government is under pressure - with only 8% finding jobs after completing courses- to work with employers and to gear courses more closely to the labour market.

With their experiential background, it is well worth students comparing their experiences with the "official" categorisations of skills:

CORE SKILLS
Communication skills:
develop communication skills in discussion and presentation
respond effectively to written information.

Working with others:
> develop skills in planning and carrying out projects in small groups
>
> sharing out tasks and responsibilities.

Numeracy:
> learn to be comfortable with numbers and with graphs, symbols, diagrams and calculators.

Problem-solving:
> develop skills in critical thinking, planning, organising, reviewing and evaluating through a series of projects.

Information Technology:
> get to grips with basic terminology of computers; learn how to make effective use of software and develop skills in the effective use of the internet.

As students get older, their thoughts naturally turn to life after school. Good careers advice should be available to help them decide which 14-19 areas they wish to specialise in, with the spurious vocational/academic divide dissolved. Formal courses with well-defined bodies of knowledge will now be available. With students now well initiated into processes of learning, there will be a sound foundation on which to build.

---

(2) PERSONAL WELL-BEING

In response to the growing concerns about a delinquent youth culture, PSHE – personal, social and health education - was bolted on to the national curriculum as a non-mandatory subject, specifically to include drugs, smoking and sexual health. More recently and with the growing crisis in schools, involving disruption, violence, truancy and widespread substance abuse, the government has been obliged to turn to the teaching of other, broader topics, some of which I deal with below.

Emotional Health

The Education Department's "Personal Well-being" document (9) is presented in conventional curriculum form:

curricular aim: successful learners, confident individuals etc;
key concepts: personal identities, healthy lifestyles etc;
skills and processes: developing relationships;
range and content: body image, mental and emotional health disorders.

Further study of the document suggests, as with previous official documents, that it is located within the technical mode of curriculum development: for example,

" the skills of self-awareness and managing feelings" and "delivery of the skills identified",augmented by the language of the objectives model"pupils should be able to ….."

This technical approach to subjects like emotional health and emotional intelligence raises a fundamental philosophical issue. As Patrick Turner puts it:

"The whole 'skills-based' emotional literacy calculus beloved of policy-makers seeking to heal family and community breakdown, makes a profound category mistake. The provision of 'training' in anger management, assertiveness, listening, cost / benefit analysis, openness and flexibility, is the futile application of an instrumental rationality to realms properly governed by volcanic emotion, fellow feeling and sentiment." (10)

In other words, emotional maturity is more likely to come - if it is to come at all in a selfish individualist, materialist society - from discussion of relevant experiences both in and out of the classroom, and dealing with issues in an open, critical and democratic atmosphere, than from any explicit attempt to "deliver" appropriate skills. But educational documents seldom take account of context. For example, the assertion:

"As pupils learn to recognise, develop and communicate their qualities, skills and attitudes, they build knowledge, confidence and self - esteem,"

takes no account of the ethos of the average school operating within the competitive constraints of league table and parental choice. How, for example, can a pupil be expected to gain self-esteem in an individualistic competitive school environment, where he / she constantly fails the grading system? And how can a pupil be expected to become a more responsible person in the conventional classroom, where the teacher represents the voice of unquestioned authority and the pupil the passive recipient of the "goods" being dispensed?

The argument here, then, is that the mainstream culture of the school with its structures, curriculum and assessment procedures is antithetical to the development of emotional maturity. Any realistic attempt to develop personal and moral autonomy has to take account both of the deficiencies of the present school system and pressures upon young people from the corrupting influences of the outside world. A democratic curriculum based upon the principles outlined earlier and moving from a technical, rule-following curriculum towards an empowering one would involve such shared activities as rigorous enquiry into the nature of our society, its values and abuses. Role play by students acting out social and moral dilemmas (eg in Drama) would not only raise awareness of their complexities but could lead to the development of empathy, as well as that emotional commitment leading to pupils taking up a moral position and demanding action in support of it. In the process they would become more responsible people with a clearer sense of identity, and on the way to becoming more emotionally mature persons.

Economic Well-being and Financial Capability

It is with the above PSHE document that we enter Voltaire's Panglossian "best of all possible worlds" where there are no losers, only winners; no controversy; no divisive issues. Whilst, for example, there is considerable emphasis in this document upon "Enterprise", other cultural realities such as "Unemployment" and "Survival" are totally ignored. And in a "hire-and-fire" culture we are told of the need to

> "understand that everyone has a career", and that: "young people need to develop the skills to manage their continuing career development", as well as:
> "developing a sense of personal identity for career progression".

In short, this document takes little account of the realities of the world outside the school-gates. As we saw in a previous chapter, we inhabit a consumerist society, where commercial organisations are intent on parting the client from his / her money. For this purpose all manner of seductive dodges such as loss leaders and slogans like "buy one, get one free" or "buy now, pay later" are used. More sophisticated psychological approaches are also employed in the media to appeal to the emotional rather than the rational sides of our nature. On top of these seductions young people are also exposed to peer pressure and the need to be "cool" and loyal to the group, so it hardly surprising that they sometimes succumb and become members of the debt culture. Students will doubtless have their own experiences, which they can relate to each other.

One result of all this consumerism is that 125% mortgages have been offered to potential housebuyers and UK personal debt has stood at over 1.3 trillion pounds, rising by 1 million pounds every four minutes! At the time of writing, this unsustainable culture has finally crashed, banks have become bankrupt and unemployment (especially among young people) is rising rapidly. It remains to be seen whether this crisis leads to fundamental reform or a patching-up process . So far it seems that it will be a case of "more of the same", a good case for educating people.

In our Western culture then, young people need to be reminded that taking out a loan attracts interest, usually linked to the Bank of England rate in the case of banks but varying from 30% APR (Annual Percentage Rate) in the case of the "buy now pay later" purchase - up to 1000% in the case of those "loan sharks" who are ready to "help out" with cash in hand but are also prepared to issue threats in order to recover their money. Young people need to be on their guard, then, in financial matters and resist those temptations which would plunge them into debt and threaten their credit worthiness. (11) Of course, many pupils will have enough "street cred" to find their way around this commercial jungle. Indeed, they could share their experiences with the rest of the class - including the teacher - and discuss some of the many issues which arise. Economic, as well as cultural, understanding can also be furthered by exploring the intricacies and injustices of a tax system (12) where fraud costs the country £10 billion a year, and where - not only do the poor pay proportionately more tax than the rich - but the super-rich can avoid paying tax altogether!

To provide a context sadly lacking from the government document I end this section with some detail of one of many recent financial scandals which provides some insight into the ethics of the boardroom and the naivete of consumers, and which underlines the importance of financial education. It was indeed this scandal which led to the public clamour for schools to teach financial management and the introduction of the PSHE document "Economic Well-Being".

THE FAREPAK COLLAPSE

"The Farepak Hamper Company took money from their clients on a weekly basis to pay towards a Christmas hamper made up of goods chosen from their catalogue. There were about 170,000 customers paying by 45 weekly instalments. The collapse can be traced back to a £35 million acquisition of the booksales company DMG by the parent company European Home Retail using money from the Farepak account. This was subsequently replenished by a loan from the HBOS bank. DMG made substantial losses and was subsequently sold for £5million. HBOS then called in the debt by seizing £36 million of the Farepak customers'money. Even though the Stock Exchange suspended shares in European Home Retail, Farepak continued to take its customers' money for the next three months.The customers therefore lost most of their investment and received no Christmas hamper. But the bosses paid themselves millions in salaries and bonuses throughout this period and on resigning two of the directors received large payouts and had their pensions underwritten by the government's Pension Protection Fund. No interest was paid on the instalment money paid by customers and the goods involved were worth far less than their catalogue price. Customers justified their loyalty to the firm by their long-term family connection and on the grounds of convenience, with money being taken and goods delivered at the door." (13)

Unfortunately, as can be seen from the above discussion, the PSHE document, in its blandness, manages to miss the point.

Healthy Eating

PSHE "Healthy Lifestyles" is embedded in the Healthy Schools Programme along with Healthy Eating, Physical Activity and Emotional Health. The impetus for this programme comes from mounting concern about obesity in children which, despite the various initiatives, continues to rise alarmingly from 11% to 19% for boys in the last decade, and from 12% to 18% for girls. In response to this, the emphasis in the PSHE section on Healthy Lifestyles is upon making informed choices and decisions, and considering the possible consequences of those decisions.

But it is not as simple as that. Once again the official government document fails to put its recommendations into a realistic context. "Food" is big business, with fierce "no holds barred" competition for customers. One result of this is that the food market is obsessed with innovation and novelty, with £20 million per year being spent on research. Food scientists are constantly conjuring up new seductive flavours, dyes are added to make the product more visually attractive and preservatives added to prolong shelf life. And far more (over £700 million in 2005) is spent on advertising and propaganda, increasingly targeting poorer, less well-educated areas of the world and continuing their penetration of schools. The debate has polarised into "processed" versus "non-processed" foods and opposing views can be followed in the industry-funded (and government-sponsored) publication 'British Nutrition Foundation' (14) and the independent 'Food Magazine (15).

How, then, is one to follow the advice of the PSHE and "make informed choices and decisions and consider the possible consequences of those decisions"? The Foods Standards Agency has been promoting since 2000 a policy of food labelling. It has been locked in dispute with supermarkets over the form this labelling should take, with some supermarkets apparently reluctant to disclose the precise details of additives used. There has been growing concern from some mothers about possible effects, including hyperactivity, of these additives on their children. But the emphasis has increasingly been focussed upon excessive amounts of saturated fats, salt and sugar in "junk foods" and campaigns have been launched to have these banned. The response of the government has been typically deferential: "the government intends to discuss with the food industry how it might contribute." And a new Coalition government has now announced that it will put nutritional issues in the hands of the food industry itself!

It will be recalled that the National Curriculum recategorised "cookery" as a component of Food Technology, so that instead of children being taught how to cook cheap, nutritious food, they could serve the interests of supermarkets. Now in a climate of increasing panic about childhood obesity

(1 million to be obese in the next decade) the government is re-introducing compulsory lessons in cookery! Any shift from passive consumerism to more productive activities is to be welcomed. It is now time to move one step further and introduce into schools the compulsory growing of food, bringing children closer to nature and developing their understanding both of natural processes and the various issues involved in mass food production. For example,

how was the food produced, organically or with synthetic fertilisers?
were herbicides and pesticides used in plants, or antibiotics in animals?
how much transportation and fuel was involved in getting it to processing plants and hence to the consumer?
and crucially for a democratic curriculum with its principle of "respect for others":
was there any labour exploitation in the production of the food?

All of this provides an excellent opportunity for a rigorous and relevant study of both life and physical sciences. It also offers a rich opportunity for the critical analysis of those claims made by self-styled nutritionists offering "scientific" nutritional advice. These "nutritionists" are inclined, from time to time, to make the most absurd and confident assertions without providing any empirical evidence, assertions which will raise a few eyebrows even amongst pupils merely following an elementary science course. For example, "molecules carry an electric charge", "chlorophyll will oxygenate your blood", "fatty acids are made up of carbon molecules, hydrogen and oxygen atoms" (16). These are clear factual errors, qualifying for the term "howlers". Sometimes the assertions are more mysterious. What will pupils make, for example, of:

> *"Our thoughts have powerful energy. When we write down these thoughts, and transfer them into pictures, we dramatically intensify them. You are now harnessing the thought into action. You become the creator of your own destiny" (17)*

Such claims demand both that the question "How do you know?" be asked and that evidence be provided. The fact that such questions are seldom if ever asked by either book publishers or TV producers is a sad reflection on the nature of our society, where the chief concern in a competitive materialist world is not for truth, but for publicity, viewer ratings and profit. Such is the cultural context for the teaching of "healthy eating" and for the development of critical thought.

(3) SOCIETY AND CITIZENSHIP

Towards the end of the last century concerns were being increasingly expressed about the growing disengagement of young people from mainstream society in the context of a declining social and moral fabric, and the lack of trust and respect for politicians as well as interest in the political process. More specifically, the concept of "human rights" had more fully entered the public consciousness through legislation and the activities of various pressure groups. It was in 1984 that the Law Society funded the "Law in Education" Project to introduce students to their legal rights and responsibilities and empower them to engage in the wider community. Students were encouraged, by the use of appropriate materials and teaching methods, to engage in open discussion and critical thinking.

This Project led to the establishment of the Citizenship Foundation in 1989 and the expansion into other areas of public life, but still with a continuing emphasis upon law-related education with mock trials and youth parliament competitions. Recognising the universal importance of Citizenship, the Foundation, together with other groups, lobbied the government to introduce the subject into the National Curriculum. Faced with these pressures and with the growing disconnection of young people from society, the Education Secretary in 1997 pledged to strengthen education for citizenship and the teaching of democracy in schools by setting up an Advisory Committee to cover the teaching of civics, participative democracy and citizenship, including some understanding of democratic institutions and practices. The subsequent Crick Report ("Education for Citizenship and the Teaching of Democracy in Schools") was not lacking in ambition:

> *"We aim at no less than a change in political culture of this country both nationally and locally; for people to think of themselves as active citizens willing, able and equipped to have an influence in public life."*
> (18)

In other words, it emphasised "active citizenship" and "participatory democracy" and identified three essential strands:

       social and moral responsibility,
       community involvement and
       political literacy

and four elements :

    1. concepts (" a number of key concepts provide a clear, overarching conceptual core….. pupils should come to understand how these key concepts serve collectively to underpin effective education for citizenship")

    2. values and dispositions (" pupils should be encouraged to reflect and act upon these values and dispositions")

    3. skills and attitudes ("pupils should have the opportunities to develop and apply these skills and aptitudes within pluralist contexts")

    4. knowledge and understanding ("pupils should acquire basic knowledge and understanding of particular aspects : social, moral, political, economic and environmental")

However, the Report, accepting the need to take up a pragmatic quasi-objectives stance, accepted the need to conceptualise its curriculum in terms of "learning outcomes" and to accommodate these within the following manner as Key Stages of the National Curriculum:

"By the end of KS1 pupils should be able to ……."

In the wake of this Report, the government - apparently oblivious to the fact that, because of its policies, it was presiding over a society of increasing inequality, greed and individualism - introduced "Citizenship" as a cross-curricular theme in the National Curriculum, making it mandatory from 2002 - with the primary aim of producing "informed citizens". The Qualifications and Curriculum Authority (QCA), for example, defined citizenship education in terms of:

    knowledge and understanding about becoming informed citizens;
    skills of enquiry and communication;
    skills of participation and responsible action.

It has subsequently become available as a GCSE subject (19), throwing into sharp relief the tensions between (a) the initial ambitions of the Crick Report, with its implications of a practical or emancipatory (20) mode of curriculum development, and (b) the technical interest of examination boards, with their requirements of "validity", "comparability" and reliability" and an implied pedagogy of "delivery" (the very word used by the Education Secretary of the time).

[Thus the general form of examination includes a written paper of short and extended questions (60%) and a coursework requirement (40%). The latter, which should provide the very essence of "active citizenship" (with its hypothetical exploration and unearthing of those cultural forces masquerading as God-given and natural) is placed within a technical framework of (1) knowledge and understanding; (2) planning and evaluation; and (3) explanation and interpretation. Furthermore, certain topics for investigation are suggested, and whilst some of these are enlightened there is the possibility - given the authority of examination boards - that these suggestions can further limit the autonomy of the student.]

Evidence about the actual substance of citizenship activities is sketchy, given the paucity of field-based research. But, depending upon the role played by the teacher, there are, on the surface, opportunities for a practical, rather than a technical approach. Thus, students are required to provide reasoned arguments, interpret texts and use their judgment in various areas. Such departures from the technical curriculum provide a serious challenge to the teacher. Teaching must now be dialogic, rather than expository, fresh values must be internalised and the art of negotiation acquired. At the risk of repetition, it must be emphasised that fundamental problems are posed for Teacher Training courses, and the implications are that these have not yet been taken seriously by the Education Department. Indeed, Citizenship has been labelled by Ofsted the "worst taught subject in secondary schools". Which is hardly surprising, given its lowly status, the fact that it is foreign to teachers' own educational upbringing, and that no-one has been effectively trained to teach the subject. And developments in teacher training described elsewhere are travelling in the opposite direction.

This specific example, then, contains several salutary and general lessons for curriculum developers:

the constraints that are placed upon any progressive project when necessarily placed within a framework of state control and its concern for the maintenance of "standards" and the reproduction of the structural elements of society;

the need to adequately educate (as opposed to train) intending teachers and to supplement this with continuing professional development;

the relative strength of private curriculum initiatives which are able to run counter to state hegemony.

This chapter provides ample illustration of the constraints placed upon teachers wishing to develop critical thinking in their students, when faced with the bland documents provided by officialdom aimed at blind acceptance of the status quo. This is just one more constraint placed upon teachers attempting to provide genuine educational alternatives for their students in the face of such obstacles as the following:

the state-controlled technical curriculum (in positivist mode) described earlier aimed at the reproduction of the socio-economic order;

a corporate hegemony providing an instrumental, consumerist, materialistic, culture, with instant gratification and - with its short attention span - providing an obstacle to the development of sustained learning .

Given that governments have never taken state education seriously and provided adequate resources, particularly in deprived areas, progressive teachers would appear to face an impossible task. But there are counter-cultural elements here and there (as witness the resistance to state - provided education by school "failures" mentioned earlier) and this interplay of hegemony and counter-hegemony will provide the context for the initiatives described in the next chapter.

NOTES AND REFERENCES

1.Oborne,P. (2007) "The Triumph of the Political Class". Simon and Shuster.London

2. Cited in Furedi op cit

3. Thomas and Pattinson (2008) How Children Learn at Home. Continuum.

4. Apple and Beane op cit

5.Connell op cit

6. QCA 14-19 Learning

7 .C.Leadbeater op cit

8 .J.Cruddas "The Knowledge Economy" Renewal vol14. no1

9.QCA PSHE Personal Well-being

10.http://www.culturewars.org.uk/2004-02/weatherill.htm

11.www.direct.gov.uk/MoneyTaxAndBenefits/Taxes/BeginnersGuide

12.www.direct.gov.uk/MoneyTaxAndBenefits/ManagingDebt/DebtsAndArrear

13.thisismoney.co.uk

14. www.nutrition.org.uk

15. wwwfoodcomm.org.uk/fmag.htm

16. see www.badscience.net/ for more examples

17 .G.McKeith(2006) Ultimate Health Plan. Michael Joseph. London

18 .www.qca.org.uk/qca_4844.uspx

19. www.qca.org.uk/14655.html

20. S. Grundy op cit

CHAPTER THIRTEEN

CHALLENGES TO CURRENT ORTHODOXY

> *"Each particular way of constructing the curriculum (organising the field of knowledge and defining how it is to be taught and learned) carries social effects. Curriculum empowers and disempowers, authorises and de-authorises, recognises and mis - recognises different social groups and their knowledge and identities." (R.E. Connell "Poverty and Education)*

Educational Features of the Status Quo
Making Waves - or Ripples?
> *(1) Challenging the Technical "Delivery" Curriculum:*
>   *"Opening Minds"*
> *(2) Challenging the IQ myth*
> *(3) The "Closed School": Citizenship: the Student Voice*
> *(4) Challenging Fixed Term Schooling: lifelong learning*
> *(5) Representative Democracy: representing whose interests?*
> *(6) Participatory Democracy: the lessons from Porto Alegre*
>   *Hegemonic Barriers:*
> *Consumerism and Corporatism*
> *Technicism; psychometrics and neuroscience*

Where Now?
> *Failures in Delivery*
> *Internal Contradictions: Ideologies in Conflict*
>   *the corporatist approach*
>   *the humanistic approach*

Educational Features of the Status Quo

The government is fond of telling us that "the status quo is not an option". But this narrative has shown how stable is the socio-economic order, capable of recruiting significant allies into the dominant class whilst making concessions which do not fundamentally affect the "natural order of things", all justified by the arts of legitimation. What then are the more obvious educational features characterising this status quo and manifesting the state interest?

(i) a selection process favouring the upper and middle classes, either through

(ii) parents buying a private education or gaining access to the more successful state or faith schools, a procedure which is justified either in terms of parental responsibility or through an assumption of social differentiation of intelligence and aptitude, and

(iii) reinforced by a curriculum based upon middle class language and values and with "high status" reified content linked to positions of power and thus largely irrelevant to the lower classes, lending itself to

(iv) objective individualised competitive assessment procedures, providing the necessary legitimation both for social differentiation, and for

(v) an education which is longer for successful than unsuccessful candidates,

(vi) taking place for a fixed term in a closed institution.

The argument that the programme of academies and trust schools does in fact represent fundamental educational change can be dismissed on the grounds that any changes are peripheral and do not affect the basic order of things; that is, education remains untouched as a vehicle for social stratification, and the transmission of high and low-status knowledge, to be uncritically accepted by the student. It is clear, then, that the goal of producing moral, critical and autonomous students in a democratic society characterised by social justice and freedom is as far away as ever. Despite this, I have selected below for your consideration, various innovations which may still mount challenges of some potency to the status quo, reflecting in their particular way the criteria above. But it cannot be stressed too often that all educational initiatives will be liable to failure if they do not produce superior results as judged by conventional social and economic and subject-based criteria. New initiatives must, for example, include the rigorous application of disciplined thinking to problems as experienced by students - and hence be resistant to dismissal on the grounds of being a "soft option". And such an ambitious approach will require extensive teacher training, more favourable pupil-teacher ratios and the recruitment of the highest teacher material. All of which will in turn demand massive injection of financial resources, to be expected only when a crisis of sufficient magnitude compels the state to take education seriously.

(a) MAKING WAVES – OR RIPPLES ?

(1) Challenging the Technical "Delivery" Curriculum

<u>The Royal Society of Arts: "Opening Minds"</u>

The technical curriculum, it will be remembered, is characterised by a content of objectified (factual) knowledge, a monologic pedagogy and a graded, individualised assessment scheme. A challenge to this conventional wisdom is provided by the Royal Society for Arts' "Campaign for Learning" project launched in 1996 (1). This has a vision of an inclusive society in which learning is understood, valued and is accessible to everyone as of right, and where learning is seen to be a process of active engagement with experience. An investigation into the way young people were educated led to the conclusion that the national curriculum was:

> *"information-driven, unlikely to equip young people for*
> *adult life in a new century... neglecting the development*
> *of competences and skills young people will need to*
> *survive and succeed in their future world" (2)*

This apparent neglect of "competence" in the school curriculum led to the launching in 1999 of the RSA Opening Minds project with an emphasis upon the following key competencies:

> citizenship,
> learning,
> managing information,
> relating to people,
> managing situations.

As far as substance is concerned, existing subject content is used as a basis for developing these competences. Key features in the implementation of this alternative curriculum which are of relevance to a democratic approach are:

> teachers must share a common understanding of the competencies,
> the competences must be made explicit to the students,
> each school develops its own vision.

The number of schools using this approach had grown from 8 in 1999 to 50 by 2003, chiefly with Year 7 pupils. The evidence so far obtained indicates considerable progress in terms of student attendance, behaviour and achievement. That this achievement is not at the expense of what has been claimed as "an overcrowded curriculum" is given credence by reports from practitioners showing that performance exceeds that of "normal" classes. One head, for example, claims an "outstanding success" for the "Opening Minds" project and support for the hypotheses that:

(a) the National Curriculum could be taught in a shorter space of time and
(b) learners could become more effective if the constraints of the National Curriculum were removed. (3)

THE "OPENING MINDS" EXPERIMENT

A pilot group of 85 Year 7 pupils out of a total of 250 began the competence-based approach in 2000 and, in 2002 not only achieved results which were between 12% and 15% better than the control group but were completing Year 11 coursework in Year 9. The ultimate accolade for these remarkable achievements is provided by Ofsted, which declared the project an outstanding success:

"the innovative approach in Year 7 provides integrated work across subjects, developing personal skills and competencies excellently. This has a particularly strong impact on the performance of boys and has encouraged high levels of self-confidence and enjoyment."

The implications from this innovation confirm those common sense impressions which somehow escape the experts:

students learn better when work is found to be enjoyable;
when they are treated with respect and:
when there is some freedom of choice .

In this particular case there is both peer and self-evaluation (from time-to-time together with the tutor) as well as freedom of choice, within a common framework, both in terms of content and timescale.

Student perceptions

having more say in what you do;
not being rushed;
not having too many teachers;
being able to work through breaks;
giving presentations to parents and staff.

Teacher perceptions

much greater opportunity to get to know the students really well;
better working relationships;
more work completed to a higher standard;
improved motivation and better behaviour.

A further important point should be added - both governors and parents were kept fully informed both of the intended innovation and the progress being made; being invited, for example, to student presentations. "Opening Minds" is being thoroughly disseminated through its communication network, including newsletters and regular meetings. Interestingly, in view of its radical approach, it is being partially funded by the Education Department.

What can we make of this development in curriculum innovation? Although "Opening Minds" does not set out explicitly to provide a democratic curriculum, there are several relevant features, as well as a clear challenge to the status quo:

emphasis upon student choice (admittedly within a teacher-specified framework)
self and peer evaluation
respect for students and their opinions
the student voice is heard
involvement of the local community. (4)

In fact it might have been said to have occupied Gramsci's "War of Position" (S. Grundy op cit). That is, its practical and democratic curriculum is morally

272

and socially superior to the current technical variety whilst producing superior results as measured by the criteria of the existing system. So far, the evidence suggests also that it leads to an improvement in pupils' behaviour and promises to meet those "needs of industry" which are apparently becoming increasingly attitudinal and based upon personal attributes rather than skills. What is of immense significance, in line with the hypotheses of the headmaster above, is that there is the possibility of resolving the inevitable tension between the education and State interest, by meeting the latter's demands through improved motivation, leaving time for educational pursuits. There is the further advantage that the qualitative evaluation by portfolio complements the quantitative assessment required by the State.

It must be stressed, however, that "Opening Minds" is not a scientific experiment with a representative sample of schools, and the schools involved may well be high-performing and have more responsible and enthusiastic pupils and parents than many others. [It will also be interesting to see how this innovation can be reconciled with the restrictive demands of the New Public Management approach to teacher training (see later)].

(2) Challenging The IQ Dogma - Alternative Pedagogies

We have dealt earlier with some of the problems arising out of attempts to define and measure "intelligence". Our concern here is the hegemonic notion that intelligence is distributed along class lines; put simply, that the upper classes are cleverer than the lower - a useful device for justifying social privilege and injustice. Here are two examples which provide an empirical counter to such a myth, first with the emphasis upon social context; secondly, in terms of alternative pedagogies.

The Royal Wanstead Children's Foundation

This charitable foundation has a tradition of placing poor, vulnerable children in independent boarding schools, staying during term time and being fostered out in the holidays. Recently the Foundation decided to track 97 children from single - parent or care homes through their boarding-school careers, 60% having been exposed to violence or abuse and 70% with significant emotional problems. On admission 27% were rated at or above average for their peer group on cognitive and affective criteria. Within three years 85% had reached this level whilst 35% were in the top quarter in terms of school performance. Perhaps the most surprising feature was the speed with which these children settled into their new culture.

Not surprisingly, in view of these results, the Foundation urged the expansion of the scheme into the state sector. Colin Morrison, chair of the Foundation called on ministers:

> *"to provide means-tested grants to enable more children who are not in local authority care to attend boarding school. We calculate that within the existing boarding school provision in the UK there is capacity for an extra 2000 vulnerable children who could be accommodated with just a little additional funding." (5)*

In response, the government has made encouraging noises and has begun talks with state and private boarding schools. The scheme certainly provides a possible solution for the severe educational problems of children from dysfunctional families caught up in a culture antagonistic to schooling. But the chief and exciting implication of this initiative is that there is a much higher ceiling for the learning potential of disadvantaged children than was hitherto thought possible.

Montessori and Gorton Mount Primary School

Further evidence for the above is provided by an alternative pedagogy being applied with remarkable success in a failing primary school in Manchester. Gorton Mount Primary School has what might be thought to be insurmountable problems:

37% special needs;
36 languages;
71% free meals.

In an imaginative attempt to solve these problems, the school head, who was already sympathetic to Montessori methods, arranged a meeting with the Montessori Schools Foundation. This led to a joint proposal being put to the governors and trustees that Montessori methods be tried in the school "to add value to the children's educational experiences".

Maria Montessori showed true respect for children in several ways:

they were seen as competent beings, capable of self-directed learning and with limitless motivation to perfect skills and understandings

they learnt best in their own way and at their own pace through discovery and by interaction with the environment

they had both freedom of choice and freedom of movement

it was for the teacher, through close observation and in a 1:1 situation, to capitalise on the stage of development of the child and on the child's interests by preparing an appropriate learning environment and by guidance in practical life skills

there was to be no punishment or grading by tests. The child's portfolio would be available for evaluation.

The proposal was accepted and agreement subsequently reached both by the Montessori Schools Foundation and the Minister of State for Children that there should be joint funding of £60,000 for a six-month trial, involving 100 nursery and reception pupils aged 3 to 5.

Sarah Rowledge, head of a Montessori school in Essex, oversaw the project, which included training the teachers in Montessori methods. She described a very tough first term, the teachers:

"not knowing what had hit them. I have never seen anything like it.....children all spontaneously holding pencils and writing. Now whatever hell they are going through at home, they are leaving it at the door when they arrive at school" (7)

Ofsted inspected the nursery and reception classes at the start of Sarah Rowledge's second term and gave a positive reaction to the emerging benefits of this project, with the majority of children reaching the national average in maths (a unique achievement for the school). Subsequently, the project was formally evaluated by a member of the London Institute of Education, using standard - and possibly inappropriate - measuring instruments against a control school. The overall findings suggested that whilst there might be no outstanding or significant cognitive gains in what after all was a very brief experiment, good affective progress had been made, with sociability and self-esteem improving a great deal.

A significant finding for future work was that parental perspectives on the whole were not generally found to be favourable, attributed to the exclusion of parents from the classroom and their poor understanding of the approach - a salutary reminder that, not only do parents need to be educated in terms of fundamental innovations affecting their children, but that a "democratic school" implies this. (8)

On the whole, what evaluations have been carried out imply an emphatic vote of confidence. Other struggling schools unsurprisingly are looking with interest at this experiment and Gorton Mount and the Montessori Foundation have requested matching funding. Currently 14 staff are undergoing training to full Montessori Diploma level at the Montessori Centre and another school has now become the second "Montessori state primary school". The Montessori Schools Association is also planning to set up a bespoke state primary school with its own teacher training wing, using £5 million from its own funds, plus support from a local authority or the private sector.

What is of particular significance about these developments is that, whereas Montessori schools generally thrive in the private sector (631 registered primary and nursery schools) here the method is being tried with some success in a most difficult inner city school. It adds, on balance, to the growing body of evidence that given adequate resources and an appropriate pedagogy in a democratic climate, children are capable of much greater achievement than has hitherto been thought possible. Both of these initiatives undermine the claim that intelligence is fixed and non-contextual.

[Oliver Sacks in his book "The Man who Mistook his Wife for a Hat", provides some highly significant examples of unimagined human capabilities found in the "mentally defective"; qualities of mind other than the conceptual, with enhanced powers of concrete imagery and memory. These capabilities are contextually - related and can be revealed when a testing regime is replaced by music or drama, with music having the power to organise what previously were "uncouth movements" and drama providing the capacity to perform, to "be". Sack's work reminds us of the great unsolved mysteries of the mind, as well as the contextual nature of human behaviour.]

(3) Challenging the "Closed" School: Citizenship Revisited and the Student Voice

It is true that schools are now much more open than they were a few decades ago, but the open - ness is still narrow (e.g. parent helpers, governors or the occasional outside speaker). In other words, pupils have seldom been encouraged to regard the outside world as an extension of school and a place of learning. But with the advent of Citizenship and Work Experience in the school curriculum, this situation is possibly due to change.

I have already described the setting up of the Citizenship Foundation with the chief aim of empowering individuals to engage in the wider community through education about democracy and the development of critical thinking through democratic discussion. It was influential in persuading the government to introduce Citizenship into the school curriculum.

Since then the Foundation has become the leading source of support for teachers through its training courses and the provision both of textbooks and CD's as well as speakers and workshops, and guidance from experienced teachers.

There are now several examples of the results of such citizenship education, where the student voice is acknowledged as both a valid component of "Citizenship" and as a contributor to community projects.

(a) one school in Essex discovered that there are now fewer Thames boat builders because that part of the Thames Estuary is too shallow and that, because of this, an old shipbuilding barn had remained vacant for years. A needs assessment was carried out by the pupils to find out how the area could be developed most effectively and the results submitted to public, democratic discussion, with pupils making their views known, and attending public meetings to talk about what they think needs to happen to that space;

(b) pupils in one borough set a budget, involving the allocation of finance for education, crime prevention, housing, street cleaning etc. and presented it for discussion to the local councillors responsible for financial affairs;

(c) one school coordinated an awareness and fund-raising campaign to help Kosovan refugees (with whom it has emotional attachments). Pupils organised assemblies at which Kosovan refugees spoke of their experiences, mounted an exhibition and made appeals to the local press and shops for donations. As a result of their efforts, £1800 was raised. (9)

But most of these activities are at the local level and do not deal with representative democracy at the national level. The Institute for Citizenship, a charity set up to "promote informed, active citizenship and greater participation in democracy" is particularly concerned with current public indifference to representative democracy and has developed a "Learning through Elections" pack containing lesson plans, activities and background information to provide a framework to help pupils understand the various processes taking place during election time. The Institute has also managed a "Democracy through Citizenship "project funded by the Joseph Rowntree Trust to provide opportunities for young people to get involved in real political decision-making.

"Democracy through Citizenship"

Students from a sixth form college organised an event around local government elections to encourage young people to register on the Electoral Register and actually vote.

Publicity was provided through posters and leaflets as well as the local media and radio. Representatives from the major political parties attended the event, which was provided with information stalls.

In addition to registering, young people were able to take part in informal discussions with the political parties.

"Young People's Question Time Challenge"

The Institute for Citizenship has also developed a competition between schools involving a Young People's Question Time (based on the BBC versions) where pupils are required to carry out the necessary organisational tasks:
>   finding and booking a venue;
>
>   agreeing on a chair and panellists and sending out invitations and guidelines;
>   deciding on the audience and the involvement of other schools;
>   gathering and selecting questions;
>   publicising the event;
>   holding a dress rehearsal. (10)

The BBC has become involved in this competition, choosing the four best schools to work alongside David Dimbleby and a BBC production team in producing a special Question Time programme. A panellist is also selected to appear on a real "live" BBC Question Time.

It may be asked "What are the students actually learning?" The simple answer is: "They are learning to act democratically". But claims are also made for the acquisition of certain competencies:

> working effectively as a team;
> learning about citizenship;
> decision-making;
> dealing with people in authority;
> improving their speaking and listening skills;
> developing organisation skills etc.

The term "curriculum = course of study" is no longer applicable to such activities, raising the question of how it is to be conceptualised. The government's approach of regarding "Citizenship" as a subject, to be examined and graded on an individual basis, invalidates it as a serious contribution to critical democracy. The private sector, free from such constraints, might be expected to adopt a more practical approach, with its dialogic discourse, interpretation of situations and events, generation of meaning, and practical judgment. Our interest here is focussed upon the student voice, the opportunities for its expression and its potency. In the absence of detailed case studies, one is left with surmise but it seems safe to make the following observations to illustrate the prevailing tensions between the State and the Education interest:

> the attempt to articulate the projects with the key stages of the national curriculum and the provision of teacher plans and kits suggests a slide towards the technical mode:

> the involvement of students in both decision-making and development, the move into the community and the emphasis upon interaction with people rather than with a product, provides a sound basis for a practical and democratic "curriculum", as well as for the development of personal autonomy.

It remains to explore the possibility of an emancipatory approach to the development of a dialogic learning community in our schools and to the exposure of apparently natural oppressive structures as merely social constructs - and hence open to change. It is worth mentioning at this point that a recent Ofsted report, whilst complaining that not enough schools were taking Citizenship seriously, rejects the idea that lessons should be about compliance, good behaviour and the acceptance of values. Instead it claims that "best practice" focuses on "challenging and promoting a critical democracy!" So at least the concept of "critical democracy" has entered the education lexicon. But in the absence of examples, it is difficult to know what this might imply. Michael Fielding (11) does provide an interesting example of how students can bring about changes to curriculum structures, starting initially with 13-17 year-olds, assuming the role of researchers. (but, so far as I can find out, when key personnel left, the school moved on to other, possibly more pressing matters.) Fielding ran an introductory session involving a joint exploration of both research intentions and procedures. One result was that the school assessment system was changed in ways which explicitly acknowledged the students' work. Fielding described the overall impact thus:

> *"(students) highlighted an overdidactic pedagogy that gave students little room to get involved in more active and engaging forms of learning. Lastly, and most radically, they challenged the whole model of curriculum that underpins current thinking and practice in the UK.........led to the emergence of new organisational structures which incorporated students as equal partners in the process of curriculum renewal." (12)*

The student voice described here would appear to have an authentic quality and potency to it, as it expresses its concerns and interests to a sympathetic staff. But there are some situations when the student voice is perhaps not all that it seems:

tokenism: the student is not in control of either the content or the style of communication;

manipulation: the student voice is used to carry the teacher's message.

The student voice can also be used mischievously by the student. The fundamental requirement, as usual, is a democratic ethos, where there is mutual trust and respect and openness to other points of view.

(4) Challenging Fixed-term Schooling: Lifelong Education and The Learning Society

Conventionally "education" has been conceptualised in formal terms as taking place only in institutions set aside for the purpose, and ending on leaving such an institution. Looked at in these terms, lifelong learning and the notion of a learning society represents a threat to the status quo. On the other hand, "lifelong learning" would appear to be a redundant concept, since an innate property of homo sapiens involves constant adjustment to a changing environment and the ability to learn from it. It only begins to make sense when placed within a particular material and societal context.

For example, from the point of view of the European Commission on the Learning Society, the "learning society" involves the following lines of action:

- bringing school and the business sector closer together;
- treating capital investment and training on an equal basis;
- encouraging the acquisition of new knowledge;
- combating exclusion (13)

In this country, the government has published a Green Paper giving its recommendations for the Learning Age. In a foreword to this document the Education Secretary made the following points:

> *"Learning is the key to prosperity.....Investment in human capital will be the foundation of success in the knowledge - based global economy of the twenty - first century." (14)*

It is clear from these examples that the driving force behind bringing lifelong learning on to policy agendas is the concern to improve workers' employability in a rapidly changing economy and hence the general material well-being of the state. In this connection, the Learning and Skills Council was set up by the government in 2001 to plan and fund education and training for over 16-year olds so that by 2010:

> *"young people and adults in England will have knowledge and productive skills matching the best in the world".*

But the introduction of "14-19 Learning" into schools has necessitated a fundamental structural change. Local authorities will be responsible for commissioning and funding training for 16-19 year olds, and will receive £7 billion per annum for the purpose, whilst a Skills Funding Agency will be established to ensure that public money is routed swiftly to further education colleges and providers. Hovering in the background, of course, is the Leitch Report: "to identify the optimal skills mix for 2020 to maximise economic growth, productivity and social justice". And dominating the foreground is the current deep recession which threatens large cuts in public expenditure.

The basic principle behind these initiatives is the expansion of both further and higher education and it will be instructive to learn what distinctions are being made between the two.

Further Education

- set up individual learning accounts……..
- invest in young people…….
- double the help for basic literacy and numeracy skills…..
- set and publish clear targets…..
- work with business, employees and their trade unions to support and develop skills in the workplace
- build a qualifications system which is easily understood.

This, then, is the Further Education Learning Age for those who might have been perceived as "academic failures" at school, and gone down the vocational route. As far as the government is concerned, it involves no more than continuous instrumental vocational training, with an upgrading of skills as necessitated by technological change.

Now compare the above with those principles of the Dearing Report set up to consider *Higher Education*:

- be at the leading edge of world practice in effective teaching and learning,
- sustain a culture which demands disciplined thinking, encourages curiosity, challenges existing ideas and generates new ones,
- be part of the conscience of a democratic society, founded on respect for the rights of the individual and the responsibilities of the individual to society as a whole,
- be accountable to students and society and seek continuously to improve its own performance. (15)

What does this say about the government's conception of the Learning

Society? It tells us that the state maintains the two-tier academic/vocational separation beyond the compulsory stage of schooling. This Learning Society, then, will be made up of sheep and goats, representing a continuing separation of "mental" from "manual" labour and providing unequal provision for different sectors of society. And the constant ruthless erosion of the budget for the funding of intrinsic post-school learning in the Arts and Humanities, confirms the view that education for the masses is now increasingly defined in instrumental, economistic terms.

So much for the present government's assured, unreflective approach to the Learning Society. Elsewhere, there has been considerable critical debate, often harking back to the days of ancient Athens, where citizens had the right - indeed the obligation - to participate directly in state decision-making through argumentation and communities of discourse, and where the Learning Society would take on a fuller meaning. But the contemporary debate spreads its wings widely (probably too widely) with a conceptual spectrum stretching from a "skills revolution" to "a society which must learn how it is changing". In what is a contested concept, attempts tend to be confined to the categorisation of necessary criteria, the formulation of strategies and learning networks - and the resolution of the many contradictions. At the moment conceptual confusion reigns.

Stewart Ranson, as a result of his research into variants of the Learning Society comes to the inevitable conclusion:

> *"The conditions for a learning society are, in the last resort, fundamentally political, requiring the creation of a polity which provides the foundation for personal and collective empowerment........Without political structures which bring together communities of discourse, the conditions for learning will not exist: it is not possible to create the virtues of learning without the forms of life and institutions which sustain them........A different polity, enabling all people to make a purpose of their lives, will create the conditions for motivation in the classroom. Only a new moral and political order can provide the foundation for sustaining the personal development of all." (16)*

(5) Representative Democracy: representing whose interests?

Thus, according to Ranson, such challenges to the status quo are, in the final analysis, political. But our political system seems incapable of providing those structures deemed necessary by Ranson. I earlier drew attention to some of the symptoms:

a general indifference to political issues on the part of the electorate, resulting in extremely low turn-outs at election time, with the result that governments have dubious legitimacy to run the country;

a "legitimacy deficit", with the main concern of government being to reflect, not the interests of the majority of the people, but those of big business;

emasculation of the authority of the Commons, with cabinet government beingeroded in favour of a presidential style;

disproportionate social mix of MP's, with a majority having come from privileged backgrounds, unrepresentative of most of the electorate;

a predominance of "career politicians" i.e. MP's going into Parliament straight from university - with little or no experience of the outside world and its deprivations.

Little can be expected from such a situation in terms of radical approaches to education. However, one might examine the manifestos of the major political parties to see if there any radical elements present, which might suggest at the very least a questioning of the fundamentals of our educational system - and so move beyond empty rhetoric. Such an examination indicates that the dominant educational priorities hardly appear in their present form to contain the seeds of fundamental reform, or to get at the roots of our educational malaise :

Labour Party: "personalised learning; fulfilling potential; more academies and trust schools; closure of local schools not meeting expected standards; expansion of free nursery places for 2-year-olds; education or training guaranteed up to age of 18"

Conservative Party: "parental choice; teaching by ability; more good newschools; smaller classes and raised standards; restoring order and discipline"

Liberal Democratic : "smaller class sizes; more specialist teachers; more money for teachers working in poorest areas; parity of financial support for state and public schools; improving discipline and confronting bullying. "

That such changes, whilst thought to be electorally popular, are anything but radical – and unlikely to challenge the status quo - is hardly surprising, given that no party has sought to question the fundamental assumptions of mass state education. What, then, of the Cooperative Movement, given that its ancestry lies with Robert Owen, whose remarkably enlightened and humane curriculum provided the first example of curriculum design in this book, at a time when only the most rudimentary utilitarian mass schooling was being provided for working-class children? It is fitting that towards the end of this book we should return to Owen and his revolutionary educational principles, in an effort to find out how far the Cooperative Movement has remained faithful to them, and how far state education has progressed in the last two hundred years.

ROBERT OWEN'S VIEWS AND PRINCIPLES

On Learning

"To train and educate the rising generation will at all times be the first object of society, to which every other will be subordinate.......Where are these rational practices to be taught and acquired ? Not within the four walls of a bare building, in which formality predominates....but in the nursery, play-ground, fields, gardens, workshops, manufactures, museums and class-rooms.... The facts collected from all these sources will be concentrated, explained, discussed, made obvious to all and shown in their direct application to practice in all the business of life"

Poor and Disadvantaged Children

"They would receive the same care and attention as those who belong to the establishment.....I would prefer to receive the offspring of the worst (parents) because they require more of our care and pity and by well-training these, society will be more essentially benefited."

On Childcare

"The Institution has been devised to afford the means of receiving your children at an early age, almost as soon as they can walk. By this means many of you, mothers and families will be able to earn a better maintenance or support for your children."

On Parenting Classes

"One of the apartments will also be occasionally appropriated for the purpose of giving useful instruction to the older classes of the inhabitants. For believe me, my friends, you are yet very deficient with regard to the best modes of training your children, or of arranging your domestic concerns"

On Women's Rights

"Women will be no longer made the slaves of, or dependent on men.....They will be equal in education, rights, privileges and personal liberty"

On Work

"The working classes may be injuriously degraded and oppressed in three ways:

when they are degraded in infancy
when they are overworked by their employer
when they are paid low wages for their labour.

Eight hours' daily labour is enough for any human being and under proper arrangements sufficient to afford an ample supply of food, raiment and shelter…. and for the remainder of the time he is entitled to education, recreation and sleep" (17)

In the light of this potential legacy, what is the Cooperative Party's current approach to education? Their present initiative is the:

"sponsorship of specialist schools; strategic intervention into education to introduce cooperative learning in schools. The Cooperative Movement recognises that it needs to inspire young people through its values to get involved and help build the future of their businesses. The "Business and Enterprise" option provides a unique opportunity to do this."

This initiative tells us that the Cooperative Movement has rejected the educational legacy of Robert Owen for the economic one of the Rochdale Pioneers. Thus, it has agreed to sponsor a number of schools seeking to become specialist schools in Business and Enterprise, and incorporating the values of self-help, self-responsibility, democracy, equality, equity and solidarity; and with learning activities involving role - play, decision - making activities, data interpretation and analysis. But there seems to have been little attempt to operationalise the various aspects of cooperative learning. This will not just happen out of the blue, but will require the development of various social and communicative competences, and, at least in the early days, appropriate structuring of activities to ensure the productive engagement of each student.

The former Education Minister (like his Prime Minister a member of a Cooperative Party affiliated to Labour) was full of praise for what he calls the "collaborative culture" of cooperative schools, and was aiming to have at least 100 cooperative trusts up and running in the next two years, with this collaborative culture embedded in the local community. And the Prime Minister had promised to put cooperative values and mutualism at the heart of the forthcoming election manifesto. At the same time, the Tory Party had launched a Conservative Cooperative Movement to provide a resource for local community groups, including the provision of worker cooperatives in the public sector. "Collaborative learning" and "Cooperation" are clearly the buzzwords of the time.

What might all this sudden activity add up to? It is evocative of those past agonised discussions over "Reform or Revolution?" questioning the future of those reforming activities lacking a basis in an established political movement. For example, twenty years ago, the National League for Nursing launched a "Curriculum Revolution" involving a fundamental transformation of the educational processes in its nursing programme. Now, twenty years on, it can be seen that this "revolution" involved no more than an addition or rearrangement of content, rather than a paradigmatic shift. One also wonders about the future of "collaborative learning" when it enters the competitive world of neo – liberalism, in the absence of well-established political roots..

It is clear that fundamental educational changes to the status quo can be expected only when embedded within mainstream culture or the coherent ideology of a political movement. Where might we look for such political or cultural support?

(6) Participative Democracy: the lessons from Porto Alegre

I have been concerned in previous sections with the possibilities of a Learning Society producing autonomous citizens in a functional democracy. But present societal indicators are not particularly propitious. For all the talk of Britain becoming a classless society, the nation is as divided along class lines as ever, with the concept of "social mobility" becoming increasingly redundant. The rich continue to reproduce their privileged position through the private schools system, where students are five times more likely than the national average to gain entry to the top 20 universities (the Russell Group) and from thence occupy powerful positions in the social hierarchy. And the rest of the middle classes adopt all sorts of strategies to ensure that their offspring gain access to well - performing comprehensive schools. As for the lower class, they are left with what have become "sink" schools, leaving a rejected underclass to develop oppositional practices – most dramatically a black youth gang culture. As a result of these dysfunctional and divisive forces, the government has been obliged to make some sort of response and there is increasing reference in official circles to "community empowerment".

287

But before I look at this in some detail I want to explore the possibilities raised by what is generally regarded as the classical example of community empowerment, that provided by the Brazilian city of Porto Alegre.

PARTICIPATORY DEMOCRACY IN ACTION (18)

The classic example of participatory democracy in action is provided by the city of Porto Alegre, capital of a Brazilian state. Brazil had been ruled by a military dictatorship for twenty before being replaced in 1985 by a neoliberal government, which among other things decentralised the education system. The immediate context for radical change was provided by a declining economy with a third of the population in poverty. The Workers' Party in Porto Alegre was established in 1981 with a pledge to bring about popular democracy. Conditions for such a change in Porto Alegre were favourable, in that there was a democratic tradition, a history of collective resistance and the existence of well-organised popular movements. By 1989 it was the major party in a left-wing coalition in what was styled "popular administration", motivated by a redistributive logic and pledged to use the knowledge of the community as a resource for action. In the field of education, this resulted at the regional level in a series of democratic participatory processes, with the overall objective of education as a human right, producing autonomous, critical and creative citizens, with the central values of liberty, justice and respect for others as well as for nature. At the state level, the "School Constituency" process involved a thorough and comprehensive analysis of all existing educational practices including teaching methods, the evaluation of learning, and alternative knowledge areas. This extensive process resulted in the production of a draft "base text", which was discussed and amended in almost 200 municipal conferences involving 60,000 people, before final revision by a State Conference of 3,500 elected delegates.

The starting point for the production of curricular knowledge was an analysis of methods of teaching and evaluation, an exploration of the culture of the local communities, and the specification of emergent main themes. These themes from each community were then incorporated into an interdisciplinary, thematic complex. Eventual study areas included biological, chemical and physical science, social history, mathematics and social expression, directly linked to the interests of both students and the community and raising crucial issues. As far as teacher education was concerned, seminars were held twice annually with progressive education researchers. Motivation for what originally was a reluctant teaching force in the face of demanding new roles, was provided by raising what were initially poor basic salaries. It is also important to remember that these initiatives are never final but subject to constant evaluation.

But more tangible than educational developments are the benefits resulting from participatory budgeting. The principle involved was that the sharing of political power implied a redistribution of wealth by opening up the budget to the community. What is a complex procedure involved annual assemblies at which elected delegates, having sounded out the people on what they considered important issues, would agree financial priorities for the following financial year (having acquired "budget literacy" by attending training sessions). An important aspect of this procedure is its transparency: through an open process of negotiation and reporting back, the overall budget is drawn up and presented to the mayor and the municipal council for final agreement. As a result of this budgeting procedure, involving a budget of $230 million in 2001, 50 schools have been built in the last ten years (and truancy reduced from 9% to less than 1%) and people provided with brick housing, clean water and sewage treatment.

Participatory budgeting has now spread to almost 200 Brazilian municipalities as well as several other countries. The International Observatory of Participatory Democracy was set up in 2001 by cities in over 20 countries to exchange information, experiences and ideas. And a recent study commissioned by the Inter-American Development Bank has demonstrated that participatory budgeting is an effective way for empowerment as well as enhancing social equity. But so far these have been local initiatives and tensions can eventually be expected with national governments committed to a neo-liberal agenda.

It is naïve to imagine that a culture can be transplanted from one country to another: the history and current circumstances in Porte Alegre were in many ways both exceptional and propitious. The nation had decentralised education, a Workers' Party had been set up pledged to develop popular democracy and some well-organised political organisations and pressure groups already existed. But given these reservations, there are several important features, not unlike those behind those principles informing this book. Education was taken as a human right, concerned to develop autonomous citizens, and based upon principles of liberty, respect and social justice; instead of dismissing community knowledge as irrelevant to education, it was taken as a vital resource for curriculum construction; the needs of the community, the interest of the student and crucial issues were discovered empirically and taken into account when constructing interdisciplinary themes as the basis for a curriculum; the emphasis throughout was upon democratic and transparent processes.

Even here, in the United Kingdom, there are some signs of movement towards a popular democracy with the retiring government finally acknowledging the repeated expressions of discontent that local people had no control over community affairs.

Community Empowerment Plan

In October 2007 the Communities and Local Government Department published a Community Empowerment Action Plan with 3 key areas:

widening and deepening empowerment opportunities locally;
supporting and enabling people to take up empowerment opportunities;
strengthening local representative democracy.

So much for the rhetoric. A 23-point Action Plan was also produced, including:

the transfer of more assets to communities;
the development of community kitties;
giving tenants a greater role in housing management.

That same year a "Participatory Budgeting Unit" was set up "to empower communities through the development of UK models of participatory budgeting" trialled in six local authority areas.

The Communities Minister has since announced a pilot scheme whereby 10 councils will be provided with up to £2 million to enable local residents to decide on financial priorities. She also made it clear that she wants every neighbourhood to have control of some of the council's cash within five years and that councils will have to hold ballots before deciding where money should be targeted. She added:

> *"The purpose of the pilot projects is to show that this (PB) can be done and you get better decisions. Participatory budgeting is not just consultation. It is where people come together, set priorities and vote on what is going to happen. It means giving them the choice over whether they want to prioritise street cleaning, leisure facilities for young people, traffic calming or whatever the local concerns might be. (But) councillors must not feel their democratic mandate is by-passed and instead recognise that it will strengthen their relationship with their local community." (19)*

When one considers the radical nature of participatory democracy in Porte Alegre, this clarion call to the people by a government obsessed with centralisation is not without its black humour - and is entitled to be greeted with scorn. There is a huge, and presently insurmountable conceptual gap between the concerns expressed here, with such issues as traffic calming and street cleaning; and concerns with constructing local democratic curricula along the lines of Porte Alegro, with its emphasis upon the needs of the community, the development of personal autonomy and social justice. At the moment local democracy hardly exists here, ignored by the people at election time and manifested in the autocratic enforcement of petty rules by faceless bureaucrats. As Simon Jenkins puts it in the Guardian of Feb.18 2009:

> *"Ministers such as Hazel Blears put on smocks, stuck straw in their hair and talked of parish forums and kitties*

and stakeholders. They were all hardcore centralists who have given themselves the greatest concentration of state power in Europe".

suggesting that talk of "community empowerment" is little more than high-flown rhetoric.

Genuine commitment to community empowerment and local democracy would in the first place be expressed in financial terms with real tax-raising powers giving some autonomy over local decision-taking. But despite the rhetoric of "localism" and "people power" the current move to centralisation of school funding and the emasculation of local education authorities underlines the contradictions of current political power. For example, in the absence of public discussion about the nature and purposes of mass education, we are left – bereft of principles – to drown in a sea of slogans. Thus, we have pupil-parent guarantees, self-regulated schooling, supply-side revolutions, cooperative learning and – inevitably – "freedom and choice"; as well as academies, trust schools and, more recently, free schools (free to spend tax-payers money and free to accept the diktat of the Education Minister). What could it all mean in practice? Significantly, such key concepts as accountability, transparency and democratic decision-making (judging from the evidence provided earlier from existing academies and trust schools) are generally absent. The minimum demand from state-funded schools must be a detailed public statement of its education programme, including its conception of education, as well as its curriculum aims and procedures, together with its policies on such matters as selection and evaluation. But, given all this, to whom should the school be accountable? In the light of current rhetoric on the Big Society, one would expect the community to be primarily involved. But the new Academies Bill renders the notion of "community" schools invisible, and the new schools planned and set up by the government are anything but community schools.

There is however one recent development which may provide the opportunity to give some of these abstractions and speculations concrete reality and provide a basis for substantive analysis. It concerns the building of Elmgreen School, in Lambeth, the first parent-powered comprehensive school in the country. The initial motivation arose from a shortage of secondary school places in Lambeth, with as many as 50% of children having to go to schools outside the borough, so up to 500 parents petitioned Lambeth Council for a new school. But the parents wanted, not another academy with its financial seductions, but a non-selective, non-denominational comprehensive school, to be an integral part of the community. It was the strength and determination of these parents, together with their organising ability - setting up a Parent Promoter Foundation and subsequently an educational trust - which marks out this particular initiative. The overall outcome of the pressure brought by the parents and its determination to overcome the many bureaucratic obstacles standing in the way, was a grant of £25 millions from the "Building Schools for the Future" programme and the granting of Specialist (humanities) schools status. Although the school is still being built, it opened its doors to its first intake last year and provides visible evidence of "parent-empowerment". It will be interesting to see how this school develops - from our particular perspective, how well it promotes personal autonomy and contributes to participatory democracy.

We have dealt in this chapter with some of the more visible challenges to the status quo. But underpinning all this are deeper, less visible reactionary forces at work, which represent perhaps the greatest obstacle of all to change, and which I shall look at now.

(b) BARRIERS TO CHANGE

We have mentioned the term "hegemony" several times in the course of this narrative in referring to a particular culture which has become so dominant that it saturates our consciousness and takes on the quality of the natural order of things, to which there appears to be no alternative. We have also seen how in recent times a hegemonic corporate message has been reinforced by positive support from the state, providing what might be seen as an irresistible force of indoctrination or "brainwashing", as with the hidden curriculum of the school, to which several references have been made already.

CONSUMERISM

This hidden curriculum can be seen as one manifestation of corporatism, where the values, processes and structures of corporate capitalism are accepted uncritically and implicitly. Thus knowledge is commodified and packaged as objectified (reified) subjects in accordance with an objectives model based upon specific targets, for delivery to students / consumers in exchange for future qualifications, obtained through graded external quantifiable examinations. In accordance with market principles, this exchange takes place in a competitive environment characterised by such criteria as examination success, displayed by "league tables", to facilitate parental choice. In such situations learning is essentially instrumental, in terms of exchange value, rather than intrinsic to the learner.

A fundamental dilemma facing corporatism is the constant need for capital accumulation. Thus, once most basic needs of the developed world are met, it is necessary to change the emphasis from the manufacture of goods to the manufacture of needs in order to expand profitable markets, a process which leads inexorably to a consumerist culture. Making use of various psychological theories, corporations have launched a massive campaign of marketing and advertising, in order to penetrate the consciousness of the potential consumer. For example, humanistic psychology is applied to the exploration of emotions and fantasies, as well as TV product placements as a basis for subsequent viewer discourse. And psychoanalytic theory has been employed in subliminal advertising, where the message was transmitted to the subconscious, by-passing the conscious mind.

Even "psychographics" has been invented to enable the categorisation and hence the exploitation of consumer values and motivations. Some idea of the intense nature of competition in the commercial world is provided by what until now has been the surreal possibility of using "neuromarketing": tracing brain activity in response to various marketing stimuli and hence giving a competitive advantage.

We saw earlier how business, with the active encouragement of government, has sought to extend its penetration of every corner of society to schools, with sponsorship deals, vending machines and with the provision of business–friendly teaching materials. Schoolchildren have been seen as a captive audience with considerable spending power and hence as valuable consumers. But at a deeper level, there is the more sinister prospect of children's consciousness and identity being subverted by exposure to this corporatist culture. Thus, advertising propagates a particular life style, so that nowadays one of the worst things that can happen to a young person is to be labelled "uncool". In the words of 8-year-old Robert:

> *"If you were like going out with your mates you'd probably want your cool stuff because you don't want your mates to say you're rubbish". (20)*

More specifically, advertising aims to develop brand loyalty which provides an important symbolic representation of group identity (and has been compared by anthropologists to tribalism with its totems.) Identities often become extensions of corporate logos, whilst human worth is seen, not in terms of personal qualities ("being") but more in terms of material possessions ("having"). As one perceptive 10-year-old puts it:

> "People see what you look like before they realise what you are like. So you show your personality in what you are wearing". (21)

Or in the words of one psychologist:

> "In my practice I see kids becoming incredibly consumerist. The most stark example is when I ask them what they want to do when they grow up . They all say they want to make money. When they talk about their friends, they talk about the clothes they wear, the designer labels they wear, not the person's human qualities." (22).

Not only are pupils corrupted by such commercialisation, but schools themselves (as well as the academies being run by unaccountable businessmen) are being converted into agencies for the propagation of corporatist values, with the emphasis upon the instrumental rather than the intrinsic. This corporatist curriculum teaches young people the values - amongst other things - of instant gratification, materialism and individualism. It denies the existence of a moral commitment to society, with the functional citizen described earlier and prized in the Learning Society being replaced by the passive consumer. Whilst there is an illusion of freedom in a world of plenty, in reality it provides a covert means of social control and acts as a barrier to the development of personal autonomy.

TECHNICISM : PSYCHOMETRICS AND NEUROSCIENCE

Another ideology which is increasingly entering our mainstream culture and gaining uncritical acceptance is Technicism, which promises to meet all our needs and solve all our problems. It is concerned to reduce human realities and experiences to technical terms, and to explain them by such devices as categorisation and measurement. And with its potential for social control it is of great interest to state apparatuses. Our first encounter with technicism in this book came with the psychometric movement and its definition and measurement

294

of intelligence, encapsulated in the concept of "intelligence quotient", a term which has unproblematically entered mainstream language and has been used by governments to legitimate various selection procedures in both education and business. ("Metrics" is now common currency among bureaucracies and is used extensively by the Healthcare Commission for the measurement, not just of physical properties like blood pressure, but of more elusive human qualities such as "compassion"). More recently, psychometricians, in a climate of growing clinical depression and social breakdown, have turned their attention to emotional aspects and have now produced a quantified "emotional quotient", which we have dealt with earlier, and which the Education Department has begun to employ in its "positive psychology" lessons in school. [This urge to measure everything has not only led to the establishment of personality quotients in the past for selection purposes in business and education but is leading into ever more exotic areas like "humanity quotients" - testimony to the growing potency of the "metric" movement].

Another potential weapon in the armoury of technicism comes with the rapid advances in neuroscience accompanying the increasing sophistication of brain scanners. These reveal not only the structure of the brain but networks of neurons responsible for different patterns of brain activity, each particular pattern indicating what a person is thinking about. A particularly revealing discovery concerns the way that the destruction of a brain circuit (as in a stroke) leads to the formation of new neural connections. In other words, the brain is not rigid and immutable, as was previously thought, but highly plastic. Whilst this idea of neuroplasticity can have valuable pathological applications, it has alerted many researchers to possible educational implications with its potential for "rewiring" the brain. It is this feature which is of particular concern here.

Centres for Education and NeuroScience are springing up in our universities and, given the potential for fundamental reworking of the brain, we need to know not just how radical are their intentions but also what is their conception of education. One neuroscientific definition of Education, for example, is:

> "a process of adaptation such that learning is guided to
> ensure proper brain development and functionality",

whilst:

> "a better understanding of the neural underpinnings of
> behaviour and learning will also help tailor pedagogic

curricula towards pupils' individual neurocognitive resources". (23)

And the Oxford Cognitive Neuroscience Education Forum presents as its two main objectives:

> *"1. to design cognitive neuroscientific experiments that could address important educational concerns;*
> *2. to inform the education profession of relevant cognitive neuroscientific research." (24)*

Initially educational neuroresearch has been confined to cognitive disability and has merely provided a physical explanation for such conventional wisdom that intense practice improves mechanical performance. For instance, dyslexia has responded to 100 hours of instruction through its rewiring of the brain. But some researchers are anxious to move beyond such traditional or pathological approaches. For example, Uta Frith, of University College, London, makes the really bold confident prediction of the impact of neuro - science on education, even suggesting that micro - chips might be implanted into the brain to enhance cognitive function:

> *"Neuroscience techniques will be available to track the effects of learning in the developing brain of individual children . We will be able to decide which teaching method, or indeed which teacher, is best suited to each child.....Neuroscience will reveal the basis of academic skills such as reading, writing, or maths and what to do about children at risk of failing to learn these skills.......*
> *By 2020, neuroscience will have revealed the brain basis of our emotions, our sense of justice and our moral sensitivity." (25)*

None of the above is to suggest that psychology is necessarily a sinister science in the pay of ambitious governments, or that technology is without its beneficial aspects. For example, there are soft-liners as well as hard-liners in neuro-science. It is the latter who deny the existence of human consciousness, of human intentionality, desires and belief - as well as the separation of physical and mental activities. Given their potential for social control it is imperative that initiatives such as those described above be carefully monitored and open for inspection by the community. At the moment evidence for the effects of conditioning is fairly sketchy. What can be claimed, though, with some confidence, is that these ideologies are the very antithesis of humanistic education. They provide additional resources for a Brave New World, and as they become hegemonic they are increasingly accepted into the collective consciousness.

(c) WHERE NOW ?

The dehumanising hegemony of "techno-corporatism" described above paints a bleak picture of the prospects of breaking down the status quo and educating for personal autonomy. It promises a self-reinforcing hierarchical "delivery" system whereby the alphas, betas, gammas, deltas and omegas are selected to perform their allotted tasks for a capitalist economy, whilst all are indoctrinated into the business values of materialism, individualism and self-interest - and where the state endorses the technical manipulation of human behaviour.

It is not surprising then that, given all these obstacles to radical change, mere reform is often thought to be inadequate. Instead, there are increasing calls for revolutionary movements. But revolutions are unlikely to happen in the modern capitalist state with its monopoly of social and political control - and the record of revolutions in the past is hardly encouraging. So we must consider other alternatives. Fortunately the persistence of such a hegemonic culture depends upon certain key features. The system must continue to deliver on its promise of ever-increasing personal wealth, and the underpinning ideology must be free from internal contradictions. I shall look at these two features in turn.

Failures to Deliver

What might appear to be a solid ideological barrier to reform is not all that it seems. Capitalism has often been thought to contain the seeds of its own destruction - not least because of its pillage of finite resources. As I write this, its financial system is in self-destruct mode, taxpayers the world over are being obliged to bail out privately-owned banks, and there is a rapid increase in unemployment. "Experts" are scratching their heads in attempts to explain this phenomenon, questioning the authenticity of theories of equilibrium and market fundamentalism, the lack of regulation in a neo-liberal climate, or blaming excessive self-interest on the part of executives. Some previously successful capitalists are even arguing that a new world order is needed. Certainly the present consumerist culture is under threat and losing the gloss accompanying claims of ever - increasing wealth and well -being.

So this barrier is not as impregnable as it once seemed. Connections are also being made between corporate capitalism and the increase in clinical depression, due either to the decline of genuine human relationships in a materialist, individualist culture or to growing inequalities.

And the Education Department, locked into this ideology, is not without its problems of legitimation:

> 23 out of 53 targets, including literacy and numeracy standards, set in 1998 are still being missed;
> a quarter to a fifth of pupils are functionally illiterate when they enter secondary school;
> it is estimated that there are about 10,000 regular and 60,000 casual truants, resulting in 30,000 penalty notices being sent to parents. (There is even a special category NEETS for those school-leavers in neither work, further education or training.);
> international comparative tables invariably show UK pupils in a poor light and there is widespread disaffection among those "bright" students succeeding within the system.

It is hardly surprising, given all this that the Education Department is on the defensive and in some ideological disarray, as the following two important accounts reveal only too clearly. They show (ostensibly) two opposing ideologies operating in the same government department. I have tried to keep the detail to a minimum but I regard the contradictions as potentially so significant that they deserve close scrutiny.

Internal Contradictions: Ideologies in Conflict?

I have drawn attention earlier to the absence of a consensual operational definition of state education, which not only allows the state interest in the reproduction of the socio-economic order to go unquestioned, but allows bureaucratic agencies to travel along different paths, two of which are followed below.

(a) *The Corporatist Approach: "Command and Control" Teacher Training*

Previously......

> During the period covered in this book, the training of teachers has developed from the apprenticeship system of "on-the-job" pupil-teachers (learning through practice) to a theory / practice separation provided respectively in higher education institutions and teaching practice schools. The institutions involved were relatively autonomous (subject to general university oversight) and free to develop their own solutions to what were perceived as the problems of a broad teacher education (as opposed to a limited teacher training)

"Education", then, was seen in the liberal terms of overall human development, so that intending teachers were introduced to the major related disciplines of philosophy, sociology, history and psychology.

The Move towards Centralised Control of Teacher Training

But with what was perceived as the emerging threat of globalisation and inefficient public services, came a more economist view linked to the New Public Management model described earlier, and demanding centralised control. Pupils were seen in terms of "human capital" and economic progress was linked causally – and with spurious evidence - to educational development.

In 1984, the Teacher Training Agency, an arm of the Education Department and since renamed the Training and Development Agency (TDA), was set up, ostensibly to bring coherence to what was seen as a fragmented system, both by exerting more centralised control and by limiting the influence of the universities. Since then there has been a continuous movement by the State to exert increased control over the entire education system, from teacher training to classroom practice. "Potential new providers" (PNP) of courses (which could vary from large universities to groups of schools) were now required to submit proposals meeting over 150 assessment criteria! Accompanying this formidable list of requirements was also the implied threat of closure for non - compliance with the assessment criteria. It is clear that, apart from the content of the academic component of the degree, control of training courses has passed from university to central government, with a corresponding decline in academic freedom.

So much for the centralisation of control. The intending teacher usually then embarks on a series of stages on the way to becoming a qualified teacher:

(1) Initial Teacher Training (ITT). The minimum entry requirement to this course is the equivalent of grade C in GCSE English and mathematics, coupled with the extraordinary requirement that students should be able to read effectively and communicate clearly and accurately in written and spoken English.

(2) Newly Qualified Teacher (NQT). On successful completion of the course – which demands the passing of skills tests in numeracy, literacy and ICT - trainees acquire the status of "newly – qualified teacher" (NQT)

(3) Qualified Teacher Status. They then enter a one-year induction period, before acquiring qualified teacher status (QTS) by reaching recommended standards in professional attributes, skills, knowledge and understanding.

There is subsequently a series of thresholds which provide, on crossing successfully, performance-related pay.

Professional Development and Performance-related Pay

It was now that the Rewards and Incentive Group, an offshoot of TDA, came on to the scene to tighten this control even further by developing new Performance Management arrangements (due to come into force in September 2007). These are of such profound significance for the future of a democratic curriculum that they need to be looked at in some detail. The NUT expresses its concerns as follows:

> "Performance management, classroom observation and performance related pay are hitting the profession with a pace and purpose that could bring a sea change in the work of teachers and to relationships within the staff rooms of schools

across England.....Guidance is being promulgated even before the consultation period is completed....The new arrangements could treble the amount of time and numbers of visits to which reviewees are subjected for classroom observation for performance management purposes." (26)

New teachers with QTS status now enter a framework of progressive professional standards underpinned by performance-related pay, related to the sequential levels of "threshold", "excellent" and "advanced skills". In other words they have now passed through the portals of "Performance Management", based upon the processes of :

> planning (in terms of objectives)
> review (of progress over the year, against stated objectives)
> monitoring (progress kept under review by teacher and team leader).

The Reward and Incentive Group have recently taken upon themselves the task of providing guidance on "continuing professional development", with the disarming comment that they seek to "remove the burden from local authorities". In introducing their performance management scheme, they claim - without apparent irony - that they are seeking to develop a "non-bureaucratic streamlined and multipurpose arrangement". How well they succeed is revealed by studying the document itself. (27) For example, the category "performance management process" comprises 49 prescriptions, and includes "classroom observation". As this is likely to be the most revealing and contentious part of the document, I will look at it in a little more detail.

PERFORMANCE MANAGEMENT: CLASSROOM OBSERVATION

The procedure involves both a reviewer and reviewee; the reviewer is ideally the head (if an "excellent" or "advanced skills" teacher) or line manager .

(1) the regulations specify a limit of three hours in the "review cycle".
(2) the reviewer and reviewee agree plans for the observation which should be realistic and manageable and include rigorous objectives.
(3) classroom observation should be supportive and developmental, followed by a short, written record, with feedback.
(4) any voluntary peer observations initiated by the teacher are not part of management performance arrangements;

(5) Ofsted observations are also not part of performance management.
Where the reviewee is eligible, assessment may lead to a recommendation for pay progression.

Analysis

The relationship between policy initiatives and educational research appears to be virtually non - existent. Any problems of lack of evidence are easily resolved by a bureaucracy regarding curriculum development as a logical, rather than an empirical, exercise. In this spirit I will deduce what conclusions follow logically from the above document:

> (a) it clearly comes within the instrumental conception of teaching, with observation linked to the teacher's pay prospects.
> (b) the entire programme is atheoretical, without any reference to pedagogic principles or theories of learning;
> (c) there is no explicit notion of accountability - only implicit accountability to the state.

Thus, neither the pupils' nor parents' interests / values are taken into account;

> (d) the prescriptive, objectives model on show represents a technical approach to teaching, involving the delivery of a sequenced package of unproblematic knowledge. There is no allowance for teacher judgment to take account of contextual variables - nor for the pupil voice to be heard
> (e) nowhere can reference to justification be found.

In short it is a totalitarian document, completely at odds with a democratic education and promising to produce a divided individualistic teaching staff. It is indicative of the profound cultural shift taking place in the country, as a corporate capitalist hegemony takes a stronger hold on our lives and such words as "solidarity" and "cooperation" vanish from our working vocabulary. From this point of view, the challenge facing the introduction of a democratic education is, to say the least, daunting. There is the hope, however, that "reflective" teachers, with a sense of mission and with their own prior experiences and education, will tend to engage in professional discourse at odds with the technical rationality implied in this new approach to professional development and distort, if not actually subvert, its central message.

So much, then for this example of the application of New Public Management to the training of our teachers. Let us look now at some initiatives more directly linked to relationships in the classroom and potentially at odds with the above ideology.

(b) The Humanistic Approach: Conversation Pieces: Personalised Learning

(i) the National Conversation

In sharp contrast to the totalitarian tone of the above document is the invitation from the Education Department to practising teachers to hold a "National Conversation":

> "We would like you to join a national conversation about how personalisation can be used to drive success in every school. It is a conversation that has already started.....We would like you to take a further step in the conversation by visiting the personalised website....where you will be able to discuss with a system-wide audience:
>   how you are personalising learning in your school.....
>   whether the resources for progress we are providing are helpful...
>   what more the DfES can do to help.
> We look forward to working with you to make it a reality."
> (29)

The contrast of what is, prima facie, a humanistic approach, to that of the "Command and Control" of the corporate management model described above could hardly be starker. Instead of a prescriptive approach to the curriculum, we now have in principle a shared cooperative model implying a practical rather than a technical curriculum. Admittedly it is constrained by a bureaucratic definition of "personalised" but it still represents a sufficient contradiction to warrant the question "Who is deciding education policy"?

(ii) <u>the Learning Conversation</u>

The previous "conversation" is between the Education Department and teachers. The Learning Conversation, on the other hand, is intended to be between teachers and pupils. In 2005, the DfES funded the Learning Conversation Research Project as part of the initiative into personalised learning. Five LEA's were nominated as pilots and were each required to appoint two consultants to "create the framework for Learning Conversations" and provide "training to develop facilitators' skills". Pupils were selected by project leaders and were expected to hold at least three learning conversations a term outside the classroom during lesson time. The student voice was at last to be heard as mentors opened dialogue with them.

The following student aims were proposed by the national team:

> clarify their understanding of learning and of themselves as learners and so take greater control over their learning;
> make informed choices about the curriculum and learning;
> express preferences and opinions about learning;
> negotiate targets for learning;
> transfer and apply their learning better across subjects and contexts and so improve their rate of progress. (30)

This formalised innovation appears to at least provide the foundations for student autonomy and a democratic curriculum, with the "student voice" finally taken seriously in the context of dialogic teaching. And although the Education Department's version of "personalised learning" is not to be equated with democratic "person-centred education" as I have indicated before, it conceivably represents a possible evolutionary move in that direction. And the recent Secondary Curriculum Review by QCA (Qualifications and Curriculum Authority) ostensibly carries this shift to a democratic curriculum a stage further:

> investigate and reflect on the social, moral and political problems and ethical issues they encounter in life, the media and through learning;
> engage with those in authority, challenge injustice and make a difference to things they feel strongly about;
> enable greater flexibility and creativity (including creative partnerships with artists).

But there are timely reminders of the need to locate such initiatives within a material context. For example:

> *"It is important to resist illusions that these curriculum reforms and the other associated changes can be the basis of a new and unambiguously progressive consensus. These reforms do not contradict the neo-liberal function of the school system. The underpinning rationale remains the production of an economically competitive workforce". (31)*

To which one could add a culture of targets, league tables, managerialism, rote learning and individual quantitative competitive examinations, all within a technicist framework.

We are left with a sharp reminder of the forces supporting and underpinning the status quo and resisting change. Whilst, for example, on the one hand Ofsted (and more recently the Secondary Curriculum Review) has called for authority to be challenged and social injustice to be exposed; on the other there is the rigid production line of "Command and Control" for the preparation of future teachers working within a technical "delivery" mode, which highlights the immense difficulty facing teachers wishing to enter a practical or emancipatory mode. Fortunately the work of imaginative teachers and their subject associations over the years has produced a more enlightened, interesting and relevant curriculum, whilst "Rethinking Education" (32) produces both radical and practical ideas for the classroom. A further problem concerns the transient nature of many curriculum initiatives which die with the innovator. But what is perhaps most frustrating is the ability of neo-liberalism to capture and pervert radical innovations; for example, making Citizenship an examination subject, emphasising the difficulty of unearthing the deeper implications of government initiatives.

With a new government comes a new Education Minister, an innocent unburdened by a knowledge of education history and oblivious to the machinations of those reactionary forces which have been the focus of this book. He cheerfully clears away what he regards as unnecessary clutter, in a context of the ideology of the privatisation and marketisation of schools and universities, with league tables to assist in "freedom of choice". "Choice", however, will be confined to utilitarian, commercial subjects, needed by students to pay off their debts, in the absence of funding by the State. We await events with interest.......

SUMMING UP

Insofar as people ever think of the State, they probably entertain an avuncular image of a benign institution acting for the common good. Aristotle, for example, thought that the state existed for the sake of a good and happy life, with the best form of government being that which promoted the well-being of all. "All" for Aristotle, however, excluded slaves and women. And this narrative has shown how the modern State has also operated in an exclusive capacity. Throughout the period of our enquiry it has acted exclusively in the interests of the privileged and powerful, initially the interests of the ruling class by sustaining the social order and latterly in the Business interest through a redefinition of education as commodity and the active encouragement of the penetration of schools for commercial purposes, both short and long-term.

Its actions have here been shown to be profoundly undemocratic. As the "Making of the National Curriculum" has indicated (see Appendix) ministers became increasingly indifferent to the views of the working committees in imposing unilaterally their own untested ideas. On the level of policy-making on other hand, the recent Academies Bill (for all its talk of "parental choice") denies parents any consultation, whilst only one school governor (and no parents) received a formal invitation for its school to become an academy. In attempting to defend those academies already functioning, the government has shown a lack of transparency in the publication of their examination results, whilst, despite repeated contradictions, there has been "cherry-picking" of students in order to boost examination performance. We have also seen unsavoury creeping in at the level of the shop floor, with Ofsted reports being ignored in order to show that successful schools were in fact failing, in order to justify their transformation into academies.

The selective favouring of corporate capitalism by the State also leads to profound changes in the values and processes of education. The second part of this book has in fact described in some detail this process of incorporation and capture. Education has been redefined in economic terms and subject to market forces, with consumer choice being exercised in terms of spurious objective criteria, such as league tables, resulting in schools set against schools in competition. Meanwhile, the curriculum has become increasingly unbalanced, with the relative exclusion of humanities subjects in favour of those with direct economic potential (STEM - Science, Technology, Engineering and Mathematics). Overall, the chief role of the State, instead of being concerned with the educational and common interest, is now focussed upon the reproduction of the socio-economic order.

The net effect of all this on the education of future generations is the development of consumers rather than citizens, with diminished critical awareness and a limited knowledge and understanding – not only of our heritage - but of the environment . Politically, these products of our education system are typically naïve, lacking social solidarity and the will to protect our civilisation - with the possibility of our current social malaise and cultural impoverishment deepening, threatening our way of life and even our security. The notion of "community" has all but vanished from our vocabulary. And recent actions taken by the State with respect to mass education can only be a further divisive step, emphasising inequalities in our society, with poor, unmotivated families being left at the bottom of the pile, whilst "outstanding" schools are given extra resources.

Such is the grip of corporate hegemony on our society that it would seem that we are condemned to act as passive robots, further sustaining the system. But arguments are increasingly made for the transfer of power from a centralised State down to local level. And while the present government's talk of a Big Society may be little more than a visionary flourish, an impressive report "From Social Security to Social Productivity" from the Commission for Public Services (2020 Public Services Trust 2010) attempts to reconceptualise and operationalise the relationships between centre and periphery:

> *"We need a new deal between citizen, society and the state. This rejects old models of universal service delivery and the new public management models of consumerism…..Our approach is bottom-up. The means of achieving it we call social productivity………our goal must be a new culture of democratic participation and social responsibility…..public services must engage and enrol citizens, families, communities in creating better outcomes as partners……..Parents and local communities should be free to agree educational outcomes to develop*

*curriculum with local schools......**but this freedom must come with a responsibility to shape local strategies around a set of strategic principles"**.*

Here we come to the heart of the matter. For too long the educational interest has been subordinated to other interests. We have seen in this narrative how in the early stages of mass education poor children were given a manual/practical curriculum to meet the perceived needs of industrial capitalism, whilst the sons of the rich enjoyed a non-utilitarian classical education to cement their position in the social order. The latter was taken as the holy grail by a working-class movement demanding equality of educational opportunity. The futility of this position was revealed with comprehensivisation which showed all too clearly that a grammar/public school curriculum was rejected by a majority of working-class children. Since then, the education system has remained fragmented, with "bright" children following an academic curriculum to ensure examination success and improved career prospects, whilst the rest were left alienated and rootless, subjected to various offers of vocational education. The opening up of schools to external sponsors, with their own interests, has led to further chaos. So the time is long overdue for a working towards a national consensus of basic and essential educational principles, within which teachers are free to operate, depending upon the particular needs and interests of their charges. At least, in this situation, the State could be said to be furthering social justice, with an equalisation of educational opportunity.

But all this is to ignore the reactionary forces currently prevailing in our society, ready to counter what might be seen as the awakening of possible destabilising forces, or useless attempts to turn a sow's ear into a silk purse. The later chapters of the book do in fact provide illustrations of attempts to counter the totalitarianism of a corporate hegemony, by emphasising in their different ways humanising and democratising alternatives. But it has to be admitted that history is not on the side of these Davids in their struggle with Goliath.

Make of all this what you will. I leave the last word to Michael Pollan:

> *"Sometimes you have to act as if acting will make a difference, even when you can't prove that it will. That, after all, was precisely what happened in Communist*

Czechoslovakia and Poland when a handful of individuals such as Vaclav Havel and Adam Michnik resolved that they would simply conduct their lives as if they lived in a free society. That improbable bet created a tiny space of liberty that, in time, expanded to take in, and then help bring down, the whole of the Eastern Bloc". (33)

NOTES AND REFERENCES

1. www.thersa.org/newcurriculum
2. RSA Opening Minds Home
3. RSA Journal – Curriculum for a New Century. The pilot group achieved results between 12% and 15% better than the control group. The coursework for Biology, Chemistry and Physics normally undertaken in Year 11 was completed in Year 9.
4. Pupils are required to take responsibility for their own learning, to indicate which tasks will be performed within the framework laid down by the teachers, and which competences will be developed, together with evidence of attainment:

    Scheme: my life

    Unit: going places

    Activity: making a travel brochure

    Competences developed: learning to think, using my creative talents, using ICT

    How the competences were developed: "I had to decide what to put in the booklet, plan the layout, put it together on the computer and print it" etc

    Evidence: booklet in my "Going Places" folder etc
5. Garner, R. in The Independent Nov 26 2007.
6   Dr. Maria Montessori invented her radical teaching approach in 1907 in order to teach the poor children of Rome.
7. www.montessori.org.uk/GortonMount
8. http.//www.Montessori.org.uk/pdfs
9   www.politics.co.uk.
10 op cit.
11 Fielding, M. (2001) in J.of Educational Change 2. 123-141
12 op cit
13 European Commission (1996) Teaching and Learning: Towards the Learning Society. Luxembourg: EC
14 http://www.lifelonglearning.co.uk/greenpaper/
15 Dearing Report (1997) "Higher Education in the Learning Society "HMSO.London
16 Ranson,S.(ed) (1998) Inside the Learning Society. Cassell. London
17 www.robert-owen.com/quotes.htm
18 Wainwright, H. (op cit) and others
19 Blears, H. BBC News July 5 2007
20. www.consumer.bbk.ac.uk/research/pole.html

21. op.cit.

22.http://www.globalissues.org/article/237/children-as-consumers

23. 9134 TLRPLearn4.stg.6

24.Oxford Cognitive Neuroscience- Education Forum

25. J.Educ. for Teaching vol 31 no4

26 NUT on the Web, January 19 2007

27. www.dfes.gov.uk.consultations. The document includes the following categories:

    i. roles and responsibilities: 21 recommendations

    ii. preparing for performance management: 15 prescriptions

    iii. the performance management process: 49 prescriptions

    iv. specific issues for groups of teachers:19 suggestions

28. literacy trust.org.uk

29..DfES The National Conversation:Schools Leading Reform

30. www.pupil-voice.org.uk/conference-2006.html

31 .her,R. J.C.E.P.S. vol5 no2

32. www.rethinkinged.org.uk

33. Pollan,M Guardian June 6 2008

POST SCRIPT – THINKING OUT OF THE BOX

In one sense this narrative can be seen as a modest attempt to rehabilitate the history of education. And how much educational history is in need of rehabilitation can be gauged from the blistering comments by Robin Alexander in the course of his analysis of the Education Department's Primary Strategy. Claiming that the government does not so much rewrite history as ignore it, he goes on :

> " It (the Primary Strategy) shows little awareness of evidence from outside the charmed circle of government and its agencies; and no awareness of what even previous governments and government agencies did before 1997, the year in which, apparently, history and real education began. .... Quite apart from its disparaging view of the competence of teachers and the quality of teacher training before 1997 (the year of New Labour's election) its sweeping dismissal of this period as one of 'uninformed professional judgment' or at best 'uninformed prescription' simply ignores the vast body of information of which many in the education world were acutely aware: HMI Reports on individual schools, HMI national surveys.....major independent Reports on primary, secondary, further, higher and teacher education.......
> HMI documents on the curriculum; local evidence on standards of attainment ...... national evidence on pupil attainment from the sampled assessment programmes of the Assessment of Performance Unit; reports from Commons Select Committees; the accumulated body of curriculum guidance and materials from the Schools Council; and of course research. "

The seriousness of the educational implications following from this airbrushing out of history by an arrogant government can be easily illustrated. At the macro-level, this "living for the present" with no historical perspective, leads to educational practices being carried out in total denial of those momentous world events which threaten to render such practices redundant. Whilst at the micro-level, the a - historical approach of New Labour to the National Curriculum gives a picture of sterile unchanging God - given knowledge, leading to the packaging of inert subject matter transmitted from teacher to student without entering the minds of either. On the other hand an awareness of the politicking taking place in the course of the construction of the National Curriculum, as described earlier, reveals subjects to be social constructs, constantly contested by different interest groups and based upon living disciplines.

So much for the relevance and importance of educational history. The particular historical dynamic of this narrative has revealed a variety of interests and forces (political, economic, religious etc.) acting in various ways upon the education system: defining education, controlling access or stipulating the form of curriculum, pedagogy and examination. According to the Whig interpretation of history, "better ideas" replace poorer ones over time, so that the historical record is one of continual human progress. The need for better ideas is indicated by the current dehumanisation of society resulting from a corporate hegemony, with its hierarchical division of labour, alienating relations of production and a fierce competitive climate.

But, by its nature, capitalism exploits not only human beings but also natural resources. By regarding resources like oil and mineral as "income" rather than "capital" items, modern industries pillage them without a thought for the morrow. In the process they pollute the atmosphere with greenhouse gases and various toxins, and degrade the water supply with mineral waste, rendering it undrinkable and less suitable for food production. This is eco-vandalism on a massive scale, leading to a degradation of 60% of the world's ecosystems over the past quarter of a century, threatening the future of our civilisation and putting millions of lives at risk.

What might the "better idea" be, then to counter these effects? E.F. Schumacher in his book "Small is Beautiful: a Study of Economics as if People Mattered " (1974 Abacus) suggests that human relationships would be improved by the development of what he calls "intermediate technology", not involving mass production but production for the masses:

> *"making use of the best knowledge and experience conducive to decentralisation, compatible with the laws of ecology, gentle in its use of scarce resources, designed to serve the human person instead of making him the servant of machines.....mobilising the priceless resources which are possessed by all human beings, their clever brains and skilful hands, and supporting them with first-class tools"*

Schumacher also advocates a fresh direction for education, with the restoration of ethics and values to the curriculum at the expense of value-free positivism:

> *"The task of our generation is one of metaphysical reconstruction.....We are suffering from a metaphysical disease and the cure therefore must be metaphysical. Education which fails to clarify our central convictions is mere training or indulgence. For it is our central convictions that are in disorder and as long as the present anti - metaphysical temper persists, the disorder will grow worse. Far from ranking as man's greatest resource, education will then be an agent of destruction." (op cit)*

But an a - historical society, concerned only with the present and with material prosperity, is not listening. It is in denial, seduced by the god of economic growth. Even its financial system ensures that the rich get richer and the poor get poorer, with 20% of the world's population earning just 2% of global income, leading to a highly unstable and dangerous situation, threatening conflict as nations fight for scarce resources and living space, exacerbated by a sharply rising population. So not only is the system unsustainable ecologically and economically, but also politically. Still, we remain in denial, and as this narrative has shown, carry on with business as usual, as though all is well with the wider world.

What, then, are the implications of this bleak view of the future for our young people? In the absence of successful counter - hegemonic movements it will be necessary at some point to challenge the "curriculum for socio-economic reproduction" with a "curriculum for survival", repairing as far as possible the ravages inflicted upon humanity by corporate capitalism. In other words, by re-integrating the human personality and emphasising

314

the intrinsic rather than the instrumental - together with a shift from commercial to humanistic values, such as cooperation, respect for others and compassion. But the "better idea" referred to above, demands much more than this. For example, educational activities should:-

be collective rather than individual,

involve democratic decision-making, with an awareness of the political dimension,

have a cooperative ethos, involving as far as possible job-sharing and rotation,

be productive - involving, for example, the growing, preparation and cooking of food stuffs, as well as the construction and improvisation of relevant, simple structures and implements, meeting the basic needs for food, water and shelter, integrate mental and manual labour by setting practical activities within a framework of the understanding of important theoretical principles, (environmental, biological, physical etc.)

be sustainable, by ensuring that any use of the earth's resources can be replenished,

be "adventure" based, with the overall aim of developing personal qualities of self-sufficiency, resourcefulness and adaptability.

It is, in short, a curriculum for survival in an uncertain future, redolent of Herbert Spencer's efforts recounted earlier, but in a more collective context. Whilst it may be seen in one sense as a preparation in readiness for future crises, it can also be seen as no more than an obvious approach to the development of personal autonomy – and a reminder of how out-of-touch traditional curricula are, when dealing with problems of the real world. It stands in contrast to the National Curriculum's "Survival Guide to the Teenage Years" which is rooted firmly in the educational status quo with its "the development of appropriate skills and values to cope with the changes, stresses and responsibilities of adolescence" - with no reference to the social context for these problems, or the possibilities of future seismic change.

These recommendations take it for granted that the political system and the basic infrastructure remain intact, and ignore the possibility of apocalyptic change, such as that accompanying nuclear war, natural disaster, disease – or even collision with an asteroid (possibilities which captivate both religious cults and creative writers). It is impossible to prescribe an educational course which might cover all eventualities, but it would seem safe to claim that those who have followed survival courses will cope better than those who have stayed with the National Curriculum or Business Studies.

There is still one final possibility: to join the Survivors Club (www.survivorsclub.org)! According to the author Ben Sherwood, people divide into three groups when confronted by an emergency (the "10-80-10" theory of survival). 10% recover their poise quickly, 80% remain bewildered, while 10% lose their mental grip. Neuro - scientists tell us that these differences are due to the pre - frontal cortex of the brain, which can be rewired as we all learn to be survivors. Ben Sherwood also tells us how we can obtain our own Survival IQ from a Survivor Profile:

> *"The Survivor Profile is an exclusive internet - based questionnaire that was developed……(it) reveals your survivor personality and top three strengths. In just a few minutes online you'll discover what you've got to handle adversity. The test is fun, quick and produces a customised profile of your unique Survivor IQ."*

It is reassuring that, at the end of this narrative, we should be reacquainted with those visitors from the Brave New World : Neuro - science and Metrics.

APPENDICES

APPENDIX 1 ALIASES OF THE DEPARTMENT OF EDUCATION: 1833 –2008

1833– Committee of the Privy Council on Education

1856- Education Department (by absorption of the above)

1899 – Board of Education (combination of Education Department, Science and Art Department and Charity Commission)

1944 - Ministry of Education

1964 – Department of Education and Science (DES)

1992 - Department for Education (DFS)

1995 - Department for Education and Employment (DFEE)

2001 – Department for Education and Skills (DfES)

2007 – Department for Children, Families and Schools (DCFS)

2010 – Department for Education

APPENDIX 2: MAKING A NATIONAL CURRICULUM"

Subject Working Parties: Acrimony And Resignations

Kenneth Baker, as Education Minister in the process of making a National Curriculum, set up a National Curriculum Council with Duncan Graham (formerly chief education officer for Suffolk) as chief executive. He was soon to find himself embroiled in disputes both within and without the subject working parties, as the following extracts show.

MATHEMATICS: TRADITIONAL OR PROGRESSIVE?

Differing ideologies informing the teaching of mathematics were visible as far back as the sixteenth century, with abstract mathematics for the privileged and "more able", and practical mathematics (including arithmetic) for the rest, a practice which has continued to the present day. Differences could therefore be expected between various members of the maths working party. So it was not long before the group had split into two factions, roughly traditional and progressive. For example:

traditionalists:

> a thousand long divisions a day;
> the learning of tables;
> calculators not to be used before the age of 16.

progressives:

> solving real-life problems using modern aids like calculators;
> opposed to attainment targets, programmes of study and testing at the ages of 7 and 11.

Such polarisation of views led to acrimonious discussions and an absence of consensus. Under the circumstances the interim report the working party produced was lacking in coherence. As Baker himself puts it in his memoirs:

> *"The Group's interim report was disappointing and I was astonished to find it reflecting the deep doctrinal divisions that exist in maths.......The Group had not begun to address the task of setting out a progressive programme of study with clear attainment targets at each level.... This*

made me exasperated. I had a frank and angry meeting with the Maths Group in September 1987, when I made it clear that their work had turned out to be an academic exercise with no practical outcome". (8)

He decided to replace the chairman with Duncan Graham, who was also chief executive. The bad feeling in the group also led to the resignation, in rancour, of the emergent leader of the traditionalists. According to Duncan Graham:

"Baker and the civil servants then began a process of softening up the working group although many of them probably thought they were being roughed up. (They) told the working group that from now on things would have to be done their way...I became acutely aware that in its implementation and substance this was a Civil Service driven curriculum and not the property of the HMI. This was the first evidence of a huge de facto power shift in the way education was controlled in England and Wales ....the first major education reform in Britain that had not been created by the educational professionals....At this point the national curriculum hung by a thread. Kenneth Baker made it clear that we simply had to deliver if the national curriculum was to be saved.....I found to my relief that there was a tremendous desire to get on with it......One of the first and most difficult tasks was to arrive at a reasonable number of attainment targets ..we pinned all the attainment targets we had unearthed so far.... there were 354 which were eventually whittled down to 14 and were at that time state of the art.....Although a close run thing, the final report was delivered on time and to everybody's relief was generally well-received." (9)

As Kenneth Baker himself put it, "at last we had our first subject in place".

SCIENCE - BUILDING AN EMPIRE

Meanwhile, the Science working party was making good and relatively uncontentious progress. School Science was by now the very model of an academic subject. It had "evolved" over time from practical to academic concerns, and there was a well-established base in universities, where pure/ basic science possessed all the requisite criteria of a "form of knowledge", with distinctive conceptual schemes, coherent theoretical frameworks with wide-ranging explanatory powers informed by consensual methods of investigation (the so-called "scientific method"). Full of the self-confidence coming from their acknowledged place in both the academic and commercial worlds, the working party approached their task with what Duncan Graham thought was "messianic zeal" in taking the opportunity to make science "king of the curriculum" (and colonising part of Geography as "Earth Science" on the way). Their report recommended a balanced science course (in the process upsetting the independent schools, who wished to retain separate science subjects) taking up 25% of the school timetable and leading to a Dual Science award at GCSE. The NCC, fearing the emergence of an overcrowded curriculum, recommended two options: 20% for Dual Science and 15% for Single Science. As the science group reported on the same day as the maths group, August 16, 1988, teaching of these two subjects could begin in September 1989.

ENGLISH; FORMAL OR INFORMAL ?

The consensus established among members of the Science working party was to prove the exception. "English" was to divide rather than unite: the Secretary of State himself had particularly strong views on what comprised an English syllabus:

> "In the 1960's and 1970's the teaching of English had fallen victim to left-wing dogma. This meant that little was taught about formal grammar and punctuation, legibility was not important, spelling mistakes were frequently not corrected...It was because I love the English language and literature so much and had drawn so much pleasure from it in my own life, that I wanted everyone else to have the chance of enjoying it...Teaching had to convey the magic and power of the English language...I appointed a Working Group to draw up the curriculum on English under the chairmanship of Professor Brian Cox...given the task of drawing up a teaching programme to ensure that all school-leavers would be competent in the use of

320

*written and spoken English by the time they left school.
I also asked the Group to include recommendations on
what books children should have been expected to have
read by a certain age." (10)*

Cox had been co-editor of the Black Papers and it was widely assumed that Baker was ensuring that the English curriculum would be free of "left-wing dogma". But the interim report could hardly be described as right - wing or traditional, stressing that grammar was only one part of language and should be taught in context, not as a labelling exercise - "it is not sensible to propose a definitive list of terms." With regard to a book-list the Group believed the important thing was that books selected must be those children enjoy. In the end the idea of a definitive list was dropped.

The Prime Minister expressed her disappointment with the report, whilst Mr. Baker found it "woolly" and told the NCC to consider redefining the attainment targets so that they were sufficiently precise and reflected the importance of grammatical structure and terminology. The primary English curriculum which was eventually presented laid down that children should be taught certain grammatical terms and memorise the spelling of words, as well as learning poetry by heart – in deference to the Minister's wishes. As Duncan Graham put it "Baker's intervention was the first indication that ministerial whim could be enshrined in law" – but it was not to be the last. The subsequent secondary English report underlined the indivisibility of language and literature, leading to one GCSE. Children should have an acquaintance with the heritage of English literature as well as having access to modern material. But it was clear that a consensus had not been reached on whether grammar should be taught formally or whether the structure of language should be acquired through usage.

TECHNOLOGY: WHOSE NEEDS ?

Technology was a new developing subject still grappling with the prospect of deserting practical skills for the world of academia. In fact two curriculum groups had approached the problem of "School Technology" from two directions, one from the "craft" angle and one from an "applied Science" perspective, without either becoming the dominant model. What were the Secretary of State's thought on the matter?

"I had always believed that there was an overwhelming need for all children to be trained in the practical skills of computing, design, engineering, and business studies. Some schools were already teaching craft design technology, which had developed partly from woodwork, metalwork and art. Often alongside this was home economics. Many of these subjects were popular since they seemed to have greater relevance to their lives after school than the more academic subjects they were studying...To bring all this under the umbrella of the National Curriculum we appointed a Technology Working Group under the chairmanship of Lady Parkes, a governor of the BBC with a strong technological background...She had the task of creating an entirely new curriculum subject and stood up well to the various pressure groups of teachers who were all demanding more time for their own subject specialisms." (11)

The Working Group sought coherence for this new subject through a common set of procedures. Children had to:

first identify a problem or need;
then design a solution:
make whatever was required and
evaluate the outcome in aesthetic, commercial and environmental terms.

As Duncan Graham puts it:

"Here at last was a school lesson concerned with generating ideas, making and doing. Industrialists could hardly contain their approval as they saw this as the basis for all commercial enterprises." (12)

The National Curriculum could be described as a traditional grammar school curriculum, made up of "pure" subjects. In this sense Technology was an intruder, conventionally seen as an "applied" subject, using pure knowledge as a basis, in Graham's words, "for all commercial purposes", and hence serving the business - rather than the academic - interest. Whilst this is not necessarily anti-educational, it is instructive to note the impact of this particular conceptualisation on the fate in our schools of one particular subject, Home Economics, which now comes under the umbrella of "Technology". Whereas in the past as the name suggested, the focal point of this subject was the home, with children being taught how to make cheap and nutritious meals in specially - equipped cookery rooms, pupils were now to be initiated into a consumerist society serving a capitalist economy. (Although as I write this, it is becoming apparent that the demand for reversing this procedure and re-installing cookery rooms is becoming increasingly vocal) This change from "maker" to "consumer" is quickly revealed by inspection of current examination papers. In one recent GCSE examination on "Food", for example, out of seven questions, five are devoted to the commercial problems of food manufacturers. For example:

"A manufacturer wishes to extend the range of his ready-made pizza products. The test kitchen works to the following design criteria:
The successful product will:

be an AB product
use fresh vegetables
be served in individual portions
be eaten hot or cold
have a variety of textures.

(a) (i) with the aid of notes and sketches, produce two different design ideas which meet the design criteria
(ii) choose one of your design ideas for the manufacturer to develop

(b) (i) write a product specification for your chosen design idea
(ii) list the ingredients needed to make the chosen design idea in the test kitchen
(iii) produce a plan for making your chosen idea in the test kitchen."
(13)

Technology, then, as it is being conceptualised here is clearly out of step with the other subjects in the National Curriculum in having obvious commercial and exploitable potential. It is therefore important that clear guidelines are laid down. As far as educational potential is concerned it is also important to explore the relationship between theory and practice. Is "theory" closed and purely practical or can it lead to intellectual development? Both the working party and Duncan Graham seem unaware of these aspects. In fact Graham's comments on "rigour" are intriguing, to say the least:

> *"Technology leavened a subject-oriented curriculum and is most closely related to vocational qualification...The introduction of technology also led to facing up to the fact that there would have to be a certain abandonment of standards and rigour which were the driving forces of all the other subjects." (14)*

As is often the case, political implications of curriculum development are ignored. In view of future developments to be described later, it is important to see how Technology comes to be (re)defined, whether as a vocational or an academic subject.

HISTORY: KNOWLEDGE OR SKILLS?

History has few, if any, vocational aspirations. But there have been several different interpretations and definitions of history, chiefly concerned over whether history should emphasise factual knowledge or methods of historical enquiry. Ministers claimed therefore to have taken great care over the membership of the Working Group to ensure that there was wide representation from education and industry although the choice of chairman was both ideosyncratic and - in terms of the arbitrary manner in which power is sometimes bestowed - very revealing. As Duncan Graham put it:

> *"The appointment of Commander Michael Saunders Watson...was extraordinary. He appeared to be an eccentric choice inspired by Baker after the two men had met at a reception and found they had a mutual interest in history. Saunders Watson's only obvious credentials were that he ran a stately home which was used by many schools...He appeared to everybody to be a peculiarly Tory choice and looked to many as the first overt political appointment." (15)*

Both the Prime Minister (and Kenneth Baker) had decided views on what constituted history: the acquisition of historical knowledge:

> *"Though not an historian myself I had a very clear idea of what history was. History is an account of what happened in the past. Learning history, therefore, requires*

knowledge of events. It is impossible to make sense of these events without absorbing sufficient factual information and without placing matters in a clear chronological framework – which means knowing dates." (6)

Once again, it was a case of "traditionalists" versus "progressive". In setting up the working group in January 1989 the Minister made it clear that the programmes of study should have at the core the history of Britain, the record of its past and in particular, its political, constitutional and cultural heritage. When he saw the first draft from the working group he expressed his disappointment with the lack of emphasis on the teaching of hard facts and their chronology.

But the working group had come to the conclusion that it was impossible to accommodate hard facts within the attainment targets, a view shared by the chairman, who, like Professor Cox with the English working group, proved he was not the right-wing ideologue he may have been expected to be. On the contrary, attainment targets should specify skills such as interpretation, understanding and critical awareness. The reaction of Margaret Thatcher to the interim report was unequivocal:

"I was appalled. It put the emphasis on interpretation and enquiry as against content and knowledge. There was insufficient weight given to British history. There was not enough emphasis on history as chronological study...I considered the document comprehensively flawed and told Ken that there must be major, not minor, changes. (17)

John MacGregor had by now replaced Kenneth Baker as Secretary of State. He asked the working report to include more chronology, more British history and to incorporate historical knowledge in the attainment targets. Eventually, after much argument, MacGregor proposed that the original attainment target of "understanding history in its setting" be changed to "the knowledge and understanding of history" and that it be given higher weighting.

By the time the final report was ready, the Cabinet game of "musical chairs" had seen John MacGregor replaced as Education Minister by Kenneth Clarke. It had been assumed by the working group that the study of history continued to the present day. But Clarke assumed otherwise, believing that "history" would be confused with "current affairs". After much argument he agreed that history was to end twenty years previously. He had already decided that compulsory history should finish at the age of 14 and that modern history would be studied only beyond this age. According to Duncan Graham this was the first political intrusion into what was taught in the country's schools.

GEOGRAPHY: A QUART IN A PINT POT

One of the difficulties facing those working groups beginning their work later concerned the amount of time left for them in the curriculum. The Prime Minister had insisted that the national curriculum should occupy no more than 70% of school time. There was talk of the "overcrowded curriculum" and "half-subjects". Despite this, the geography working party produced a very weighty interim report, with seven attainment targets, and with the emphasis upon skills rather than facts. But the Minister argued that geography had moved away from its real purpose of a systematic study of one's own country. He also wanted "knowledge" to be brought into the attainment targets and a reduction in the number. He got his way: the original attainment targets 2, 3 and 4 were collapsed into "knowledge and understanding of places" and the emphasis to this day is upon "knowledge and understanding". (I sometimes wonder what "knowledge without understanding" is worth.)

MODERN LANGUAGES: WHICH ONE?

A problem facing this working group, apart from constructing attainment targets and programmes of study, was that concerning which languages to study. (Despite this Kenneth Baker found it to be the least controversial of the groups.) It was decided that if only one language were to be studied it must be a European one. The initial attainment targets agreed upon were:

> the ability to understand spoken languages of various kinds;
> to express oneself effectively in speech and conversation;
> to read, understand and respond appropriately to written language of various kinds; and
> to formulate, record and convey meaning in the written language being studied.

The NCC simplified these to listening; speaking; reading; and writing! (A case of the mountain bringing forth a mouse and a reminder that skills in the absence of substance are empty, whilst substance without skills is dead) The final report was not received with universal acclaim: according to Duncan Graham, some language teachers seemed keen to preserve the elitist flavour of the subject, making it the only group which claimed that its subject was unsuitable for the less able.

THE REST: BOTTOM OF THE PILE

Art, Music and Physical Education

These three subjects come at the fag - end: so much for the rhetoric of a broad and balanced curriculum. By way of confirming their lowly status – if such confirmation were needed – no guarantee was given that the subjects would be compulsory beyond the age of 14, nor how much time in the curriculum they would be allocated. As if further humiliation was in order, John MacGregor even suggested that the needs of Music and PE could be satisfied through out-of-school activities, whilst the Art working group claimed that "design" had been captured by Technology (now labelled "Design and Technology") By the time the final reports were produced, Kenneth Clarke was the Minister and he reduced the attainment targets to: "the knowledge and understanding pupils are expected to have at each key stage". As Duncan Graham puts it:

> *"Art and Music are the ultimate expressions of the government's determination to reveal the pure streak that had existed in the beginning - knowledge was more important than skills". (18)*

To which might be added "And knowledge with economic potential is most important of all".

APPENDIX 3 ADDRESSES OF RELEVANT AGENCIES

Action Aid: fighting for a world without poverty and a life of dignity
 ActionAid UK
 Hamlyn House, McDonald Rd
 Archway, London N19 5PG

Amnesty International: protecting human rights; campaigning for release of prisoners of conscience and for fair trials
 1 Easton St
 London WC1X 0DW

Citizens Advice Bureau: problems of debt, housing benefits, employment etc
 Myddleton House
 London

Friends of the Earth: protecting and improving conditions for life on earth
 26-28 Underwood St
 London N1 7JQ

Greenpeace: positive change through action; confronting environmental abuse
 Canonbury Villas
 London N1 2PN

Oxfam: putting an end to poverty
 Oxfam House, John Smith Dr
 Cowley, Oxford OX4 2JY

VSO: volunteering to fight global poverty
 317 Putney Bridge Road
 London SW15 2PN

World Development Movement: campaigns for action on climate change, access to water and fairer world trade
 66 Offley Road, London SW9 0LS

BIBLIOGRAPHY

Apple,M. (1979) Ideology and the Curriculum. Routledge. London

Apple,M. and Beane,J. (1995) Democratic Schools Heinemann London

Baker,K (1993) The Turbulent Years. Faber and Faber. London.

Bantock,G.H, The Times Educational Supplement 12 and 19 march 1971. "Towards a Theory of Popular Education"

Barrow,R. (1976) Common Sense and the Curriculum. Allen and Unwin. London

Barrow, R. and White,P. (eds)1993 Beyond Liberal Education. Routledge. London

Benn,C. and Simon, B.(1972) Half Way There (2nd.ed.) Penguin Harmondsworth

Beckett,F. (2007) The Great City Academies Fraud. Continuum. London.

Bennett,N. (1976) Teaching Styles and Pupil Progress. Open Books. London

Berman,M (2000) The Twilight of American Culture. Duckworth .London

Board of Education (1927) Educating the Adolescent. HMSO London

Board of Education (1931) The Primary School. HMSO London

Braverman,H. (1974) Labor and Monopoly Capital Monthly Review Press. New York

Briggs,A. (1954) Victorian People. Odhams Press. London

Bobbitt,P. (2002) The Shield of Achilles. Allen Lane

Bookchin,M. (2005) The Ecology of Freedom. A.K. Pratt.NY

Bowen, J.A. (1981) A History of Western Education vol.3 Methuen London

Bowles,S and Gintis.H. (1976) Schooling in Capitalist America, Routledge and Kegan Paul. London

Broadfoot,P. (1979) Assessment, Schools and Society, Methuen…

Brown,P. Green,A. Lauder,H. (2001) High Skills. Oxford University Press. Oxford.

Callahan, R.E. (1963) Education and the Cult of Efficiency. Univ. Chicago. Press. Chicago

Cannadine, D. (1992) The Decline and Fall of the British Aristocracy. Pan Books. London

Chitty,C. (2002) Understanding Schools and Schooling. Routledge. London

Chitty,C.(2004) Education Policy in Britain. Palgrave. MacMillan. Basingstoke

Cole, G.D.H. and M. (eds) (1944) The Opinions of William Cobbett. The Cobbett Publishing Co. Ltd. London

Cole G.D.H. and Filson,A.W. British Working Class Movements, Selected Documents 1789-1875

Crosland, C.A.R. (1964) The Future of Socialism. Jonathan Cape. London

Cruddas,J Neo-classical Labour in Renewal vol.14 no.1

Denham, A. and Garnett,M. (2001) Keith Joseph. Acumen . Chesham

Edwards, A.D. & Furlong, V.J. (1978) The Language of Education. Heinemann. London

Entwistle,H. (1979) Antonio Gramsci. Routledge. London

Eraut,M. (1994) Developing Professional Knowledge and Competence. Falmer. London

Furedi,F. (2005) The Politics of Fear. Continuum. London

Golby,M. et al (eds) (1975) Curriculum Design. Croom Helm. London

Goodson,I.F. (ed) (1985) Social Histories of the Secondary Curriculum Falmer Press. London

Graham, D (with Tytler,D. (1993) A Lesson for us All. Routledge.London.

Grundy,S. (1987) Curriculum: Product or Praxis. Falmer Press. London

Harvey,D. (2005) A Brief History of NeoLiberalism. Oxford

Himmelfarb,G. (1984) The Idea of Poverty. Faber and Faber. London

Hobsbawm,E. J. (1962) The Age of Revolutions. Weidenfeld and Nicolson. London
　　　　　(1997) The Age of Capital. Abacus. London
(1984) Worlds of Labour. Weidenfeld and Nicolson. London

Hodson,D. and Prophet R.B. (1983) Why the Science Curriculum Changes – Evolution or Social Control? School Science Review, Sept. 1983

Hoggart, R. (1958) The Uses of Literacy. Penguin. Harmondsworth
Illich,I (1973) DeSchooling Society Penguin Books

Kogan,M. (1971) The Politics of Education. Penguin

Kogan, M.(1978) The Politics of Educational Change. Collins. Glasgow.

James, O. (2007) Affluenza. How to be Successful and Stay Sane. Vermilion

Laslett,P. (1983) The World we Have Lost- further explored. Methuen. London

Layard,R. (2005) Happiness- Lessons from a new Science. Allen Lane

Lawson,J. and Silver,H. (1973) A Social History of Education in England. Methuen. London

Layton,D. (1973) Science for the People. Allen and Unwin.London

Leadbeater,C. (2000) Living on Thin Air. Penguin. Harmondsworth

McCulloch, G. et al (1985) Technological Revolution ? Falmer Press. London

McKeith,G. (2006) The Ultimate Health Plan. Michael Joseph. London

McSmith, A. (1994) Kenneth Clarke: a Political Biography. Verso. London

MacRae, D. (ed) (1969) Spencer: the Man versus the State. Pelican. Harmondsworth.

Major, J. (1999) John Major. Harper Collins.London.

Milliband, R. (1969) The State in Capitalist Society. Weidenfeld and Nicolson. London

Monbiot,G. (2000) The Captive State.MacMillan. London

Monbiot,G. (2006) Heat. How to Stop the Planet Burning. Allen Lane. London

Morton,A.L. 1962 The Life and Ideas of Robert Owen. Lawrence and Wishart.London

Mumford,L. (1934) Technics and Civilisation. RKP London

Oakeshott,R. (1978) The Case for Workers Coops. RKP. London

Oborne,P. (2007) The Triumph of the Political Class. Simon & Schuster. London

Peston,R. (2008) Who Runs Britain? Hodder and Stoughton. London

Peters, R.S. (1966) Ethics and Education Allen and Unwin. London

Ranson, S. (ed) (1998) Inside the Learning Society Cassell.London

Rogers, C. & Freiberg H.J. (1994) Freedom to Learn. McMillan. Ohio

Rose,J. (2001) The Intellectual Life of the Working Classes.Yale Univ. Press. London

Sacks,O. (1986) The Man Who Mistook his Wife for a Hat. Picador. London

Salter,B. and Tapper,T. (1981) Education, Politics and the State.Grant McIntyre.London

Sampson,A. (2004) Who Runs this Place ? John Murray

Sandler,M.J. (2009) Justice. What's the Right Thing To Do . Allen Lane. London

Schon,D. (1971) Beyond the Stable State. Norton. NY

Seddon,J.(2003) Freedom from Command and Control . Vanguard Education. Birmingham

Seligman, M. (2002) Authemtic Happiness. Free Press . New York

Sennett,R. (2006) The Culture of the New Capitalism. Yale Univ. Press

Silver,H. ed. (1969) Robert Owen on Education CUP Cambridge

Simon,B. (1960) Studies in the History of Education 1780-1870 Lawrence and Wishart.

Simon,B. (1965) Education and the Labour Movement,1879-1920, Lawrence and Wishart

Simon,B. (1991) Education and the Social Order, 1940-1990. Lawrence and Wishart

Stuart MacClure,J. (1965) Educational Documents. Methuen

Tallis, R. (1994) Why the Mind is not a Computer . Imprint Academic. Exeter

Thatcher,M. (1993) The Downing Street Years. Harper Collins. London

Thompson,D. (1993) Outsiders. Class, Gender and Nation. Versa. London

Thompson, E.P.(1963) The Making of the English Working Class. Penguin

Tyler,R.W. (1949) The basic Principles of Curriculum and Instruction. Univ. Chicago Press. Chicago

Wainwright, H. (2003) Reclaim the State. Experiments in Popular Democracy.Verso

Walden,G. (2000) The New Elites. Penguin

West, E.G. (2003) E.G. West on Education. Inst. Economic Affairs. London

Wheen,F. (2004) How Mumbo-Jumbo Conquered the World.4th Estate. London

Wiener, M.J. (1985) English Culture and the Decline of the Industrial Spirit. Penguin. Harmondsworth

Williams,R. (1961) The Long Revolution. Chatto and Windus. London

Willis.P. "The Significance of School Counter-culture" in Hammersley.M. and Woods,P.(1976) The Process of Schooling Routledge and Kegan Paul. London

Wilkinson, R.G. (2005) The Impact of Inequality. Routledge. Abingdon

Wilson, P.S. (1971) Interest and Discipline in Education. Routledge and Kegan Paul.London.

Winter,J.(1976) Robert Lowe.Univ. of Toronto Press. Toronto

Young,D. (1990) The Enterprise Years. Headline. London

Young, M.F.D. (ed) (1971) Knowledge and Control. Collier-MacMillan. London.